THE
SACRED BOOKS OF THE HINDUS

VOL. 28

AMS PRESS

NEW YORK

THE
SACRED BOOKS
OF THE
HINDUS

TRANSLATED BY

VARIOUS SANSKRIT SCHOLARS

EDITED BY

Major B. D. Basu, I. M. S. (Retired).

VOLUME XXVIII.

INTRODUCTION TO

THE MIMAMSA SUTRAS OF JAIMINI

BY

Pandit Mohan Lal Sandal, M. A., LL. B.

PUBLISHED BY

Major B. D. Basu, I. M. S. (Retired), at the Panini Office,

Bhuvaneswari Asrama, Bahadurganj, Allahabad.

Library of Congress Cataloging in Publication Data

Sandal, Mohan Lal.
    Introduction to the Mimamsa sutras of Jaimini.

    Original ed. issued as v. 28 of The Sacred books of
the Hindus.
    Intended as an introd. to The Pūrva mimāṃsa sūtras
of Jaimini and The Mīmāṃsā sūtras of Jaiminī, issued as
v. 10 and v. 27 of the series.
    1. Mīmāṃsā.   2. Jaimini.   I. Title.   II. Series: The
Sacred books of the Hindus, v. 28.
B132.M5S28   1974   181'.42   73-3821
ISBN 0-404-57828-4

Reprinted from the edition of 1925, Allahabad
First AMS edition published, 1974
Manufactured in the United States of America

International Standard Book Number:
Complete Set: 0-404-57800-4
Volume 28: 0-404-57828-4

AMS Press, INC.
New York, N.Y. 10003

INTRODUCTION TO
THE
MIMAMSA SUTRAS
OF
JAIMINI

BY

Pandit Mohan Lal Sandal, M. A., LL. B.

PUBLISHED BY

Major B. D. Basu, I. M. S. (Retired), at the Panini Office,

Bhuvaneswari Asrama, Bahadurganj, Allahabad.

[1925]

FOREWORD.

When this work was undertaken, it was intended to form a part of the Mîmâmsâ sûtras of Jaimini. Accordingly the pages were printed with Roman figures to distinguish them from those of the main book. As the bulk of the main book exceeded beyond expectation and the introduction also assumed a decent form of a book, it was, therefore thought advisable to issue the introduction in a seperate volume giving its pages the number of a separate volume.

ALLAHABAD
10th July 1925.

EDITOR.

V

Addenda Et. Corrigenda.

Page	Line	Read	For
i	7	'atomic'	atomis
ii	1	कर्तुरेहरत्मायात्	कर्तुरहत्मायात्
ii	6	'founder'	fonnder
vii	4	'in'	n
xvi	12	'following'	fallowing
xx	10	अग्नि	न्नि
xxix	1	सर्वमेवाप्नोति	स्वमेवाप्नोति
xxix	32	insert 'need of an'	after 'in'
xxxiv	21	„ to वैश्वानर:	after pans
xxxiv	25	„ 'ten' after	baked on
xxxvii	9	ब्राह्मण	ब्रामण
xxxvii	10	मर्यंका	मर्यं या
xli	21	पत्नीसंवाज	क्तीसंवाज
xliv	34	शुक्राग्यात्	शुक्रयात्
li	27	आर्षं बसजत्ति	बर्षंबिसर्जति
lix	19	पुरोडाय	पुयोडाय
lx	14	माचित्र	चित्र
lxviii	3	is to be	to is be
lxxviii	23	आतिथ्येत्ति	अग्नीषोमीव
lxxxi	20	वाजपेयेनेष्ट्वा	वाजपेयेनेष्ट्वा
lxxxiv	14 (margin)	Krama	Karma
lxxxvii	2	तदादिन्वाथ	नदादिन्वाथ
lxxxvii	last	मद्गण	मद्म्ख
xci	20	secondly	second
xci	29	earrying	carring
xci	last	no	eno
xciv	2	Delete	'and'
cxvi	last but one	Vaisvadevi	Vaisvadavi
xcix	last but one	ऊर्ववधान	ऊववान
cvi	4	and	ond
cvi	25 'margin)}	not having	having not
cvii	27	Pârasava	Pararava
cxvi	1	cxvi	cvi
cxvi	35	Anvâdhana	Anvadana
cxvii	17 (margin)	सन्नायी	सन्मायी
cxxv	1	Ṣadahas	Sadahes
cxxvi	1	o	of

cxxviii	22 (margin)	delete is	
cxxxv	2	' carry '	carrying
cxlv	3 (margin)	षट्त्रिंशरात्र	दत्रिंशरात्र
cxlviii	33	after ' verse ' insert no act is possible without an object	
clii	23	asamavetavachana for asamaveta &c.	
cliii	32	Yajñayajñiya	Yajnayajui
clviii	25 (margin)	यज्ञायज्ञीय	यषावज्ञीय
clviii	15	मौद्गं	मौदंग
clix	36 (margin)	माधव	मधव
clx	30	मेघक	मधव
clxi	22 (margin)	when	where
clxi	23 (margin)	delete ' where '	
clxi	23	' more goods '	' goods more ''
clxii	15	द्विपज्ञयदनयोबङ्क्रय:	द्विपज्ञयदनयोबङ्क्ष
clxxi	8 (margin)	कृष्णाल	कुष्णाल
clxxxvii	15	author	auther
clxxxvii	34 (margin)	सम्ूढ	सँमूढ
cxc	6 (margin)	Insert ' and ' bet: कूइट and रबंतर	
cxcix	8	songs	soma
cc	1	the	he
ccx	20	सदा	सघ
ccxiii	2 (margin)	सुब्रह्मएव	सुब्रह्मणाच
ccxvi	11	delete ' where '	
ccxvi	11	are	ar
ccxxii	12	अग्नीषोमीय	आग्नीषोमीय
ccxxii	21	the	ths
ccxxiv	32	इंद्रीसुब्रह्मएया	इंद्रीब्रह्मएया
ccxxv	30	sacrificial	secrificial
ccxxvi	23 (margin)	द्यावापृथिबी	धावापृथिबी
ccxxvii	11	option	optin
ccxxvii	22	निऋसत्य	निऋसल्बल्ब
ccxxviii	22	should	shauld
ccxxix	4 (margin)	बसेधारर	वसेधार
ccxxix	21	when	where
ccxxxi	18	be	he

Introduction.

The word मीमांसा is derived from ' मान ' meaning ' determination, '
' measure, ' by adding अ as an affix in the सन् form of the
verb. It therefore means determination or discrimina-
tion. It is one of the six systems of Hindu philosophy.

Derivation of ' मीमांसा '

The first and the oldest is वैशेषिक of कणाद who is the first to start the
atomis theory of creation ; his system contains both the
mental and natural philosophies. The second school is
known as the न्याय school founded by गौतम. Both of
these two systems come under one group ; the न्याय being

Six schools of philo- sophy.

subsequent to the वैशेषिक and is an improvement on the latter as it does not
deal with the physics and confines itself to mental philosophy generally and
logic specially.

In the second group comes सांख्य and योग. The former was founded
by कपिल whose views are embodied in the प्रवचनसूत्र which I hold to
be older than the *Karika*. I have written a separate thesis showing
that the प्रवचन सूत्रs are the oldest in the सांख्य school and cannot be
assigned the date which the European scholars have done. As it is
a subject foreign to the present, I cannot deal wfth it here. It is an
agnostic philosophy and paved the way to the found\ition of the hetero-
dox or heritical schools of philosophy which became fossilised in the
shape of the two well known religions of India *viz.* Budhism and
Jainism. The traces of agnosticism are found in the Rigveda X: 129
verses 6 & 7. See छांदोग्योपनिषत् chapter VIII. 8. 5, where वैरोचन is said
to have come to the conclusion that it was the body that was the ' self. '
Subsequently वृहस्पति, चार्वाक and जावालि became the well known leaders
belonging to the athiestic school of philosophy. (See सर्वदर्शनसंग्रह). The
योग system of philosophy belonging to the 2nd group is subsequent to the
सांख्य system and is called सेश्वर in contradistiction to the अनीश्वर (athiestic
school) of कपिल. I hold सांख्य group to be posterior to the वैशेषिक as कपिल
has criticised the वैशेषिक system (See 1. 25.)

The last group consists of the पूर्व and उत्तरमीमांसाs. The पूर्व मीमांसा
school with which we have to deal was started by जैमिनि and उत्तर मीमांसा
which is popularly known as वेदान्त by बादरायण. The former is also called
कर्म मीमांसा or shortly मीमांसा.

The founder of the मीमांसा school of philosophy is जैमिनि a mythical saint
about whom we know nothing. There is a verse quoted in

जैमिनि's life

पञ्चतंत्र in the 2nd तंत्र at p. 8 of the Bombay Sanskrit series.

II.

सिंहो व्याकरणस्य कर्तुरहरत्प्राणान्प्रियान् पाणिनेर्मीमांसा कृतमुन्ममाथ सहसाहस्ती मुनिं जैमिनिम् । छन्दोज्ञाननिधिंजघानमकरो वेलातटे पिङ्गल मज्ञानावृत्तचेतसा मतिरहषां कोऽर्थ स्तिरश्चांगुणैः ॥

"A lion deprived पाणिनि the writer of grammar of his dear life; an elephant trampled the sage जैमिनि the founder of मीमांसा suddenly and an alligator devoured पिङ्गल the great writer on the science of prosody on a bank. What have the ferocious animals filled with ignorance to do with the merits?" We find that जैमिनि the writer of the मीमांसासूत्र met his death at the feet or trunk of an angry or wild elephant. We know for certain that he was the disciple of बादरायण व्यास, the founder of the Vedanta school of philosophy and it is also certain that he had founded his school of philosophy before his preceptor did. He has been referred to and criticised by his preceptor in more passages than one in the वेदान्तसूत्र s. There is no doubt that जैमिनि has also referred to बादरायण in his सूत्र s with great respect.

Jaimini, the writer or the founder belongs to the Sûtra Period which roughly extends from 600 to 200 B. C. according to Max Muller. There was a period in the history of the Vedic literature when people took to writing scientific treatises in the pithy and mnemonic sentences called सूत्र or thread. We have कल्पसूत्र a treatise on the sacrifices, astronomy, orthoepy, grammar and prosody and the whole of the philosophical literature. This must have extended over a vast period in the history of the Vedic literature. It is not of a spontaneous growth. It is by evolution that the philosophical literature came to the present state in course of several centuries. There must have been an interchange of thought and attack on the views of the rival schools. This is why we find reference to one another in the philosophical literature. We also find that the sceptical school of philosophy which once existed side by side with the orthodox philosophy has disappeared and its literature most probably destroyed in the post—Budhistic period of the Hindu revival. We find the sceptic views of the great sages of the philosophical age fossilised for ever in the Budhist and Jain literature in the प्राकृत languages. This explains why in सर्वदर्शन संग्रह and शङ्कर's commentary on वेदान्त, we do not find any reference to the प्रवचन सूत्र s but only to ईश्वर कृष्ण's कारिका. माधव and शङ्कर both flourished in Southern India, the strong hold of Hinduism; it is highly probable that they would be the last people to refer to कपिल's सांख्य सूत्र s which were not studied there and which must have therefore, fallen into disfavour of the public. This must have been several centuries before the rise of Budhism and Jainism. In my opinion, it must have been several centuries before Christ. I cannot guess any exact period and the internal evidence referring to the rival school of philosophy is not satisfactory as each school developed and came to the present state in the long period extending over several centuries.

According to the orthodox Hindus, Jaimini lived at the time of बादरायण who is otherwise known as व्यास, the son of पराशर. He lived in the beginning of कलि or the end of द्वापर. The present कलि era is 5025 in 1924 and accordingly जैमिनि lived about 3101 B. C. which to a European scholar sounds absurd. If the Hindu view is on one hand extreme, the view expressed in Beni Prasad *versus* Hardai Bibi. I. L. R. 14 All. 67 at 70 to the effect that Jaimini lived in the 13th century of the Christian era is, on the other hand, simply absurd and is based upon the ignorance of the counsel in the case. The learned luminaries in the case and the learned judges did not know Sanskrit. It is very strange that Knox. J. who pretended to know Sanskrit by quoting original Sanskrit texts was a party to the full bench decision. In the separate judgment which he delivered at length he has, however, refrained from expressing such an absurd view. about the age of जैमिनि.

Mimansa is a science of judicial interpretation of the sacrificial portion (कर्मकाण्ड) of the Veda just as वेदान्त is that of the ज्ञानकाण्ड. It is an exegesis or science of interpretation. It is distinguishable on one hand from कल्पसूत्र which purely deals with the complicated procedure of the sacrificial rites and ceremonies and on the other from निरुक्त which explains the Vedic words and their bearing on the Vedic texts. The मीमांसा therefore partakes of the nature of both of them as it undertakes to interpret the Vedic words and describe the ceremonies in connection with them. It is both a philosophy and logic and *sina qua non* for the study of the sacrificial portion of the Veda.

What is Mîmânsâ ?

There is a vast literature which has gathered round the Mîmânsâ sûtras. The first commentator is उपवर्ष who is called वृत्तिकार* and भगवान् by शबर (see the commentary on सूत्र 5 of chap I).

Mîmânsâ literature.

उपवर्ष

We have not got the वृत्ति of उपवर्ष but we know from the reference made by शबर more than once in his learned commentary known as भाष्य that he had the advantage of the वृत्ति. It is useless to discuss about the life and writing of the वृत्तिकार as we have already a very learned commentary ¡on the मीमांसा सूत्र.

Next comes शबर who plays an important part in the Mîmânsâ literature. He had preceded शंकर who referred to him in his learned commentary on the Vedânta (see III. 3. 53.) His commentary is indispensable to the study of the Mîmânsâ Sûtras. He has divided the book into अधिकरण s and has given the head notes of each

शबर

---

* Some are of opinion that भवदास is the वृत्तिकार referred to by शबर but it is not supported.

अधिकरण. He has further given lucid and copious notes on each सूत्र. He has explained each अधिकरण in a logical way. He has discussed the *pros* and *cons* and the author's view; in a word he has left nothing undone. This is a perfect commentary on the मीमांसासूत्रs. The translation and the commentary of the present work are both based on शबर. It is useless to enquire into the life and time of the learned commentator as everything is enveloped in mystery and darkness.

We come to प्रभाकर who wrote a commentary on शबर's भाष्य. It is called बृहती. There is no printed edition of the work, but Prabhâkar only an incomplete manuscript in the library of the Asiatic Society of Bengal. Dr. Ganga Nath Jha has given a detailed account of it in the Prabhâkar school of Pûrva Mîmânsâ. Salik Nâth has commented upon प्रभाकर in his प्रकरणपञ्चिका. प्रभाकर is a desciple of भट्ट कुमारिल and had perhaps written his बृहती long before कुमारिल wrote his तंत्रs. Rijuvimala is a commentary on the बृहती by the same auther Salik Nâth. We can learn the view of प्रभाकर from these two works of Salik Nâth. He has started his own school of Mîmânsâ philosophy.

We now come to कुमारिल. If प्रभाकर is the founder of one branch of Mîmâ- Kumârîla nsâ school of philosophy, कुमारिल is the founder of another branch. He lived about 700 A. C. according to Keith. He was contemporary of Śankara Âchârya*; he had perhaps a great polemical discussion with the great *Achârya* in Allahabad. Read Mâdhava's शङ्कर दिग्विजय canto VII, verses 61 to 119. Ultimately कुमारिल bowed to the superior knowledge and ability of Śankar and advised him to go to Benares to मंडनमिश्र to win him over his side. In stanza 77 प्रभाकर is mentioned as a disciple of भट्ट surrounding his funeral pyre. The tradition as handed down to the time of माधव and preserved by him in the दिग्विजय may be taken to be correct, though it is clothed in poetical language unworthy of belief.

कुमारिल directed his attack on the different schools of Budhism and as Śankar was a great enemy of Budhism, he naturally became his friend They admired each other for their great work as it was expected from them. कुमारिल wrote his वार्तिक on the भाष्य of शबर; he has dissented from him at many places and rearranged the अधिकरणs (topics) at places in his own way. He has not followed शबर slavishly but deviated from his commentary wherever it was found necessary.

---

* Śankerâchârya is mentioned to have lived in 3889 of the *kali* era or 788 A. C. See शङ्करमंदारसौरभ.

प्रासूततिष्य शरदामतियातवत्या मेकादशाधिकशतोन चतुसहस्रयां ॥
"Was born in the year 3889 in autumn in पुष्य".

He divided his वार्तिक into three parts; the first consists of श्लोकवार्तिक which is a commentary in verse up to the 1st पाद of the first chapter. It is a voluminous work. The second part consists of तंत्रवार्तिक in prose bringing down his commentary to the end of the third chapter. The 3rd part is तुप्टीका which is a short commentary on the remaining chapters. Like Sankar, he has founded his own school of मीमांसा philosophy which is very different from that of the founder. As said above he wrote mainly against the different schools of Budhism which existed during his time. His main object was to save the orthodox religion of India from the attack of the athiests and to keep the old rituals of the Vedas alive.

माधव was the greatest philosopher, writer and statesman. It is said that he lived in 1336 during the reigns of Bukka and Harihar. He made the kings of Vijayanagar independent of the Mohammadan rule. The following is the geneological tree of this great writer as given in परशर's commentary.

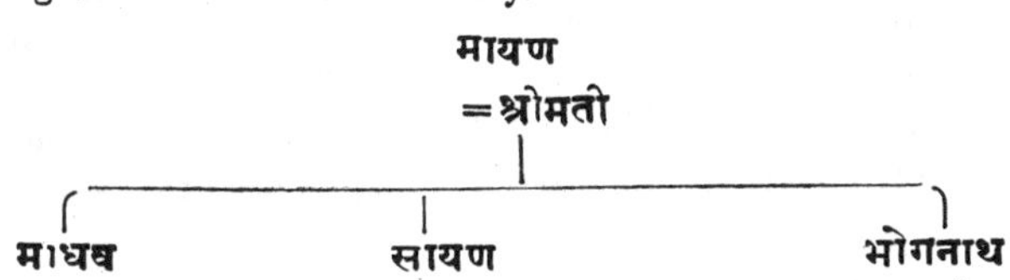

He belonged to the भारद्वाज gotra; his Veda was यजुर्वेद and the सूत्र was बौद्धायन. There is a town in southern India which is still known as माधवपुर in memory of his conquest. He conquered Goa 107 years before Vasco de Gama, the well known Portuguese discoverer of India in the Indian history.

He was the Prime Minister and Commander-in-chief of बुक्क and his nephew or son हरिहर. He is reputed to be the commentator and author of several Sanskrit works. During the reigns of these kings of Vijayanagaram, there was a revival of Sanskrit learning and several works were written. सायण the younger brother of माधव was a Sanskrit scholar; he wrote all the works in the name of his elder brother माधव. All the Vedic works were commented upon by सायण. माधव ultimately became a सन्यासी and was known as विद्यारण्य. He is the reputed author of पञ्चदशी a treatise on Vedânta. माधव was a man of versatile genius and made his mark in every department of his life.

He has written a commentary on the जैमिनि सूत्रs and called it जैमिनीय न्यायमाला. He has commented upon each अधिकरण and has given the objector's and the author's view. He has not however commented upon each सूत्र as was done by शबर and कुमारिल. This work is very valuable and ranks first amongst the works of those writers who commented upon the अधिकरणs as whole but not each sûtra separately. Mâdhava does not belong to any particular school of the Mîmânsâ.

The writer of याज्ञदीपिका is पार्थसारथिमिश्र. He has also commented upon the श्लोकवार्तिक and has called his commentary न्याय रत्नाकर. If धनपति सूरि the commentator on शङ्करदिग्विजय is to be relied on, पार्थसारथि was the disciple of कुमारिल. While commenting on प्रभाकरादयः in verse 77 canto VII, of Śankar digvijaya he says "आद्यपदेन मंडननिश्रेतर मुरारि मिश्रपार्थ सारथि निश्रादय एव ग्राह्याः" " By the word ' etc ' मुरारि मिश्र and पार्थसारथिमिश्र and other than मंडन मिश्र are meant." पार्थसारथि is, therefore, contemporary of कुमारिल and lived about 700 A. C. He follows कुमारिल his preceptor and has written a commentary on each अधिकरण as a whole.

याज्ञदीपिका

He is commented upon by रामकृष्ण in his commentary called सिद्धान्त चन्द्रिका and by सोमनाथ in his commentary called मयूखमालिका. The former is a commentary upto first पाद of the first chapter. The latter commences from the 2nd pada of the 1st chapter to the end of the 12th chapter.

पार्थसारथि is earlier than माधव who followed him in commenting upon the अधिकरणs as whole. The Ślokas that are quoted in the beginning of the अधिकरण by माधव are taken from याज्ञदीपिका. He is also the writer of न्याय रत्नमाला.

खांडदेव is another commentator of importance belonging to the school of कुमारिल. He wrote मीमांसाकौस्तुभ and भाट्टदीपिका. The latter is a very valuable commentary on the sûtras. He has also written the commentary on each अधिकरण. His commentary is a very valuable contribution to the मीमांसा literature.

खांडदेव

There are many other writers on मीमांसा who wrote thesis on the different subjects such as Gâgâ Bhaṭṭa and Śanker Bhaṭṭa etc., but my description will be of no use if 1 do not mention अर्थ संग्रह of लौगाक्षिभास्कर and मीमांसा न्याय प्रकाश of आपदेव.

Minor authors.

अर्थसंग्रह is a small treatise explaining the Mîmânsâ terms very lucidly. It is also commented upon by Râmeswar in his commentary called मीमांसासंग्रहकौमुदी. It is translated into English by Thibaut.

अर्थसंग्रह

मीमांसा न्याय प्रकाश was written by आपोदेव and is also known as आपोदेवी. The work is not different from अर्थसंग्रह in the treatment of the subject. It has defined the मीमांसा terms as the अर्थसंग्रह does. There is also a commentary called भट्टालङ्कार by his son अनन्तदेव. These two treatises on मीमांसा are very important compendiums for the study of the subject. In my opinion, they are good for the advanced student but not for a beginner. They give a bird's eye view of he subject.

मीमांसा न्याय प्रकाश

Mahâmahopâdhâya Paṇḍit Râm Krisṇa wrote अधिकरणकौमुदी. He
अधिकरणकौमुदी has explained the important अधिकरणs. The work is useful
n its own way.

There is a very important commentary on the सूत्रs of Jaimini by Râmes'-
सुबोधिनी war suri called सुबोधिनी. It is a short commentary on
each सूत्र and is a very valuable book for the correct understanding of the meaning of the सूत्रs. I consider it *sine qua non* for the
study of the Jaimina's work.

मीमांसा परिभाषा]   मीमांसा परिभाषा by कृष्ण यज्व is also a useful treatise.

It will be a great injustice, if I pass over Swâmî Dayânanda
Swâmî Dayâ-   Saraswatî, the great sanskrit scholar and reformer
nanda Saraswatî. of the last century. From what he says in the
introduction to the commentary on the Vedas and the सत्यार्थप्रकाश, it
appears that there is a conmentary on the sûtras of Jaimini by
Vyâsa, but no old commentator has mentioned the commentary of Vyâsa
on the Mîmânsâ. Certainly there is a commentary on the योगसूत्रs
by Vyâsa. It appears that there is some confusion or error. उपवर्ष as we
have seen, is the first commentator. There is a dispute whether he is उपवर्ष
or बौद्धायन. There are some scholars who are of opinion that the
वृत्तिकार referred to by शबर is no other than बौद्धायन who wrote a commentary on both the Mîmânsâs namely पूर्व मीमांसा and उत्तर मीमांसा. It is
possible that the learned Swâmî by mistake wrote down Vyasa in place of
बौद्धायन for he mentions the commentary of बौद्धायन on the Vedânta
sûtras of Vyâsa. Be that as it may ; I have by the bye mentioned the
fact written by this learned scholar of great roputation of our own
time.

The पूर्वमीमांसा has in view the Vedic texts of the कृष्णयजुर्वेद specially
of the तैत्तरीय branch just as the उत्तर मीमांसा has the
Quotations in   texts of the आरण्यकाण्ड of the ब्राह्मण especially the
the मीमांसा   उपनिषद्s.

The Pûrva Mîmânsâ is divided into 12 chapters. Each chapter is
subdivided into पादs, the latter being divided
Division of Mîmânsâ   into अधिकरणs or topics. There are sûtras or
into chapters etc.,   pithy sentences in the अधिकरणs.

viii.

The following table will show the number of the अधिकरण s.

पादs

Chapter.	1st	2nd	3rd	4th	5th	6th	7th	8th	Total.
I	8	4	10	19	...	...	...	...	41
II	17	13	14	2	...	...	...	...	46
III	15	19	15	17*	20	16	23	22	147
IV	17	14	18	12	...	...	...	...	61
V	18	12	15	9	...	...	...	...	54
VI	13	11	20	14	21	7	13	10	109
VII	5	1	14	3	...	...	...	...	23
VIII	19	6	5	5	...	...	...	...	35
IX	18	20	14	15	...	...	...	...	67
X	20	34	21	26	26	22	20	18	187
XI	10	15	14	19	...	...	...	...	58
XII	21	15	14	12	...	...	...	...	62

Total of अधिकरणs ... 890

From the above table we see that the chapters are divided into 4 पादs excepting the chapters III, VI and X which have 8 पादs each. The total number of पादs comes to 60.

---

* In the 4th पाद of chapter III, there are 4 more अधिकरण s given in the appendix. If they are added, the total of अधिकरणs comes to 894.

The number of Sûtras will appear from the following table :—

Chapter.	Pâda.								Total.
	1st	2nd	3rd	4th	5th	6th	7th	8th	
I	32	53	35	30	...	...	...	...	150
II	49	29	29	32	...	...	...	...	139
III	27	43	46	47*	53	47	51	44	358
IV	48	30	41	41	...	...	...	...	160
V	35	23	44	26	...	...	...	...	128
VI	52	31	41	47	56	39	40	42	348
VII	23	21	36	20	...	...	...	...	100
VIII	43	32	36	28	...	...	...	...	139
IX	58	60	43	60	...	...	...	...	121
X	58	73	75	59	88	79	73	70	575
XI	70	68	55	56	...	...	...	...	249
XII	44	38	32	40	...	...	...	...	154
							Grand total	...	2621

According to our text, there are 890 Adhikaraṇas and 2621 sûtras in the present Mîmânsâ. The Adhikaraṇas have been differently arranged by the different commentators. It is not proper to discuss their propriety. We have followed the edition of the Chaukhambha Sanskrit Series which is a reprint from the Bibliotheca Indica Series.

---

* There are six Sûtras given in the appendix at p. 139 which are not included in it.

I may here mention that there are four supplementary chapters
of the Mîmânsâ which go under the name of the
Sankarṣa kâṇḍa It consists of the chapters, Pâdas
and sûtras as follows :—

Supplementary
chapters
called संकर्षकांड

Pâdas

Chapter	1st	2nd	3rd	4th	Total
XIII	15	18	24	27	84
XIV	41	18	15	30	104
XV	25	36	20	14	95
XVI	12*	19	22	10	63
				Grand total ...	346

There are no Adhikaraṇas and the Sûtras are meagre; it is an
apocryphal portion of the Mîmânsâ most probably palmed
off as genuine by खांडदेव the writer of भाट्टदीपिका. It has a
commentary called भाट्टचन्द्रिका by भास्कर son of गंभीर.

This apocryphal portion is known under the name of संकर्षकांड and is said
to have been commented upon by शबर. No commentary of शबर has yet
been found. There is no doubt that रामानुज has referred to संकर्षकांड
while commenting upon III. पाद 3 of the
Vedânta Sûtras, He quotes "नाना वा देवता पृथक्त्वात ;"
we find this सूत्र in the mutilated form in Sûtra 15 of
chapter XIV. Pâda 2 of संकर्षकांड. The writer of the commentary called
वेदांतप्रदीप, who belongs to that school has also referred to it. It
cannot be said with certainty that the संकर्षणकांड or संकर्षकांड referred to
by the Râmânuja school commentators is the same as published in the
" Paṇḍit " the monthly publication of the Benares Sanskrit College.
What puts one in doubt is that Râmânuj has referred to बोधायनवृत्ति, has
quoted in the commentary on Sûtra 1 of the Vedânta Sûtra "संहितमेतच्छारीरक
जैमिनीयेन षोड्यलष णेनेति शास्त्रैकत्वसिद्धि:" ("This शारीरिक शास्त्र has been collected
by Jaimini and is characterised with sixteen chapters and is therefore one
Śâstra"), has said that by virtue of the Ṣaṭkas and chapters, there is a division
of the anterior and posterior Mîmânsâs and has quoted the first Sûtra of

---

* There is one Sûtra added at the end ; if it is counted, there will be 13
Sûtras in this Pâda.

the Mîmânsâ and the last Sûtra of the Vedânta in order to show that the two together form one body of the Sâstra.

Further, all the writers on the Mîmânsâ have characterised जैमिनि

No mention of संकर्षकांड by any commentator.

मीमांसा as containing 12 chapters. See माधवीयन्यायमाला, अर्थ संग्रह, मीमांसा न्याय प्रकाश, मीमांसा परिभाषा and सुबोधिनी.

मधुसूदन सरस्वती refers to it.

मधुसूदन सरस्वती the writer of प्रस्थानभेद says in connection with the twelve chapters of the Mîmânsâ after giving their contents " तथा संकर्षणकांडमप्यध्यायचतुष्टयात्मकं जैमिनिप्रणीतम् । तद्देवताकांड संज्ञया प्रसिद्धमप्युपासनाख्य कर्मप्रतिपादनात्वात्कर्ममीमांसावर्गतमेव । ' " Similarly संकर्षणकांड consisting of four chapters was compiled by जैमिनि. That being known under the title of देवताकांड and dealing with the subject of sacrifice, is included in the Karma Mîmânsâ ".

No mention of it in सर्वदर्शनसंग्रह

The writer of the Sarvadars'ana Sangraha has given a summary of only twelve chapters of the Mîmansa.

रामानुज time.

From the conflicting views, it appears that the Sankarṣa Kâṇḍa was once regarded a separate treatise but not a part of Jaimini's Mîmânsâ consisting of twelve chapters It formed a separate book and was passed off as the genuine work of Jaimini by the interested persons. Râmânuja was born in 1127 A. C. ; we find संकर्षकांड referred to by him for the first time ; मधुसूदन सरस्वती gave a detailed account of it.

Strange to say that the संकर्षकांड is not mentioned by Alberuni and Abul Fazal.

Alberuni and Abul Fazal do not mention it.

The latter has given the contents of the twelve chapters of Jaimini's मीमांसा. For these reasons, I am of opinion that संकर्षकांड is a spurious work. Further I am of opinion that the work as it exists in the

present form is भास्कर or खंडदेव appears to be the author.

either the work of खंडदेव or भास्कर. The latter after mentioning the incomplete commentary of खंडदेव says. ' आसीत् षोडशलक्षणी श्रुतिपदा याधर्ममीमांसिका । संकर्षाख्यवचतुर्भाग विधुरा कालेन साजायत ॥ गायत्री त्रिपदात्मिकेव बिधुधैरदासापि पाठ्यते । तांपूर्णामितनोच्छसेनमहता गम्भीरजो भास्करः ।'' " That धर्ममीमांसा containing the Vedic texts had sixteen characteristics ; the 4th part called संकर्षकांड was lost in course of time : even now like गायत्री having 3 feet, it is constantly read. Bhâskara, son of गम्भोर with great labour brought it to completion. " Bhâskara seems to be a great admirer of खंडदेव and dedicated the work in the name of his master and called it भाट्टचन्द्रिका after भाट्टदीपिका of his preceptor ; I think he was his contemporary.

Khaṇḍa Deva is said to be the preceptor of जगन्नाथ त्रिमूली the author of गङ्गा लहरी, रसगङ्गाधर, भामिनीविलास &c. The latter lived in the reigns of Shah Jehan and Aurangzeb. खंडदेव must have flourished

His time

in the reign of Shah Jehan as he is said to have died in 1665 by Keith.

The संकर्षकाण्ड never found popularity amongst the students of the Mîmânsâ and was therefore very properly consigned to oblivion. We do not find it mentioned in any ancient works prior to रामानुज or मधुसूदन सरस्वती. The editor of the ' Paṇḍit ' believing it to be a genuine work of Jaimini did well in publishing it and putting it before the Mîmânsâ reading public.

संकर्षकाण्ड was never popular.

The style of the so called Sûtras does not resemble that of Jaimini ; it is so very curt and mutilated that one can not make out anything without the help of भास्कर's भाष्यचन्द्रिका. There are no अधिकरण which are the peculiar characteristics of जैमिनी's मीमांसा. Each chapter has 4 pâdas as shown in the above table.

Style.

The last Sûtra in the 4th Pâda of the 4th chapter which is called the 16th Chapter in the work, ends with the word "····वमारा त्वा सन्मेव:" which has been repeated twice andimitated from the final endings in Sânkhya Pravachana or the Vedâanta Sûtras

Peculiarities.

It is a valuable work in the Mîmânsâ literature and is more in the nature of the Kalpa Sûtra. It does not discuss any general principle as is done by Jaimini in his Mîmânsa. The well-known twelve principles have been discussed in the twelve chapters by Jaimini, but in the present work under discussion, there is a simple description of the post-sacrificial minor ceremonies which really form the subject of Śrauta part of the Kalpa Sûtra. In this view which I take of the संकर्षकाण्ड, it can not be considered a supplement of Jaimini's Mîmânsâ.

It cannot be considered a supplement of the Mîmânsâ.

A pâda originally means a part of anything. There as a rule, a chapter is divided into 4 parts, each part being called a वाद the chapters III, VI and X are exceptions to the rule.

What is a पाद ?

An Adhikaraṇa is a thesis or a subject which forms part of its discussion It consists of 5 parts or अवयव Just as in Gotam's logic, there are 5 premises in a syllogism ; (1) प्रतिज्ञा enunciation ; (2) हेतु reason ; (3) उदाहरण major premise ; (4) उपनय minor premise ; (5) निगमन conclusion. There is a verse showing the parts of an अधिकरण :—

अधिकरण

विषयविशायश्चैव पूर्वपक्षस्तथोत्तरं ।
निर्णयश्चेति पञ्चाङ्गं शास्त्रेऽधिकरणं मतं ॥

" The subject, the doubt, the *prima facie* view, the reply, and the decision are the recognised five parts of an *adkikaran* in a treatise."

From the above quotation we see that in an अधिकरण which one can call ' subject ' or ' topic ' there is 1st, the proposition which one has to establish. It corresponds roughly with the प्रतिज्ञा of Gotama or enunciation of Euclid. Then follows 2ndly, the doubt arising out of it. Thirdly, an objector expresses his own view which is called पूर्वपक्ष. Fourthly, there is a rejoinder or reply ; fifthly, or last, we have the conclusion which is called सिद्धांत or the author's view. It is in the above verse, called a decision (निर्णय). In the Logic of Aristotle we have only 3 premises in a syllogism called the major premise, the minor premise and the conclusion. We have similarly four parts in a law suit in a court; the plaintiff puts forth his case; then the defendant gives his own case and lastly the plaintiff meets the defendant's case in his reply. Thereon follows the decision of the presiding judge. We have here 4 parts but in Jaimini's अधिकरण we see that there are five parts. Some मीमांसकs have given only four parts of an अधिकरण.

The word Sûtra means a thread or string. It is so called because the words are tied together as in a string to express the meaning succinctly. सूत्र It is a pithy or mnemonic sentence and helps one to remember it easily. There is a vast literature in this kind of style.

The Mîmânsâ is divided into two parts called (1) पूर्वषट्क and (2) उत्तरषट्क. The subject of मीमांसा The पूर्वषट्क consists of 1st six chapters dealing with उप-देश as explained in सूत्र 5 of the 1st पाद of the first chapter. The उत्तरषट्क consists of the last six chapters dealing with अतिदेश as explained at. p. 417. chapter 1. para 1. The Mîmânsâ mainly deals with Dharma. The very first sûtra starts with the enquiry into the nature of Dharma.

It is very difficult to translate धर्म in any other language. It is 'duty' 'virtue' 'law, and 'righteosness, It is succinctly explained in What is धर्म ? सूत्र 2. The वार्तिककार has written 286 verses on it. It is an अर्थ characterised by चोदना. It is an end in itself for the good but not for the evil and must have a sanction from the Vedas. This requires an explanation; if there is a command or law prohibiting any one from committing murder; or imposing a duty on a citizen to keep his house in a sanitary condition, no one will obey the negative or positive precepts of law, unless there is punishment provided for the non-observance of the law. The command of the sovereign authority is binding in all civil matters. Similarly in the divine or religious matters the divine command is binding, because it is accompanied by the rewards in future life. This is what the author calls 'chodanâ' the divine command which stimulates one to act or refrain from acting in a particular way. Chodanâ is therefore a Vedic order or direction embodied in a Vedic text.

In this connection, it is better to explain what Bhâvana is. The human mind according to the Western school of philosophy consists of three important phenomena, viz., cogoition, emotion and volition. भावना I see an orange in front of me and I know from my past experience that it is very sweet to eat. This is the 1st stage which is called cognition in psychology. Then there springs up a desire to take it, saliva begins to flow in the mouth and I cannot resist the temptation to taste it. This is the 2nd stage which is called emotion in psychology. Lastly 1 strech out my hand to take the orange in order to eat it ; this is the last stage called volition in psychology. Similarly in the religious matter the Vedic command holds out hopes, as for instance "यजेत स्वर्ग काम: " "Let one desirous of heaven perform a sacrifice." If one is possessed of the desire to have heavenly bliss, he shall have to perform a sacrifice The activity to perform a 'yajña' accompanied by all the psychological factors of the mind is called भावना in the language of मीमांसा. It is of two kinds. शाब्दी and आर्थी.. The former arises from the word of mouth i. e. command. When a man is told to do or not to do a thing, he does it or refrains from doing it, because he feels that he is so ordered. I order my servant to bring my horse, he is bound to bring it. In the worldy affairs, the order comes from a supesior. but in religious affairs the command comes from the Veda.

In the आर्थी भावना, the energy to act arises from a particular motive or desire to act or refrain from acting. The command has generally the लिङ् form of a verb.

The constituent parts of the भावना in the मीमांसा are साध्य, साधन and इतिकर्तव्यता which have been explained at several places. (see at p. 224.) In the शाब्दी भावना, sacrifice is the साध्य (object) and in the आर्थी भावना, heaven is the साध्य (object).

The con-tituent parts
   of Bhâvanâ

Having explained चोदना which derives its binding force from the Veda, it is necessary to explain the term *artha* which is significant. It means purpose which ends in one's good. A sacrifice which is performed to obtain heaven comes under the definition but a द्वेषयाग which ends in the destruction of an enemy is, therefore, not within its purview.

अर्थ

There are eight प्रमाणs or means of proof viz (1) प्रत्यक्ष perception (2) अनुमान inference (3) उपमान analogy (4) शब्द verbal testimony 5) ऐतिह्य history (6) अर्थापत्ति presumption (7) संभव possibility (8) and अभाव negation. They require a little explanation; anything which is an object of any of the five senses is said to be प्रत्यक्ष or perceptible. see Gotama's 1. 1. 4.

प्रत्यक्ष

The second i. e., अनुमान is an infererce. It is of three kinds (1) पूर्ववत् (2) शेषवत् (3) सामान्यतोदृष्ट. When you make an inference of an effect from its cause, it is called पूर्ववत् as by seeing the clouds, you make an inference as to the future rainfall, When you make an inference of a cause from its effect, it is called शेषवत् as by seeing the flood in a river you infer the past rainfall: सामान्यतोदृष्ट is the common experience, as when you see John in Cawnpore and subsequently see him in Allahabed, you infer that he must have come to Allahabad from Cawnpore.

उपमान is analogy. It is thus defined by Gotama in I. 1. 6. "Analogy is a means of proving a thing to be proved by the similarity with the thing already proved." Description of an unknown thing by means of a known thing is analogy. You know a cow but you do not know a गवय (bos gaveas). Your teacher tells you that a bos

उपमान

gaveas resembles a cow: subsequently you happen to see a strange animal resembliug a cow, you at once by comparison or analogy recognise it as *bos gaveas.*

Śabda or verbal testimony is of an unbiassed man, while ऐतिह्य is the record in the annals or histories.

शब्द

अर्थापत्ति is the presumption which arises under the circumstances of a case; as Deva Dutta does not take his meals during the day but in spite of his fast, he appears to be robust and healthy: the presumption is that he takes meals at night.

अर्थापत्ति

Sambhava is possibility; a seer can contain 12 chataks in other words, 12 chataks. are included in a seer but not 18 chataks.

सम्भव]

Lastly we have Abhâva or negation. When a man is ordered to bring a vessel from the house and he does not find it there, he comes and informs his master as to its non-existence. According to the *Vais'esika* school, it is of four kinds (1) प्रागभाव (2) प्रध्वंसाभाव 3 अन्योनाभाव and (4) अत्यंताभाव. प्रागभाव is the non-existence in the commencement, as a pot did not exist before its construction. प्रध्वंसाभाव is the non-existence after destruction, as a pot does not exist after it is broken. अन्योनाभाव is the reciprocal non-existence, as a cow does not exist in a horse and *vice versa* and अत्यंता भाव is an absolnte non-existence as the hare's horns, chimera and satyr etc.

अभाव

Gotama accepts only first four means of proof; the Sânkhya of Kapila accepts (1) प्रत्यक्ष (2, अनुमान and (3) शब्द only. The Mîmânsâ accepts only Śabda or word.

After explaining the means of proof we now come to explain parception.

Perception — According to Jaimini I. 1. 4., it is the contact of the sense organs with the soul. It is thus the knowledge of the things existing. Here at present I am not going to discuss the theory of percaption according to the Mîmânsâ school of philosophy but I would like to compare this definition with that given by Gotama in his Nyâya. See I. 1. 4.

"Perception is the knowledge which is produced by the contact of the senses with their object, does not arise from the word, is invariable **and** certain."

Acccrding to Gotama perception is caused by the contact of the sense organs, namely the eye, ear, tongue, nose and touch with their different objects. He further differentiates this consciousness which arises by such contact from the knowledge that arises by स्वपदेश or words. The knowledge that arises from the words of mouth without seeing the object itself is not perception. Secondly this consciousness should not be variable; as for instance, you see mirage or *fata morgana* from a distance and when you go there you do not find the object perceived This kind of false or variable perception is not within the purview of the definition. Thirdly, it should be certain; there should not be any doubt about the identity of the object perceived. Vâtsâyana the scholiast says that the soul in contact with the mind comes in contact with the sense organs which in their turn come in contact with their objects. Perception according to Jaimini is consciousness arising from the soul coming in contact with the objects in existence through the instrumentality of the sense organs. It has a wider range and is not limited. Perception of mirage is therefore included in the above definition. Jaimini is, however, not interested in it, he has mentioned it by the way, for in the fallowing Sûtra, he clearly says that in matters religious, word or verbal testimony is the only means of knowledge (प्रमाण)

Jaimini in Sûtra 5 explains Śabda. He has laid down five propositions.

Śabda

(See at P 2.) I. Every word has a meaning, that is, it has an inherent power to convey a meaning. It is called Sphoṭa which has been discussed at length by Kumârila in his Ślokavârtika. Sarvadarsana Sangraha has also discussed the doctrine of Sphoṭa in the Pâṇini's system of grammar; it is beside the point to discuss it here. (II) Knowledge derived from word is called उपदेश by the Mîmânsakas. (III) In matters religious, it is the infallible guide. (IV). In the opinion of Jaimini's preceptor, the word is authoratative and has a binding force. (V). It is self-sufficient and does not derive its authority from any other source, because it will otherwise involve one in the fallacy of *regressus ad infinitum.*

So from the above summary, we see that Jaimini accepts only verbal testimony out of 8 pramâṇas mentioned above. Savara and Kumârila have discussed the six means of proof leaving aside संभव and अभाव.

The author discusses the nature of the word, he holds it eternal.First he

Eternity of word

gives the view of the objector and then gives his reply to the objections raised by the objector to the eternity of sound. See the Adhikaraṇa VI. Sûtrâs 6-23. at pp. 3-7. In this connection, I would refer a curious reader to Gotamâ's Nyâya Sûtra II. 2. 13-54 where he holds that a word is non-eternal.

Having established the eternity of words in general, he establishes in the Adhikaraṇa VII that the words when put together in a sentence in the Vedas, have a meaning just as they have in the common language. Lastly, he discusses the divine origin of the Vedas, meets the objections of the objector and accepts the divinity of the Vedas.

According to Jaimini, the words are eternally connected with their meaning; they are eternal and put together in a sentence, convey a sense. The Vedas are divine and are, therefore, infallible in the conduct of human life.

PÂDA 2.

Before I analyse the contents of Pâda 2, I think it proper to explain certain terms used in the Mîmânsâ and which cannot be understood without explaining them before. In the foregoing Pâda, we have established the divinity and the consequent infallibility of the Veda. The question

The Veda   that naturally arises is, what is the Veda ? It is of 5 qualities.   (1) विधि, (2) मंत्र, (3) नामधेय, (4) निषेध and (5) अर्थवाद.

The विधि or injunction is a command, precept or order. The portion of

विधि   the Veda which lays down a new rule with certain object for the guidance is a विधि. It is of four kinds as will appear from the following table:—

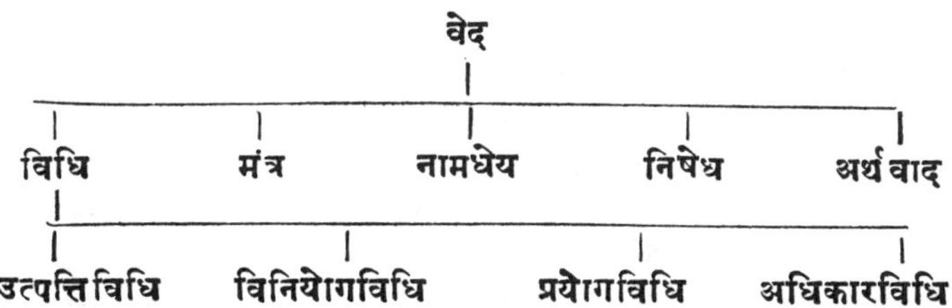

उत्पत्ति विधि lays down a command with a certain object; as for instance

उत्पत्तिविधि   "Let one perform an agnihottra, if he is desirous of heaven". If a man is desirous of heaven, he shall perform an agnihottra ; this is an originative or creative injunction i. e. it creates a desire in one to perform a sacrifice with the object to obtain heaven.

The second class of विधि is विनियोग विधि which lays down the details of

विनियोग विधि   a sacrifice. When a desire is created by the उत्पत्ति विधि, the next step is to lay down the procedure by which the object can be obtained. It comes under the head of इतिकर्तव्यता i. e. the details of the sacrifice. This kind of विधि is called विनियोगविधि or applicatory injunction, as for instance "दध्नेन्द्रियकामस्य जुहुयात्" "Let one desirous of sense-organs perform a *homa* with curd." Here the material is laid down. The first is the desire for the sense organs which is साध्य; (2) the *homa* is the means or साधन and lastly curd is the material or इतिकर्तव्यता. If a विधि lays down only material, it is called गुणविधि, as for instance "दध्ना जुहोति" "He performs a sacrifice with curd." How are we to interpret the texts that lay down the procedure ? This naturally leads us to the necessary accompaniments of the विनियोग विधि; they are six in number as will appear from the following table.

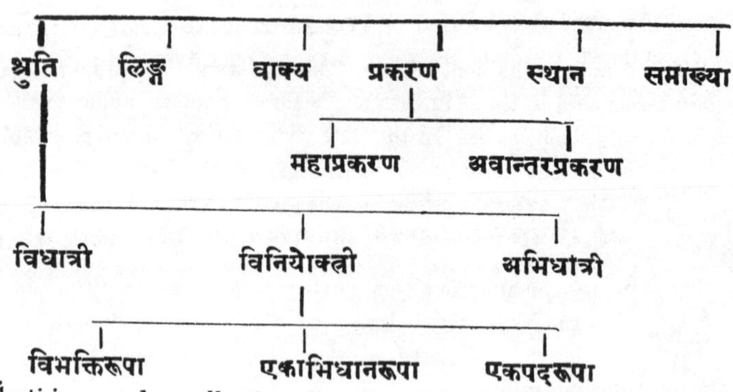

Śruti is a word or collection of words not depending on any other for its

Śruti   meaning. A word has a conventional sense attached to it; it is said to be its primary sense. Primary sense conveyed by a word without the help of any other is Śruti. It is directly heard and as soon as it is heard, a hearer understands its sense. It is of three kinds (1) विधात्री, विनियोक्त्री and अभिधात्री. The first, namely, विधात्री is indicated by the verb in the form of a विधि लिङ्; the अभिधात्री consists of the material such as wild rice etc. and the विनियोक्त्री is one on hearing which you at once see the connection of the subsidiary and the principal. The last class is also further sub-divided into three kinds (1) विभक्ति रूपा (2) एकाभिधान रूपा and एकपद रूपा The first is indicated by an affix of a declension, as for instance 'व्रीहिभिर्यजेत' "Let him perform a sacrifice with wild rice." Here the instrumental case shows that the wild rice is a part of the sacrifice. In the same way you can apply the same principle in other विभक्तिs. The एका भिधान रूपा is denoted by one word; as for instance 'पशुनायजेत, 'Let him perform a sacrifice by an animal.' Here पशुना shows that one male animal will form a part of the sacrifice; the word used shows the gender and number of the material used in the sacrifice. The word यजेत shows the भावना. The एक पद रूपा is indicated by one pada or sentence; the whole sentence in the above example shows that the animal as described above is subsidiary in relation to the sacrifice which is the principal object as indicated by the verb.

We now proceed to define *Linga* which is the second help-mate of the

Linga   विनियोग विधि. It is the suggestive or the secondary sense of a word which can be inferred from another word or collection of words. As for instance "वर्हिदेव यदनंदामि" " I cut thee O ! grass for the seat of the god. " Though वर्हि is the generic term meaning grass, yet as the मंत्र is used for cutting the *Kus'a* grass, it is used in the specific sense of *Kus'a* grass. Linga is of two kinds ; when the inferential sense can be inferred without the help of any other and secondly when it is so inferred. Kis'ori Lâl Sarkâr has explained it thus " When the meaning of a word or expression is not clear on the face of it and its latent force or suggestive power has to be brought out by the suggestive power of some other word or expression, this is called Linga." It is useless to dilate on the point as a reader of the *Mîmânsâ* will find लिंग illustrated by the author himself in the following pages.

When the meaning of a word or a collection of words is clearly gathered from the sentence in which it is used, the principle which governs it is called Vâkya. As for instance "वस्य पर्णमयीजुहूर्भवति न स पापश्लोकं श्रुणोति" " One whose ladle is made of *Parṇa* does not hear evil things. " Here पर्णमयी (made of wood) and जुहू (ladle) are two words used in their usual sense and it also appears that ' made of Parṇa wood ' is subsidiary to the 'ladle'. It follows, therefore, that the ladle can be made of any wood; then arises the question, why should there be a condition as to the ladle being made of a particular wood ? The reply is clear ; you can not achieve the transcendental result of not hearing evil things without having the ladle made of पर्ण wood. When the meaning of a word or collection of words is gathered from the whole sentence, it is called the principle of Vâkya by the Mîmânsakâs.

Vâkya

When a sentence or a clause of a sentence is not clear and its meaning cannot be gathered without the context in which it occurs, the construction is governed by the principle of Prakaraṇa; as for instance " समिधो यजति " " He sacrifices the sacrificial wood " Here the साध्य is not known. You do not know why one should sacrifice समिध् (sacrificial wood). The fruit or reward of the action in performing a sacrifice with the aid of समिध् can be known from the context in which it occurs. Take another example दर्श पूर्णमासाभ्यां स्वर्गं भावयेत्' "Let one desirious of heaven perform the new and full moon sacrifices, " Here the procedure or the subordinate parts of the दर्श पूर्णमास are not known; you can know from the context of the new and full moon sacrifices that the प्रयाज and अनुयाज are the parts of the दर्शपूर्णमास sacrifices. The Prakaraṇa is of two kinds महाप्रकरण and अवांतर प्रकरण. When the context relates to the principal भावना, it is called महाप्रकरण; as for instance, the प्रयाज and अनुयाज are the parts of the दर्श पूर्णमास sacrifices. In the अवांतर प्रकरण the context relates to the भावना of the subordinate parts ; as for instance, अभिक्रमण is a subordinate part of प्रयाज and अनुयाज.

Prakaraṇa

Let us come to Sthâna or position which is the fifth mode of interpretation. It is the location or order of words which help one in the interpretation ; as for instance, there are mangoes, guavas, oranges, apples and pears; let John, Thomas, Mathew, Jardine and Lacy take them. According to the principle of स्थान, the clauses mean that John is to take mangoes, Thomas guavas, Mathew oranges,

Sthâna

Jardine apples and Lacy pears. The following table will show the division of स्थान

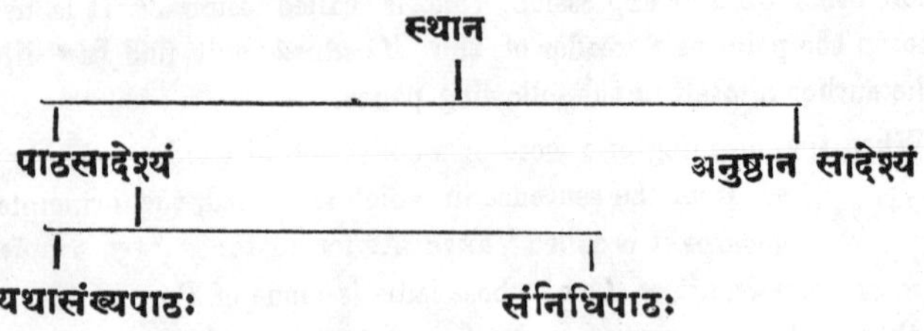

स्थान is synonymous with क्रम, (order or sequence).

पाठसादेश्य is the equality of place according to the text and is governed by the order given in a text; as for instance, "इन्द्राग्नमेकादशकपालंनिर्वपेत्" "Let him offer cakes baked on earthen pans consecrated to इन्द्र and ग्नि." Then इन्द्राग्नि रोचनादिव:" etc , सामवेद, उत्तरार्चिक 1st. अर्द्धमपाठक verse XIV, are given. Accordingly under the principle of पाठसादेश्य, the 1st. mantra will be recited with the first offer of the cake and 2nd. mantra will be repeated with the second offer and so on. But the reading in the modified sacrifice falling within two injunctions (संदर्भ) though governed by the model sacrifice, is regulated according to the principle of संनिधिपाठ i. e. by the text which is near it, as for instance the आमनहोम.

अनुष्ठानसादेश्य is the equality of place according to the performance. As for instance the details of the animal sacrifice अनुष्ठान सादेश्य are given in connection with the ceremonies to be performed on the औपवसथ्य day. The अग्नीषोमीय sacrifice is performed on the औपवसथ्य day; the principle of अनुष्ठानसादेश्य, therefore, governs it.

समाख्या is the last mode of interpretation. It is a name or denomination. It is a compound word which should be broken up समाख्या into its component parts and its meaning should be thus ascertained; as for instance, wine-cup (a cup from which one drinks wine) is distinguishable from the milk-cup. Tea-spoon, dessert spoon and table-spoon fall under this definition. It is, therefore, a name or nomenclature given by the Âcharyas to indicate divisions of the Vedas. It is of two kinds वैदिक and लौकिक; होतृचमस (a spoon from which hotâ drinks) belongs to the former class and आध्वर्यव (function of an अध्वर्वु) belongs to the latter class.

In the definition of विनियोग विधि we find two kinds of action; one is principal as the performance of la sacrifice and the other is subordinate which leads up to the completion of the former. The principal action secures the object in view as for instance स्वर्ग which is called transcendental result or अपूर्व in the language of the Mîmânsâ.

A certain action is enjoined by the Veda with a certain invisible result ; the result does not happen in one's life time but the action ceases. अपूर्व A Mîmânsaka, therefore, holds that certain invisible and transcendental *virtue* is produced in a performer by which he becomes fit for the attainment of the result or fruit in the life hereafter. This virtue or invisible or transcendental result is called अपूर्व or extraordinary principle.

The subordinate parts which lead up to the completion of the principal action are called Aṅgas and their division and subdivision will appear from the following table: —
Aṅga

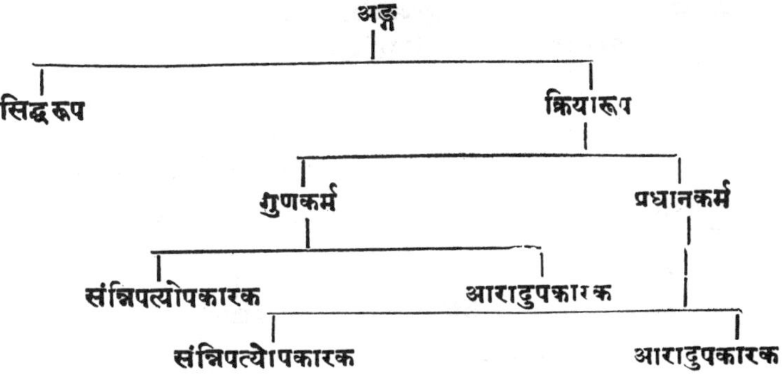

सिद्धरूप is an accomplished thing and consists of class, material number etc. It has a visible effect.
सिद्धरूप

The second class is action. It is of two kinds, it is either primary or secondary ; both of them are also of two kinds, viz. (1) संनिपत्योपकारक (2) आरादुपकारक.
क्रियारूप

The former conduces to the general result of the sacrifice through another intermediate step and the latter contributes to the general result immediately. To the class of संनिपत्योपकारक belong actions which are enjoined with respect to the substance as संनिपत्यो the threshing of the rice and sprinkling of water on it. They produce पकारक visible, invisible or both kinds of effects, as for instance, threshing of the husk has a visible effect, *viz.*, removal of husk; sprinkling of water has an invisible effect. While the offering of animal or cakes produces both kinds of effect ; because as far as the offering is concerned it has an invisible effect (अपूर्व) and as far as certain divinity to whom the offering is made is concerned it has a visible effect i. e. the remembrance of the god.

The आरादुपकारक consists of those actions which are enjoined without any reference to any substance or divinity. It leads आरादुपकारक directly to the ultimate result of the sacrifice ; it is the essence of the sacrifice in as much as it produces the transcendental result; while the former (सन्निपत्योपकारक) is the outward form of the sacrifice. The प्रयाज and अनुयाज belong to the आरादुपकारक class.

प्रयोगविधि is an injunction of performance with a view to the speedy accomplishment of the sacrifice. It consists of the performance of the main action with all its subordinate details without causing any delay. For this purpose there will be an order or succession of details that constitute the performance of the main action. The injunction that lays down the order of performance of the subsidiary or minor parts is called प्रयोगविधि.

The Krama or order is the succession or sequence. It is of six kinds as shown in the following table.

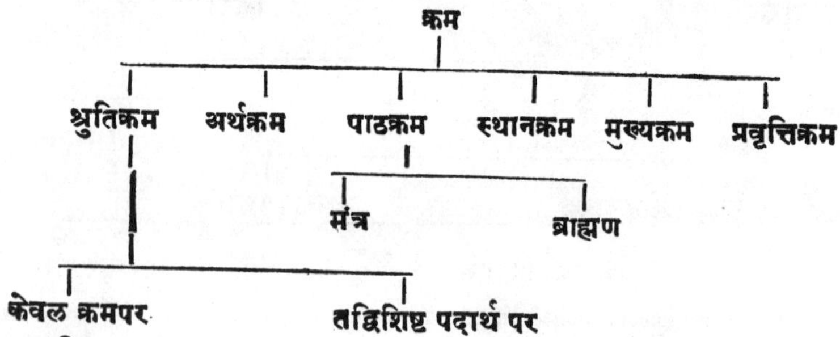

श्रुतिक्रम is the order determined by a direct text. It is of two kinds 1st. केवल क्रमपर i. e. a text indicating an order or sequence only, as for instance, "वेदं कृत्वा वेदिंकरोति" "He prepares an altar after making the Veda" The second class is तद्विशिष्टपदार्थपर indicating the order or sequence in the course of laying down certain other thing ; as for instance "वषट्कर्तुः प्रथम भक्षः" "The first drinks is of one who pronounces वषट् " The passage enjoins drinking and by the way indicates the order or sequence. The श्रुतिक्रम predominates over other kinds of क्रम ; as for instance आश्विन is third in order according to the पाठक्रम, but under the श्रुतिक्रम "आश्विनो दशमोगृह्यते" it is drunk tenth in order.

अर्थ क्रम is the order determined by the object ; as for instance, अग्निहोत्रं जुहोति यवागुंपचति " "He performs an agnihottra and cooks yavâgu. " Here an agnihottra cannot be performed without first cooking yavâgu ; though यवागु happens to be last in the above quotation, yet as its cooking is indispensable for the performance of the अग्निहोत्र it will be cooked first. The अर्थक्रम therefore predominates over the पाठक्रम.

When the order of the execution of things is governed by their order in the text, it is called पाठक्रम. It is of two kinds, it is either governed by the text of the मन्त्र or by the text of the ब्राह्मण

As for instance the offerings to Agni and अग्नीषोमौ are governed by the order of the वाक्या and अनुवाक mantras. The मंत्रपाठ predominates over the ब्राह्म texts.

स्थानक्रम means presentation. When a thing is transposed from its proper place by reasons of its being preceded by another thing which is followed by another, this transposition of the order is called स्थान क्रम An illustration will explain it better. In a ज्योतिष्टोम, there are the अग्नीषोमीय, सवनीय and अनुबंध्य animal sacrifices in their order ; but in a वाजपेय which is the modified sacrifice of the ज्योतिष्टोम the सवनीय, अग्नीषोमीय and अनुबंध्य animal sacrifices are performed, because after the drinking of the आश्विन cup the सवनीय animal sacrifice presents itself first.

मुख्यक्रम is the sequence of the subsidiaries or the subordinate parts according to the order in the principal. In it, the sequence or the order of the details in the subordinate parts is governed by that of the principal of which the subsidiaries are the subordinate parts. As for instance, when ghee is left after the प्रवाज offering, it will be first offered to Agni and then to इन्द्र because the आग्नेय is prior to ऐंद्र oblations. मुख्यक्रम predominates over the प्रवृत्तिक्रम and is inferior to the पाठक्रम.

प्रवृत्तिक्रम is the order of a procedure which once begun will apply to others as well. As for instance in a प्राजापत्य sacrifice several animals are sacrificed ; you choose one animal at random and perform certain ceremonies on it. The order in which the ceremonies are performed on the first animal will govern the order of the ceremonies on the rest of the animals.

A Vidhi or injunction which creates a right in a person is called अधिकार विधि as for instance, " स्वर्गकामो यजेत " "Let one desirous of heaven perform a sacrifice. " The vidhi text creates a right in every person to perform a sacrifice, provided he is possessed of a desire to obtain heaven. The only condition required under the text is that the person must be desirous to obtain heaven. The subject of right is fully discussed in chapter VI where the summary of it will be given.

The *Mantra* is a text which helps one to remember the procedure of a sacrifice. It is classified as follows.

Mantra

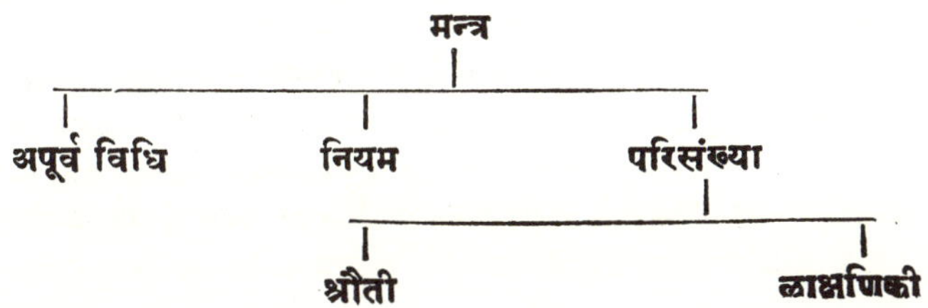

There is a well known Śloka which is on the lip of every Mîmânsâ student and which explains very succinctly all the three kinds of texts.

विधि रत्यंतमप्राप्तौ नियमः पाक्षिकेसति ।

तत्र चान्यत्र च प्राप्तौ परिसंख्येति गीयते ॥

"When it is radically non-existent, it is vidhi ; when it is partially non-existent, it is niyama ; when it can be had here and elsewhere, it is called parisaṅkhyâ " It will be now explained *seriatim.*

When a text lays down a new injunction for the attainment of our object अपूर्वविधि which you cannot know by any other means, it is said to be अपूर्वविधि as for instance " यजेतस्वर्गकाम: " " Let one who is desirous of heaven perform a sacrifice. " Here in the text we find that a new thing is laid down, *viz*, the attainment of heaven ; it is further known that you can have it by performing a sacrifice. We also further know that we are entirely ignorant whether heaven can really be obtained by the performance of the sacrifice ; it is only from the text that we know it and there is no other means to verify the statement contained in it. This is what the above Śloka calls *non-existent* because no other means to obtain heaven is known-

Niyama is a restrictive rule. When au injunction lays down one of the नियम modes for doing a thing out of many, it is said to be a Niyama. As for instance " ब्रीहीनवहति " He threshes rice. Rice is threshed by a pestle in a mortar to remove its husk ; husk can be removed from the rice grains by many other means, as for instance, by peeling it off from the rice grains, but the particular mode, that of threshing bas been laid down by the text out of many other modes. This kind of restrictive text is called *niyama.*

परिसंख्या is an implied prohibition. When both the total non-existence and परिसंख्या partial non-existence can be established by any other mode and when one of the two is excluded by the other, the injunction is called *parisankhyâ.* As for instance "पञ्चपञ्चनखाभक्ष्या: " five animals possessing five claws are fit to be eaten. " It is not an अपूर्व विधि because it is not a new thing, for the eating of the animals having five claws is naturally prompted ; it is not a *niyama*, since eating of animals and eating of animals having five claws are both naturally prompted by appetite. It is, therefore, a prohibitory text as to eating of the animals other than those having five claws.

परिसंख्या is of two kinds (1) श्रौती (2) आर्थिकी. The first is directly classification stated by some text " अत्रहृदेव गायंति" " Here only they sing. " In the text, 'only' means excepting पवमान all other songs are excluded. The second is the inferred prohibition as in the above example of " पञ्चपञ्चनखा भक्ष्या: "

The Parisankhyâ has three defects as is mentioned in the following
S'loka :—

कृतार्थस्य परित्यागादकृतार्थप्रकल्पनात् ।
प्राप्तस्य बाधा दित्येवं परिसंख्यात्रिदूषणा ॥

The *Parisankhya* has three defects by reason of losing sight of the
direct sense and putting an inferred interpretation of its own and rejecting
that which is assumed." The meaning of the verse will be clear from the
illustration of "पञ्चपञ्चनखाभक्ष्या: " Here the direct meaning is that the
animals possessed with claws are fit to be eaten ; but परिसंख्या has nothing
to do with it ; it entirely gives a go-by to it. The inferred sense that
the animals other than those possessed with five claws are excluded from
eating is assumed. Lastly the assumption which is rejected is the eating
of animals which are not possessed with five claws.

Let us now proceed to deal with the third kind of the Veda, *viz, Niyama.*

नामधेय   It is a proper noun but has a purpose in defining the matter
enjoined by it. It is of four kinds.

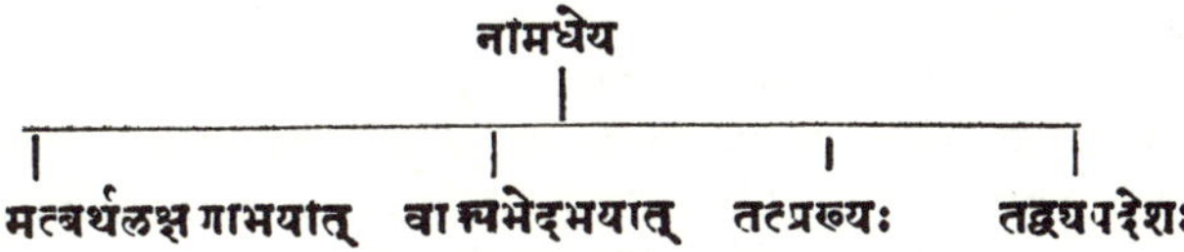

The first is a proper noun arising from the fear of using the मत्वर्थ लक्षणा.
It is a figure of speech in which you resort to the *matup* affix. As for
instance "उद्भिदा यजेत पशुकाम: " Let one perform the Udbhid sacrifice if he
is desirons of cattle. " Here in the above quotation, the *Udbhid* is the
name of a particular sacrifice and is, therefore, a proper noun. If you
resort to the मत्वर्थ लक्षणा, read उद्भिद्वता in place of उद्भिदा and interpret
it as a sacrifice in which the *Udbhid* is used ; it will be an attempt to
convert a simple sentence into two compound sentences or one complex
sentence and you will thereby commit a mistake which is called the
Vâkyabheda or splitting up of a sentence which is a serious mistake
in the eye of a Mîmânsaka.

The second class also consists of a proper noun but it arises from the
fear of the Vâkyabheda or splitting up of a sentence. As in the instance
"चित्रयायजेत पशुकाम:" "Let one disirous of cattle perform Chittrâ sacrifice ;" it can not indicate the material used in the sacrifice as there is
a passage " दधिमधुपयोघृतं धानाउदकं तंडुलास्तत्संबद्ध प्राजापत्यं. " " curd, honey,
milk, ghee, parched grain, water, rice are the mixed offering consecrated
to Prajâpati " If you take चित्रया to mean some subordinate action,
you will commit the mistake of वाक्यभेद which should always be
avoided. The Chittrâ is, therefore, the name of the sacrifice and can

not be considered to be the subordinate materials used, for fear of the split of a sentence.

Tatprakhya is a conventional name given to a particular sacrifice, the तत्प्रख्य description of which is given elsewhere in a separate treatise, as for instance " अग्निहोत्रं जुहोति " " he performs Agnihottra. Agnihottra is a name given to a sacrifice conventionally, the description of which is given elsewhere. As in ordinary language a children's play is called ' blindman's buff ' conventionally.

Tadvyapadeśa is the name given to a sacrifice by reason of its resemblance to another, from which it derives its name. As for instance, श्येनयाग which is performed to destroy one's enemy is called after a hawk, because a sacrificer kills his enemy like a hawk which pounces upon the birds and kills them. In the ordinary language a children's play is called ' duck and drake ' by reason of its resemblance of those birds.

Now we come to describe the 4th class of the Wedic texts called निषेध Niṣedha. It is a negative precept just as Vidhi is a positive or affirmative precept. It is preventing a man from doing a thing which is injurious or disadvantageous to him; as for instance, " नकलंजं भषयेत् " " Do not eat (कलंज) flesh stuck with poisonous arrow. " It is of two kinds (1) पर्य्युदास (2) प्रतिषेध. I can not do better than reproduce the language of Kis'ori Lâl Sarkâr in explaining the difference between पर्य्युदास and प्रतिषेध. " These distinctions resemble that between judgments or rights *in rem* and judgments or rights in *personam*. The former prohibitions are called Pratiṣedha and the latter Paryudâsa. प्रतिषेध is the negative precept of general applicability; as for instance, "नकलंजं भषयेत्" " Do not eat Kalañja. " It means that poisonous flesh should never be eaten. पर्य्युदास is the negative precept applicable to a person when he undertakes to perform a certain rite, as for instance नोदन्तमादित्यमीक्षेतनास्तंयंतं । एतावताहैनसाऽयुक्तो भवति । तस्यव्रतं " " Let him not see the rising and setting sun ; by this he is delivered of his sin: this is a vow ". When a man has taken a vow, then he is bound to observe the negative rule. There is a verse showing the difference between Pratiṣedha and Paryudâsa :—

पर्य्युदासस्सविज्ञेयेायत्रोत्तरपदेन ' नञ् '

प्रतिषेधस्सविज्ञेयः क्रिययास हयत्र 'नञ्' ॥

" When the negative participle is connected with the subsequent clause, it is Paryudâsa and when the negative participle is connected with the verb, it is Pratiṣedha " Take the above illustration नोदन्तमा दित्य बीक्षेत etc., here न (not) is connected with the noun उदन्तं आदित्यं

which is an objective case; it is therefore Paryudâsa. "नकलंजंभक्षयेत्" here न (not) is connected with the verb : it is therefore Pratiṣedha. When the negative precept is of general applicability, it is Pratiṣedha but when it is of special applicability, it is Paryudâsa.

Let us now proceed to the 5th and last division of the Veda. It is Arthavâda.

Passages in praise or blame are called in the terminology of the अर्थवाद Mîmânsâ, Arthavâda. They are either complements of a Vidhi or Niṣedha; as for instance, "वायव्यं श्वेतमालभेत भूतिकामः" because "वायुर्वै क्षेपिष्ठदेवता." " Let one who is desirous of prosperity " sacrifice a white animal to Vâyu because Vâyn is the swiftest of the gods." The first sentence is a Vidhi and the second sentence being in praise of Vâyu is an अर्थवाद.

Then again "बर्हिषि रजतं देयं" " Silver should not be given on the grass" ∴ "सोरोदीद्यदरोदीत्तद्रुद्रस्य रुद्रत्वं" " He wept and because he wept, therefore, there is ferocity in रुद्र. " The first is निषेध and the second sentence is अर्थवाद because it is in dispraise of the god.

Classification]   Arthavada is of three kinds.

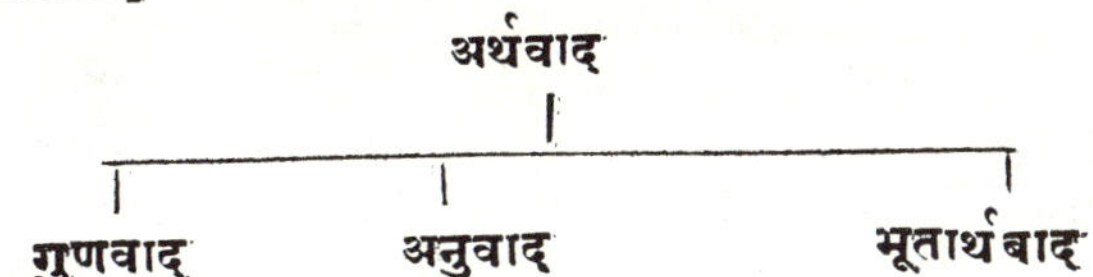

The following Śloka explains the three kinds of Arthavâda.,

विरोधेगुणवादस्यादनुवादोऽवधारिते ।
भूतार्थवादस्तद्धानादर्थवादस्त्रिधामतः ॥

" On contradiction there is Guṇavâda and on comprehension it is Anuvâda and when there is absence of both it is Bhûtârthavâda ; the Arthavâda is said to be of three kinds "

When a text makes a statement which is contradictory to the existing state of the affair and means of proof, it is said to be Guṇavâda as for instance, " आदित्यो यूपः " " The Sun is a sacrificial post. " Here in the present example, we see that the sun cannot be a sacrificial post as it contradicts the sense of perception and against the real state of facts. It is a figure of *hyperbole* meaning that the sacrificial post is as shining as the sun.

When a text makes a statement which is in keeping with the existing अनुवाद state of facts, it is said to be Anuvâda ; as for example, " अग्निर्हिमस्य भेषजं " fire is an antidote of cold." We see in the present example that fire is said to be a protector from cold; it is a fact which we can verify by our senses : so this kind of statement which is quite in keeping with the real state of the facts and can be verified by perception is said to be Anuvâda.

When a text makes a statement which is neither against the existing state of facts nor is it in conformity with it, it is said to be Bhûtârthavâda ; as for instance, " इन्द्रोद्यूत्राय वज् युदयच्छत् " " Indra uplifted his thunderbolt aganist Vrittra. " In this example, we find a statement which is neither aganist the existing facts nor is it provable by perception. It is, therefore, a statement of facts which happened in the past and is called Bhûtârthavâda.

भूतार्थवाद

Having digressed so far, let me come back to the subject of the divinity of the Vedas. In the first Pâda, the author established the divine origin of the Vedas. Now in the second Pâda, he establishes their infallibility and utility. The objector in the opening of the Pâla raises six objections to the authority of the Vedas. (I) He says that the Veda having promised heaven by means of sacrifices, it is ritualistic and anything over and above that is redundant and is, therefore, unauthoritative, as for examples " सोअरो दीत्, यदरोदीत्, तद्‌ दस्यरप्ररस्य T. S. I. 5. 1. प्रजापतिरात्मनोबपाशुदकिषदत् " T. S. II. I. I. He wept, because he wept therefore the ferocity of Rudra " " Lord of the universe removed his own omentum. ' These and similar other passages which we find in the Vedas are, therefore, of no authority.

Infallibility of the Vedas

Objection

(1). There are many things which cannot be verified by the scripture and the sensuous perception ; as for instance " स्तेनं मन: " " अनृतवादिनीवाक् " " The mind is a thief " " The tongue is a teller of lies. " " तस्माद्धूमएवाग्ने दिवादद्दृशे । तस्मादग्निदूं रानक्तं दद्दृशे " T. B. II. 1. 2. " Therefore only smoke was seen by day ; therefore fire only was seen from a distance at night. " " न चैतद्विद्भोबवं ब्राह्मणवास्म अब्राम्हणा वा " " We do not know whether we are Brâhmaṇas or not Brâhmaṇas. " Such passages are from their very nature false and the Veda which contains them cannot be authoritative.

3. The result promised by the Vedic texts does not follow as a matter of course ; as for instance " योभवतेऽस्वमुखंवयएवं वेद " " आस्रव प्रजावांवाजीबाववेद एवंवेद. " T. S. I. 7. 4. 6. ' He who knows this has a strong man amongst his descendants " These passages which promise fruits which are not realised are untrue and detract from the authority of the Veda which contains them.

4. There are passages in the Vedas which hold out promises of every thing and there is, therefore, no necessity for the performance of any

other act to achieve the desire ; as, for instance, "सर्वं वै पूर्णाहुतिः । सर्वमेवाप्नोति"
T. B. III. 8. 10, " The final oblation is all ; he obtains everything. "
" पशुबंधयाजी सर्वांल्लोकानभिजयति, तरति मृत्युं तरति ब्रह्महत्यां, योऽश्वमेधेनयजते, य उचैन
मेवं वेद. " " An animal sacrificer conquers all the worlds : he who performs
a sacrifice by means of an अश्वमेध, surpasses death, gets over Brahmicide
and he also who knows this. " If the passages are true, the result is
that one should do no other thing but to resort to the ceremonies to
achieve the desire. Such absurd hopes created by the above passages
detract from the authority and infallibilty of the Veda.

5. There are passages in the Veda which prohibit the impossible
performance of things ; as for instance, "ब्रह्मवादिनो वदंति न पृथिव्यां नांतरिक्षे न
दिव्यग्निश्चेतव्यः :" T. S. V. 2. 7. 1 " The Brahmavâdis say, the fire
should not be piled on the earth. in the sky or in the heavens. " What
is the use of such prohibitions ? Piling of fire in the sky is an impossibility. You do not require any authority for such impossible peformance.

6. There is a mention of the names in the Vedas, of persons who
were mortals; they cannot therfore, be considered eternal. There are
six objections made by the objector. The author proceeds to reply all

Reply of them *seriatim* ; he says generally they are *Arthavâdas* or compliments to the *Vidhis*. It is useless to repeat
the reply ; the reader of these pages will find it from 7 sûtra onwards
to the end of the 1st Adhikaraṇa..

In the 2nd Adhikaraṇa, the author describes Nigadas, the mantras

निगद of Yajurveda which are prononnced aloud and which
are in the nature ot injunction. In the 3rd Adhikaraṇa.
he describes those *Nigadas* which are in the nature of Arthavâda

The author proceeds to deal with the practical ulility of the Vedas

Utility of the in the 4th Adhikaraṇa. This subject is very important
Vedas and most probably borrowed from Yâska's Nirukta.
The objector asks " Do the Vedic mantras convey any
meaning"? They do not, according to the objector because they stand in
interpretation as to their practical appliciability to other works, His
second objection is that there is a complicated system of orthoepy and
grammar without which the Vedas cannot be learnt ; so it is useless to
learn them. The third objection is that they teach the very things which
we already know; their study is, therefore, unnecessary. The fourth

Objections. objection is that there are passages relating to the non-
existing thing as for example.

चत्वारिश्टङ्कात्रयोऽस्य पादाद्वेशीर्षेसप्तहस्तासो अस्य ।

त्रिधाबद्धोवृषभोरोरवीति महादेवो मत्यां आविवेश ॥ ऋ० वे० ४. ५. ८. ३.

"It has 4 horns, it has 4 feet, two heads, it has 7 hands ; the bull being tied three fold cries : the great god entered amongst the mortals." * Where is such a creature as described above in existence in nature ? It is, therefore, useless to study the Veda which contains such passages.

5. We find further that there are passages which contain an address to the inanimate objects as if they are objects possessed with life.

6. There are self-contradictory passages in the Vedas.

7. The Vedas are learnt by *rote* without knowing their meaning like a parrot This fact also shows that they have no meaning and they are useless.

8. There are many words in the Vedas the meaning of which is not known as जर्भरी and तुर्भरी

9. We find in the Vedas, the names of the mortals.

For all those reasons, the critic concludes that the Vedas are worthless and meaningless. The author proceeds to reply the objections in the

Reply.

following way ; he says that the Vedic words have a significance just as you have in the ordinary language. There are the subject, predicate and object in the Vedic sentences under the rules of grammar as it happens in the common spoken language. The repetition of the thing already known is by way of गुणवाद, परिसंख्या or अर्थवाद. Further the reading of the Vedic mantras according to the rules of orthoepy and grammar produces an Apûrva or invisible effect. The vedic *mantras* which give information of the things already known is with a view to produce invisible effect; as for instance the religious commands (प्रैष) communicated to the priests. As for the description of the bull which you say is non-existent, it is based on your ignorance. The sacrifice is compared with a bull by reason of its producing the desired effect ; it has four horns in the form of four kinds of priests; its three feet are the three libations (Savanas) ; the sacrificer and his wife are the two heads ; the chhandas are the seven hands. Being tied up by the three vedas, *viz*, the Rik, Yajus and Sâma, it resounds with the roaring sound uttered by the priests ; this great god in the form of the sacrifice is amidst the mortals. This is how Śabara has explained the Vedic verse ; but in this connection Sâyana, Patâñjali, and Yâska are also to be consulted. As to the self-contradictory passages which you find in the Vedas " आदितिर्द्यौरदितिरंतरिक्षं " यजु० वे० २५।।२३. "Aditi' is sky and Aditi is the intervening space " " एकोरुद्रो न द्वितीयोऽवतस्थे ' वै० सं० १. ८. ६. " There is only one Rudra and there is not the second

---

* This verse is very ably explained by Yâska in his Nirukta ; Patañjal in his Mahabhâṣya and Sâyaṇa in his commentary.

in existence " " असंख्याताः सहस्राणि येरुद्रा अधिभूस्वाम् " तै॰ सं॰ ४ । ५ । १३.
There are innumerable thousands of Rudras who are on the earth."

The reply is that there is no contradiction ; it is a description of a quality, as we address god " त्वमेवमाता च पिता त्वमेव " "Thou art mother thou art father also. " There is no doubt that the Veda is learnt by rote without learning the meaning for the simple reason that the performance of the sacrifice where the Mantras are recited has no connection with the meaning. If we do not know the meaning of the words, it is due to our ignorance ; जर्फरी and तुर्फरी are the names of Aświnas. These words occur in the following verse of the Rigveda : —

सृएवेव्रजर्भरी तुर्फरीतूनैतोशेव तुफरो पर्फरीका ।

उद्न्यजेव्रजेमनांमदेरूता मेजराव्त्रजरभरायु ॥

ऋ॰ वे॰ मं॰ १० सू॰ १०६. मं॰ ६.

" Let those two sons of the killer, the protectors, the killers, the accomplishers of desire, transparent like water, victorious and proud of their strength like two mad elephants make my mortal body immortal. " Then again तुर्फरी occurs in Mantra 8. These words mean 'killer' and 'protector' and are the names of the two As'winas. See its commentary by Yâska in his Nirukta in the Paris'ista I. 5. As to the address to the in animate objects, it can be explained on the principle of कैमुतिक न्याय as in I. 1. 32. As to the mention of non-eternal things in the Vedas, see Sûtra 30 of the 1st Pâda.

The author concludes that the Vedic Mantras and words have a meaning is further proved from the facts that some of the Mantras are called after the deity in whose honor they are addressed, that they are adapted by change of number and gender according to the circumstances of the case under the principle of Uha and lastly that the injunction contained therein will be of no meaning if there is no sense in them.

Pâda 3

The author having established the divine origin and the infallible authority of the Vedas, proceeds to deal with the non-Vedas.
स्मृति If the Vedas are of infallible authority then the non-veda according to the objector is of no authority. The author says that the Smritis which are the works of the Riṣis are authoritative because they are based on the Vedas. Every text of the Smriti is supported by a Vedic text ; if there is none available, the presumption is that the Vedic text supporting it, is lost provided there be no Vedic text against it. If there be any contradiction between a Vedic text and a text of a Smriti, the former prevails over the latter. If a Smriti text is based on a selfish motive it will be not binding as for instance taking of cloth by अध्वर्यु after वैसर्जन होम.

There are certain practices such as sipping of water. taking of bath and putting on the sacred thread etc. which are not found in the Vedas; but as they are not based on any selfish motive they may be accepted as authorities for our guidance. The words which are used in the non-Vedas should be taken in the sense in which they are used in the Vedas ; foreign words should be used in the sense in which they are used in the foreign language.

The author now proceeds to discuss the authority of the Kalpa Sûtras कल्पसूत्र   he says that they are not authority in themselves but derive it from the Vedas. They are authority, if they are in conformity with them.

The local customs or family customs are also authoritative in the particular locality or family where they are prevalent from time immemorial. The author bases this Adhikaraṇa, Local and family customs on the *Holi* festival, which he says was prevalent in the eastern country at the time when he flourished. Migration does not effect it.

The word of the Veda is an authority ; the next question which arises is, what is about the corrupt form of the Vedic or Sanskrit words? The author says that the corrupt forms of Sanskrit words are due to mispronunciation by reason of the difference of the countries, education and mode of living ; but as they can be corrected by the rules of orthoepy and grammar they convey the same sense as they do in the original Sanskrit. The author thinks Sanskrit to be the parent language of all the languages of the world.

The terms that convey concepts denote individuals directly and connot the quality which they possess. As for example 'Man' the word is applicable to each individual of the class 'man' ; it is called denotation in Logic, the quality of What do words convey ? 'being a man' is its connotation. The class 'man' to which John, Peter, Luke and Mathews belong is the genus (जाति) ; the individuals of which the class is made is called species (Vyakti). The form or figure of the individual by which you recognise the species or the individuals is the आकृति (figure or form). As soon as the term 'man' is uttered you have the figure of the man either 'tall' or 'small' &c. You cannot concieve a man in abstract. Now the question is whether a word denotes a form or not ; the reply of of our author in the last Adhikarana after a long discussion is embodied in the Sûtras 33 and 35 and is to the effect that it is a form.

In Gotam's Logic there is also a discussion about the denotation of a word in chap II. sec II. 56-66. The author after discussing the different views on the subject expresses his own view in Sûtra 63 that words convey genus, species and form. When the word 'cow' is uttered, you have the form of a quadruped having four feet, two horns and a tail ; you also know that it belongs to the genus of 'bovine animal' and thirdly you know the *differentia* by which it is distinguished from other species belonging to the same genus.

In the Vaisesika, we have सामान्य for genus and विशेष for species.

PÂDA 4.

The subject treated in the present Pâda properly belongs to grammar. In order to explain it, I may invite the reader's attention to the division of words indicating names according to our present grammar.

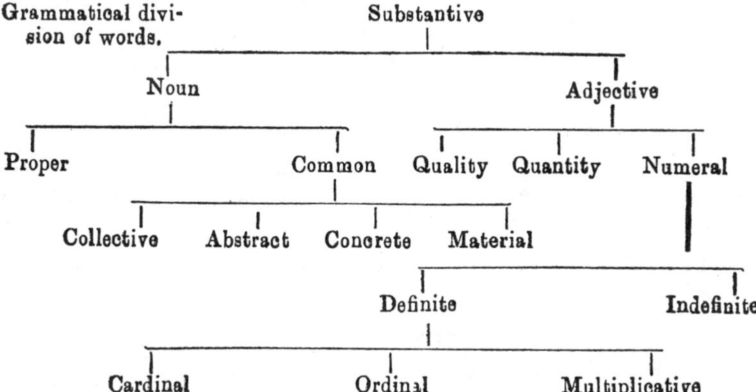

Any elementary grammar will explain the above table.

I may now proceed to explain the words meaning name according to the Sanskrit Grammarians. They are of 3 kinds. (2) रूढि (2) यौगिक (3) योगरूढि.

Device of word

A Rudhi is a root word which is not made up of any other word; it has a conventional meaning attached to it which we learn from our predecessor or preceptor. It has the inherent power to convey a sense.

रूढि

A Yaugika is a derivative word which is made up of two or three words. It is a compound word and is used in the sense conveyed by the component parts of which it is made ; as for instance राजपुरुष.

यौगिक

योगरूढि is a compound word but it has conventional sense attached to it; as गुडाकेश, हृषीकेश, पङ्कज, अलज, कमल.

योगरूढि

After clearing the ground for understanding the present subject under consideration, I must now explain नामधेय or कर्मनामधेय which is the subject of the present Pâda.

नामधेय is a proper-noun; it may be either रूढि or योगरूढि. when it is a name of an action in which certain material is used after which it is called, it is a case of वैयधिकरण as for instance let us "play at bat and ball." It is the name of a play in which bat and ball are used as a means of play. When an action is arbitrarily called

वैयधिकरण

सामानाधिकरण   by a certain name and the name is identical with the
action, it is a case of सामानाधिकरण, as for instance let us
"play blind man's buff." The former is also called भण्वर्मसिन्धया and does
not come under नामधेय or कर्म नामधेय; the latter is an example of नामधेय.
The author says that उद्भिद्युाग, चित्रायाग are नामधेयs; the former is a रूढि and
the latter is यागरूढि The author then explains तत्प्रख्य and तद्व्यपदेश the two
classes of नामधेय with examples. I have already explained them and they
do not require any further elucidation.

वाजपेय is also a proper name or यागरूढि It is, therfore, a कर्मनामधेय.

आग्नेय, बर्हि, आग्य, प्रोक्षणी, निमिंथ्य are common nouns ; they are not
कर्म नामधेय, while वैश्वदेव though a compound word, is यागरूढि and is a
कर्मनामधेय It is a sacrifice.

अर्थवाद] The author having explained कर्मनामधेय by illustration proceeds to
explain अर्थवाद by illustration.

विन्दते प्रजां वैश्वानरं द्वादशकपालं निर्वपेत् पुत्रे जातेयदष्टाकपालोभवति
गायत्रियैवैनं ब्रह्मवर्चसेन पुनाति यन्नवकपालस्त्रिवृतैवास्मिन् तेजोदधाति
यद्दशकपालोविराजैवास्मिन्नन्नाद्यं दधातियदेकादशकपाल त्रिष्टुभैवास्मिन्नि
न्द्रियंदधातियद्द्वादशकपालोजगत्यैनास्मिन् पशून् दधाति यस्मिन जातएतमिष्टि
निर्वपति पूतः ॥ T. S. II. 2. 5. 3.

" He obtains offspring ; let him offer cakes baked on twelve pans on
the birth of a son. If he offers eight cakes baked on twelve pans, he puri-
fies him with the Gâyattri metre and the Brâhmaṇik glory. If
he offers nine cakes baked on pans he puts splendour in him with
Trivrit songs. If he offers cakes baked on pans he puts eatable food
in him, with Virâja. If he offers cakes baked on eleven pans, he puts
sensory and motor organs in him with Triṣṭubh. It he offers cakes
baked on twelve pans, he places cattle in him with Jagatî. On his
birth he performs the oblation and becomes purified." The question is
whether the subsequent details of the cakes after having laid down
Dvâdas'â kapâlas nullify the Vidhi. The author says that the Vidhi
contained in the opening passage is not nullified but the details that
follow it are in the nature of explanation and are Arthavâdas. Take
for instance "Feed twelve cows ; feed 7 cows with grass and the rest
with husk." The number in the above passages is subordinate. This is
वैश्वा नर न्याय   called वैश्वानर न्याय which is fully explained in Adhikaraṇa XI and sûtras 17-22.

The Arthavâda is a praise of an individual by enlargement as "यजमानः
अश्वतरः" T. S. III. 3. 9. 3. "यजमानो वा एककपालः" T. S. I. 6. 3. 4.

"A sacrificer is a handful of grass." "A sacrificer is a cake based on a pan." It is a figure of speech. "John is a lion" meaning John is as brave as a lion.

2, It is a praise of a species as " आग्नेयो वैब्राह्मण: " T. B. II. 7. 3. 1. " ऐन्द्रो वै राजन्य: " T. S. II. 4. 13. 1. वैश्व देवादि वैश्य: " A Brâhmaṇa belongs to Agni " " A warrior pertains to Indra" " A Vais'ya belongs to विश्वेदेवा " It is also a figure of speech in praise of a class ; " the cat is a domestic lion " meaning thereby that the cat (belongs to the lionine species.

3. The Arthavâda arises by resemblance ; as " आदित्यो यूप: " T. B. II. 1. 5. 2. " The sun is a sacrificial post " It means that the sacrificial post is brilliant like the sun. It is a metaphor.

4, The Arthavâda arises by dispraising others as " अपशवोवा अन्ये गो अश्वेभ्य: T. S. V. 2. 9. 4. All others are no animals excepting the cow and the horse. " " अवगो वा एषयोत्सामा " T. S. I. 5. 7. 1. " It is no sacrifice where no psalm is sung " " अससंवा एतद्यददशोमन् " T.S.V II. 3. 8. 1. " It is not a sacrificial session where there is no दशम (extraction of soma juice on the 10th, 11th and 12th days) " It is in praise of one by dispraising others which is incidental. A curious reader can accumulate many similar examples; "It is not an assembly where there are no elderly men. " It is in praise of the elderly men.

The Arthavâda as we have seen is either an adjective or an adjectival clause ; the author says that sometimes nouns are also Arthavâdas. Take for instance the Srishti and the Prâṇabhṛit.

The Srishti is the name of a particular brick and is a proper noun but वृि as the Srishtis abound in the Agnichayana so all bricks came to be called the Srishtis. Take the example of Pandit, Seth and Thâkur. Thâkur originally applies to a warrior class but is also applicable to every landlord irrespective of caste.

The Prâṇabhṛit is also a name of a brick on which the Prâṇabhṛit verse is recited but other verses are also recited on other bricks which are also called मारुत. The मारुत therefore came to mean ' bricks of a certain class '. An umbrella bearer or the 'chhâtrin' is called a pilgrim; but some of the pilgrims do not carry umbrella but the term 'Chhâttrin' in spite of this fact, is applicable to them. Certain person by name Lynch was stoned to death by a furious mob without a trial ; now the word is used for punishing a man without trial. Boycott is another word ; Captain Boycott was shut out from all social intercourse ; now it is used generally for shutting out any person from the social intercourse. According to our author, they all come under Arthavâda.

xxxvi.

The author proceeds to discuss the principle of ellipsis, the Vâkyas'eṣa ;
Ellipsis   it is very well explained at p. 41. When the meaning
of a sentence or a clause of a sentence can be understood
by reading it with another it is called the Vâkyas'eṣa or ellipsis. As for
example, "Coachman, I am going out for a drive, bring me............"
Here the speaker means a conveyance.

Sometimes you have to fill up the ellipsis from the sense in a sentence
without the aid of any other sentence or clause. "He ate on a mat "
meaning thereby that he sat on a mat and took his food there. " He ate
in a glass plate. " He took his food in a plate which was made of glass.
Conversion of a simple sentence into a compound or a complex sentence
comes under the purview of Sûtra 30. The Vâkyas'eṣa or ellipsis of both
kinds is an Arthavâda when it is a complement of any Vidhi or Niṣedha.

CHAPTER II.

Pâda 1.

The author has explained the substantive i.e. the noun and adjective
Verb   in the preceding chapter. They alone do not convey the
intention of the speaker but require the assistance of a verb.
A verb denotes existence or action. We have nothing to do with the
verbs denoting 'being' or 'existence' in the Mîmânsâ ; we have to deal
with those verbs which denote 'doing' or ' action. ' They instigate one to
perform certain acts.

The actions are of two kinds either principal (प्रधान) or subordinate(गुण.)
When the object of an action is to produce invisible effect called
Principal   the Apûrva in the Mîmânsâ as for instance the attainment
of heaven, it is called principal ; but when the object is to
Subordinate   produce visible effect as some operation on the material, it is called subordinate. The kindling of fire, preparing of cakes and pounding and threshing of rice come under the
latter category, as the result of the various action is visible. The materials to be operated upon are in the accusative case.

The performance of the Sandhyâ, the reading of the Prayâja mantras
and repeating of prose and poetry (गद्य and स्तुत) at the time of performance of the sacrifice, come under the principal action, their object
being to produce some invisible effect (अपूर्व).

The vedic Mantras, the reading of which produces invisible effect
Division of the Veda.   naturally lead one to know what the veda is ;
it is two kinds.

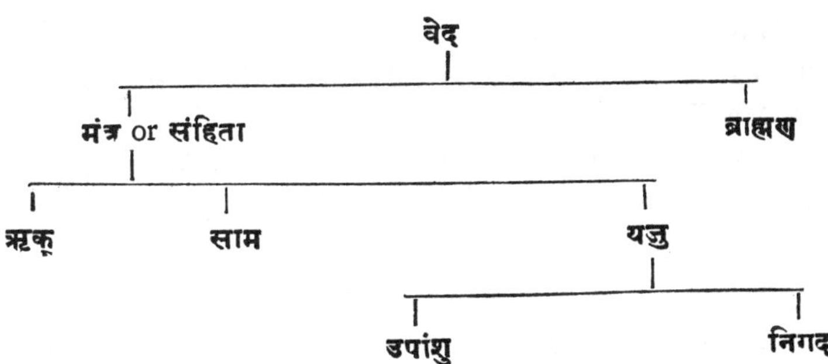

The commandatory portion of the Veda is the Mantra, but that portion which contains reason, explanation, censure, praise, doubt, command, action of a single individual or of many, taking the words in a different sense and comparison is Brâhmaṇa. It is explained in the following Ślokas.

मंत्र

ब्राह्मण

हैतुर्निर्वचनं निंदा प्रशंशा संशयाविधिः ।

परक्रियापुराकलपो व्यवधारणकल्पना ॥

उपमानंदशौतेतुविध्यो ब्राह्मणस्यतु ।

एतद्वै सर्वं वेदेषुनियतं विधिलक्षणम् ॥

1. हेतु reason ; as for instance " शूर्पे ण जुहोति तेनह्यन्नं क्रियते " " he makes an offering with a winnowing basket, because by it corn is sifted. "

2. निर्वचन explanation ; as for instance " तद्दध्नोदधित्वं " " Therefore curd is so called. "

3. निंदा Censure ; as for instance " योघमन्नं बिंदते अप्रचेता " " An unmindful person gets useless food. "

4. प्रशंसा praise ; as for instance " वायुवै क्षेपिष्टा " " वायु is swiftest of all. "

5. संशय doubt ; as for instance " होतव्यं गार्हपत्ये न होतव्यम् " "Whether it should be offered in the domestic fire or not. "

6. विधि is a command, as for instance " kindle fire. "

7. परक्रिया is the action of one individual.

8. पुराकल्प is the action of many individuals or a nation. These are the historical descriptions of one individual or many individuals and are indicated by the particles ' इति ' ' आह ' or ' ह '.

9. व्यवधारणकल्पना; when a word or a sentence means one thing but taking the surrounding circumstances into consideration, it means another, it is said to be its imagined sense ' as for instance वावदोश्वान् प्रतिगृह्णीयात् " " Let him take as many horses " meaning thereby " let him be given…....................."

xxxviii.

10. उपमान is comparison.

All these ten characteristics, says Śabara, belong to the Brâhmaṇa portion of the Veda.

The difference between Mantra and a Brâhmaṇa is better explained

Difference between मंत्र and ब्राह्मण

by the use of a legal terminology. The former is the substantive law; it is a collection of hymns which are in the nature of " chodanâ " and therefore regulate, define and create a right. The latter is what is called adjective law; it lays down *inter alia* a procedure for performance of sacrifices. It is, therefore, a ritualitic portion of the Veda full of the directions and method for the application of the hymns of the Veda.

The Mantra or Sanhitâ is of three kinds. The Rigveda is a collection

Division of the Mantra

of the verses which have metrical arrangement to convey meaning. The Sâma is a collection of those verses which are sung at the end of a sacrifice. The Yajuṣ has neither metrical arrangement nor are its verses sung. It is of

Division of yajuṣ

two kinds. The first kind embraces all those verses which are read slowly and silently and second are those which are pronounced aloud and are celled Nigada.

The author after explaining the ' Veda ' proceeds to explain a sentence

Sentence.

Simple.

Complex.

in which there is a subject, predicate and an object; such a sentence is called a simple sentence; but when there are several sentences depending for the sense on one other, it is a complex sentence.

On the other hand when there is a sentence consisting of two or more

Compound

independent sentences or clauses having no reciprocity of meaning, it is a compound sentence. Such a sentence comes under the prohibition of the Vâkyabheda or splitting up of the unity of a sentence.

The author explains the Anuṣanga (see at p. p. 54. 55). Kisorî Lâl

अनुषग

Sirkâr explains it as follows " where there is a number of incomplete clauses followed by one which is completed by a finite verbal clause, this last should be read at the end of each of the other clauses to make them complete. "

Take for example the verse quoted from the T. S. at p. 55.

" यातेअग्नेऽयाशयारजाशया हराशया

तनूवर्षिष्ठा गह्रेष्ठोऽम्वचो अपावधीं त्वेषं वचो अपावधीं श्श्वाहा ॥ "

" That body of thine, O ! Agni, which is made of iron, made of silver, made of gold is oldest and untouchable. I have killed the harsh tongue, I have killed the ferocious tongue : hail. "

In the above passage, there are three different sentences (1) That body of thine, O ! Agni, which is made of iron. (2). That body of thine, O ! Agni, which is made of silver. (3). That body of thine, O ! Agni, which is made of gold. To save the repetition of the noun body, the adjectival clauses or adjuncts are placed before the noun.

Take another example from the T. S.

" चित्पतिस्त्वापुनातु बाक्पतिस्त्वा पुनातु देवस्त्वा सविता पुना त्वच्छिद्रेण पवित्रेण वसोः सूर्यस्य रश्मिभिः " T. S. I, 2, 1, 2.

" Let the lord of mind purify thee, let the lord of tongue purify thee let the god sun purify thee with the holeless purifier (grass), with the rays of the sun, the source of life. "

There are three sentences in each ? of which the instrumental case will be repeated ; as " Let the lord of mind purify thee with the holeless purifier (grass) with the rays of the sun the source of life. " The same instrumental case will be repeated in the 2nd and the third (sentences.

When a phrase or a word breaks in the continuity of a sentence the principle of अनुषंग does not apply. As for instance, " संते प्राखो वायुना गच्छखां खंवज्ञत्रैरङ्गानि खं यज्ञपति राधिषा " T. S. I. 3. 8. 1.

" Let thy vital air unite with the air, let thy bodily|parts with the sacrifice, let the sacrificer with the hopes. "

The verbs in · the above three sentences are in different numbers ; so the principle of the Anuṣanga does not apply. It is a case of ellipses or the Vâkyas 'eṣa (see at P. 41.)

PÂDA 2.

To understand the subject of the preent Pâda, it is necessay to explain
<table><tr><td rowspan="2">Agnihotra explained.</td><td>Agnihotra. It was an offiring made to fire, the living and domestic god. This ceremony was performed morning and evening by every one after the initiation</td></tr></table>
with the sacred thre ad. Se ats made of Kus'â grass were made for sitting sacrificial fuel called Samit was brought from the jungle. The holy fire
<table><tr><td rowspan="2">Three kinds of fire</td><td>was kindled. The fire was of three kinds (1) गार्हपत्य domestic fire (2) आहवनीय fire which was produced by rubbing two pieces of wood on great sacrificial occasions</td></tr></table>
and (3) दक्षिणाग्नि the fire which was taken with the dead body for cremation ceremony. It was the duty of every one to preserve the Gârhapatya fire ; it was the duty of the master of the house to preserve it ; its extingnishment was considered ominous.

Rice was the staple food and cows constituted the wealth of the people. For the purpose of feeding the fire rice cakes were prepared and butter was extracted from milk.

The rice from which the Purodâs'a or cake was prepared was set apart and consecrated ; it was called निर्वप It was cleansed पुरोडाश and pounded with a muller ; the flour thus prepared was kneaded into balls or cakes. Potsherds or pieces of a broken pot called the Kapâlâs were arranged in a circular form as shown in the figure 3 (Frontispieca).

They were put on the burning fire in tne अष्टाकपाल offering when this earthen pan formed from the broken pieces of a कपाल pot or pots becomes sufficieatly hot, the cakcs or balls were put on it in the form of a tortoise. When the cake was sufficiently bâkad, it was put into a vessel and cut iuto pieces called Avadâna A current of ghee was poured on the pieces ; it is called Âghâra This is the way in which the Puroḍâṣa was prepared. The Kapâla is so called becanse it resembles the upper part of the human skull. The different pieces of broken pots are joined together like the skull by the sutures. The circle in the above said figure is of a diameter of six angulas. The circle is divided into three segments by drawing across two parallel lines at a distance of two angulas making the northern and southern segments equal. The middle portion is divided into three parts, the first one is in the middle, the second in the last and the third in the west of the central segment. The fourth one comes in the southern segment exactly to the south of the central square ; if the remaning Kapâlâs are of even numbers, they are equally divided into the northern and southern segments starting from the last in the southern segment and ending in the northern segment in the last, thus the southern segment having one in excess of the northern segment. If the remainder after the assignment is odd, the one Kapâla that will be in excess shall be allotted to the southern segment which shall in that case have two Kapâlâs more than the northern segment.

When one Kapâla is required, it is of the size of man's hand ; but when two are required, the circle is divided into two parts by drawing an inaginary line from south to north. When three Kapâlâs are required, the circle is divided into three parts by drawing imaginary lines from south to north. When four Kapâlâs are required you have to divide the circle into two equal parts by drawing a diameter from east to west. The southern semicircle is divided into three parts ; and the northern circle remains intact ; but if the Kapâlas required are five, the northern semicircle is then divided into two parts. thus making up the number five. These

Kapâlâs or broken pieces of the pots are joined together by rubbing their edges so as to make them resemble a skull, the constituent bones of which are joined together by sutures. The cake is made in the shape of a tortoise and is baked on ths convex side of the potsherds as mentioned above.

Milk was heated and was converted into curd by throwing some curl in it. The curd was churned and butter was extracted from it. The butter thus extracted was heated and thus clarified butter or ghee was prepared.

First of all, 5 offerings of ghee were poured in the fire by means of a ladle ; these offerings are called Pañchaprayâjas or Âjyabhâgas. Then pieces of the Puroḍâs'a were offered to अग्नि, विष्णु अग्नीषोम and इन्द्रवैधृव being the chief gods of the Dars'a Pûrṇamâsayâgas. After this, ghee was poured in the fire in honour of the Vis'vedevas ; this offering of ghee was called the Sviṣṭakrit. Then three offerings of ghee called the Anuyâjas were made to the fire. After the Anuyâjas being over, the Sûktavâk and Sanyuvâk from the Rig Veda were recited.

पञ्चप्रयाज or आज्य भाग.

स्विष्टकृत

अनुयाज

सूक्तवाक

There was a pardâ or curtain drawn between the place where there was the Gârhapatye altar and the Patnî Samyâja where the household females used to sit. The eight offerings of ghee with the Svâhâ were made in honour of the goddesses, the wives of the gods. The last ceremony was called the Patnî Samyâja.

पत्नी संयाज

We have seen how the main act is composed of the subordinate parts ; the question is whether the subordinate acts also lead to the Apurva or not. This important question is for a solution in the present Pâda.

Subordinate acts that produce the Apûrva.

The author has explained the difference between the principal act and the subordinate act in the previous Pâda ; but there are some subordinate acts though not principal yet produce invisible effect or the Apûrva He proceeds to lay down certain principles for guidance.

The verb in a sentence plays an important part in determining the Apûrva. When there are different verbs, they denote different actions and thereby so many Apûrvas, as for instance, यजति, ददाति and जुहोति Sacrifice, gift and homa which are meant by the verbs are virtuous acts in themselves and produce different Apûrvas.

Importance of the verb.

Many verbs denote many independent actions.

When there is one verb but there are different acts, they will have

A verb or a repetition of it, sometimes denotes several acts.

different Apûrvas and they, therefore, constitute independent acts; as for instance " समिधो यजति तन्नूनपातंयजति " "इडोयजति; वर्हिं यंजति स्वाहाकारंयजति " T. S., II. 6. 1. 1. 2.

" He offers sacrificial fuel ; he offers to the Tanûnapât fire ; he offers Idâ ; he offers sacrificial grass ; he offers Svâhâ " The repetition of the same verb in the above quotation shows that there are different Apûrvas involved in the different acts.

The author now proceeds to examine all those acts which are संभिपत्येप

संनिपत्येप कारक

कारक i. e. those acts which are not independent and have no Apûrva of their own but lead to the Apûrva of the principal. Take for instance a full moon sacrifice ;

Different subordinate acts under one principal.

there are different texts which describe the different parts of Pûrnamâsayâga. " यदाग्नेयोऽष्टा- कपालोऽभावस्वायां पौर्णमास्यां चाच्युतोभवति "

T. S. II. 6. 3. 3.

" आधार माधारयति " T. S. II. 5. 11. 6. आज्य भागौ यजति , स्विष्टकृते सभवदति पत्नी संयाजान् यजति समिष्ट यजुु होति " य एवं विद्वान् पूर्णमासीं यजते T. S., I. 6. 9.. 1. " य एवं विद्वान मावस्यां यजते " T. S., I. 6. 9. 2.

" The cake baked on eight pans consecrated to Agni on the new and full moon days, becomes permanent. He !sprinkles ghee. He offers two ghee oblations. He makes an offering called the Svistakrit. He performs the Patnîsamyâja. He offers समिष्टयजु. He knowing this makes a sacrifice called full moon. He knowing this makes a sacrifice called new moon. " These are different texts scattered at different places but they deal with one subject of the sacrifice having the materials, deities and मंत्र They therefore constitute one complete sentence. These subordinate acts mentioned

पूर्णमासी याग

above are not independent acts but depend upon one पूर्णमासी याग and therefore lead to one principal Apûrva.

The upâms'uyâga is an independent act because there are no scattered

Upâms'uyâga.

texts about it ; similarly the Âghâra and the Agnihottra are independent acts. The Somayâga and the Pas'uyâga are independent sacrifices though .they are called after the materials used therein.

The acts are sometimes independent by reason of enumeration, as for

ब्राजपेव

instance, the Vâjapeya where seventeen animals are killed.

वाजपेयेन स्वाराज्यकामो यजेत । सप्तदश प्राजापत्यान् पशूनालभते ।
सप्तदशोवै प्रजापति: । प्रजापतेराप्त्यै । श्यामा स्तूपरा एक रूपा । भवंति ।
एवमेवहि प्रजापति: समृद्ध्यै ॥" T. B., 1. 3. 4. 3-4.

One who is desirous of the sovereignty of heaven, shall perform
Vâpapeya ; let him kill seventeen animals consecrated to Prajâpati. The
Prajâpati sacrifice has seventeen animals to obtain the sovereignty of the
universe. They are black hornless and of one form. This is the lord of
the universe for prosperity.

The enumeration of seventeen animals of the Prâjâpatya sacrifice
in the Vâjapeya makes these acts independent. This is an example of
the numeral adjective used before the noun.

When different nouns are used in connection with any sacrifice, they

Different nouns denoting one act.
mean different independent acts ; as for instance
" अथैष ज्योति रथैष विश्वज्योति रथैषसर्वज्योतिरेतेन
सहस्र दक्षिणेन यजेत." It is ज्योति, it is विश्व ज्योति, सर्व
ज्योति ; one should perform a sacrifice with it in which the fee is of
a thousand " Here different nouns used indicate different independent
acts.

When there is a compound sentence and the acts are for different
deities, the acts are independent, as for instance, Âmîkṣâ dish for the
Vis'vedevâs and whey for the strong. See at p. 63.

When on the other hand the compound sentence denotes one act, it is

Two coordinate sentences denote one act.
one independent act though there be two or
more coordinate sentences ; as for instance अग्नि होत्र
"ंजुहोति, द्रध्ना जुहोति." " He performs Agnihottra, he offers curd." The two sentences des-
cribe one act ; the first sentence is Utpattividhi while the second sentence
is Guṇavidhi.

When the sentence is a complex sentence in which the subordinate

Complex sentence denoting one act.
depends upon the principal, the action is one
and independent ; as for instance, " अग्नि होत्रं
जुहुयात् स्वर्गकाम: " " दध्नेन्द्रियकामस्यजुहुयात् "
" Let one desirous of heaven perform Agnihottra. Let one who is desirous
of the strength of the sense organs perform a sacrifice ". Both sentences
taken together constitute one complex sentence and denote one independent act in which curd is offered (see at p. 64).

When in two or more coordinate sentences, the fruits and actions, are

Coordinate sentences denoting several acts.
described, they denote two or more independent acts ; as for instance.

त्रिबृद्ग्निष्ट दग्निष्टोम स्तस्य वायव्यसु एकविशमग्निष्टोम सामङ्कत्वा ब्रह्मवर्चसकामो यजेत ” ॥ ‘एतस्यैव रेवतीषुवारवतीयमग्निष्टोम सामङ्कत्वा पशुकामोह्योतेन यजेते ” ॥

" Agnistoma has Agnistut repeated thrice ; let one who is desirous of Brahmanic glory perform a sacrifice by making twenty one Agnistoma songs of it in honour of Vâyu." " Let one desirous of cattle perform a sacrifice by making a वारवतीय अग्निष्टोम song ending in रे, out of it.' Here in the above examples we see that two different acts with their separate fruits are described in two coordinate sentences. They are there-

When two co-ordinate sentences denote one act.

fore independent acts. But when one act accomplishes different objects though described in two or more co-ordinate sentences, it is said to be only one independent act ; as for instance.

यो वृष्टिकामो यौन्नाद्यकामोयः स्वर्गकामः यःसौभरेण स्तुवीत सर्वेवैकामः सौभरे। १। हीषिति बृष्टि कामाय निधनं कुर्थात् । उर्गि त्यन्नाद्यकामाय । उ इति स्वर्ग कामाय ॥ २ ॥

" One who is desirous of rain, one who is desirous of food, one who is desirous of heaven, should praise with a song Saubhar, because all desires are accomplished by means of a Saubhar song. Let him make a decadence with ‘हीष्’ if desirous of rain ; with ‘ उर्क् ’ if desirous of food ; with ‘उ ’ if desirous of heaven ". Here in the above example we have only one act of singing ; the different results which the act can produce by ending the song in the peculiar ways are described in the second sentence. The first sentence is Apûrva describing the all accomplishing power of the Saubhâra song, the second sentence is Niyama.

PÂDA 3.

The author after explaining the principal and subordinate acts goes

Conditional sentence.

on accumulating examples. He says that if there is a conditional sentence with the main sentence which lays down the Apûrva the conditional sentence or sentences denote subordinate action or actions ; as for instance.

“ ज्योतिष्टोमेन स्वर्गकामो यजेत । यदि रथंतरसामा सोमः स्यादैंद्र वायवाग्रान् ग्रहान् गृह्णीयात् । यदि बृहत्सामाशुक्रग्रान, यदि जगत्सामा आग्रयणाग्रान ”

" Let one who is desirous of heaven perform Jyotistoma. If there is a song in the tune of Rathantara, let him then take cups called Aindra Vâyava first ; if a song is in the Brihat tune let him take Śukra first : if a song is in the Jagat tune let him take अग्रयण first ". The first sentence laying down the अपूर्वविधि is the principal sentence and the rest of them *viz* : the conditional sentences which denote the variations of the cups in the ज्योतिष्टोम क्रतु are the subordinate sentences giving the details of the parts in the principal act.

The Aveṣṭi, though described in connection with the Râjasûya Yajña, अवेष्टि is a separate act. is a separate sacrifice as it can be performed by all the members of the twice born castes and the Râjasûya can be performed by a prince on the occasion of his coronation. Âdhâna or a ceremony for the establishment of fire being preliminary to the performance of a sacrifice is a subordinate act. The दाक्षायण, सांख्य प्रस्थायीय and संक्रम are the subordinate acts, being the modified forms of the Dars'apûrṇamâsayâga and performed on the occasions of the solastices and equinoxes.

When a sentence mentions the god, material and result by means of God, material and result denote the principal act· आलभन and निर्वाप, it is a principal sentence denoting the principal act ; as for instance वायव्यं श्वेत मालभेत भूति काम: " " सौर्यचरं निर्व पेद्‍ब्रह्मवर्चसकाम:" " द्यामालभेत " चतुरोमुष्टी निर्वपति " Let him offer a white animal to Vâyu if desirous of prosperity ". " Let him offer cooked rice आलभन and निर्वाप denote separate acts. to sun if desirous of Brahmaṇic glory." " Let him touch an axle of a carriage. He offers four handfuls ".

All these acts described above are independent acts being denoted by आलभन and निर्वाप.

There is an exception to the general rule enunciated above ; as for Exception. instance वत्समालभेत, वत्सनिकांताहि पशव: " T. S. II. 1. 4. 8. " Let him touch a calf because animals love their young ones." Here the passage indicates a purificatory rite which is a subordinate act inspite of the word ' आलभन ' used.

When an object of a material is mentioned in a text as subordinate to When a material is declared an act, it is a subordinate act ; as for instance subordinate, it is subordinate. वदेनं वत्सुपदधाति बृहस्पतेर्वा एतदन्न वह्निवारा: " " They place the boiled wild rice ; the boiled rice is the food of Brihaspati." This text occurs in the context of some sacrifice in connection with Agnichayana. The placing of wild rice is, therefore, a dependent act being for the purpose of the Minor ceremonies are dependant. Agnyâdhâna. Minor ceremonies in connection with the big ones are dependent acts ; as पर्वग्नि चरत in a त्वाष्ट्रपत्नीवत (see at p. 72).

We have seen that when the finite verbs ' यजति ' etc, are used, they

Exception to the rule that finite verbs denote a principal act. — denote separate acts; but there is an exception to the rule in the case of the soma cups which are the parts of the Agniṣṭoma. The offering of these cups is a subordinate act, though the terms यजति and जुहोति are used in the text.

"एषह्वै हविषा हविर्यजति यादाभ्यंगृ हीत्वा सोमाय जुहोति । पराचा एतस्यायुः प्राणएति योंऽशु गृह्लाति"

" He who taking अदाभ्य, offers it to सोम certainly makes a sacrifice by means of an offering. The life and breath of one who takes अंशु depart."

The taking of अदाभ्य and अंशु cups being the parts of the Soma offerings in the Agniṣṭoma sacrifice is not an independent act though the terms 'यजति' and 'जुहोति' are used.

अग्निचयन — The Agnichayana (piliug of fire) is a subordinate act being a purificatory rite and the fire being the material used there.

When the object and context of the actions are different they are

Variations in object and text indicate severality. — different acts as for instance " मासं अग्नि हो अंजुहोति; मासंदर्शपूर्णमासाभ्यां यजति " " He •sacrifices the Agnihottra for a month " He sacrifices the Dars'apûrṇa Yâgas for a month."

Description of an act without its fruit — When an act is not described but the fruit thereof is mentioned, it is a separate act, as for instance.

"अग्नये रवमवते पुरोडाशमष्टाकपालं निर्वपेतन्नरुक्कामः" तै० सं० २.२.३.३. "अग्निषोमीयमेकादश कपालं निर्वपेदुब्रह्म वर्चंलकामः" तै० सं॰ २.३.३.३. ऐंद्राग्नमेकादशकपालं निर्वपेत् प्रजाकाम :"

" Let one who is desirous of splendour, offer cake baked on eight earthen pans to the splendid Agni. Let one who is desirous of Brahmaṇic glory offer cakes baked on ten pans to Agni and Soma. Let one who is desirous of progeny offer cakes baked on eleven pans to Indra and Agni ".

In the above texts, all these acts are independent acts.

Condition attached to the rule. — The condition is that the texts must also be independent in order to make the actions independent ; as for instance.

" आग्नेयोऽष्टकपालः पुरोडाशो भवति । एतयान्नाद्यकामंयाजयेत्"

" An Âgneya sacrifice has cakes baked on eight potsherds ; let one who is desirous of eatable food be made to perform it." Here in the above quotation, the first is a principal sentence and the latter is a subordinate sentence. The text occurs in connection with the Avești sacrifice, yet as the act which is described in the first sentence which is Vidhi is inseparable from the fruit which is mentioned in the second sentence which is an अर्थवाद.

An act does not become two or more different acts by repetition; as

Repetition does not make an act several.
"for instance आग्नेयोऽष्टाकपालोऽमावस्यायां पौर्ण मास्यांचाच्युतोभवति" "आग्नेयोऽष्टाकपालोऽमावस्यायां भवति."

" An Âgneya in which there is an offering of a cake baked on eight pans on new and full moon days, becomes permanent. An Âgneya in which a cake is baked on eight earthen pans, is offered on a new moon day ". Here Âgneya is one act; it cannot break up into two independent acts by reason of the repetition which is by way of the Arthavâda.

PÂDA 4.

Repetition of an act for one's life does not make it several.
Repetition of an act though practised for one's whole life does not make it several, as for instance the Agnihottra.

Different description etc., of act in different recension of the Veda does not make an act several.
The name, form, peculiar qualities, repetition, censure, incapacity, final sentence, penance and different objects mentioned in the several branches of the Vedas, do not make an act several or independent. It is one act in spite of the different descriptions given of it in several recensions of the Veda. The subject is fully discussed in the second Adhyâya.

CHAPTER III.

PÂDA 1.

Definition of S'eṣa
The author having divided the acts into principal and subordinate proceeds to describe what S'eṣa is. S'eṣa is for the benefit or purpose of another; it is remainder. The substance, quality and purificatory rites are invariably Śeṣa but the actor, his action and the result achieved by the actor are both principal and S'eṣa according to the circumstances of the case. This distinction between प्रधान (principal) and शेष (accessory) is not arbitrary. If such distinction is not recognised, the whole theory of action falls to the ground. That which leads to the performance of the main object is principal ; every thing that leads to the accomplishment of the principal is accessory.

Every act has a purpose *i. e.* it bears a fruit ; if there is none visible,
it shall be presumed.

Presumption as to fruit

The materials that are mentioned in the text are for the purpose for which they are intended, as for example :—

The purpose of sacrificial weapon (यज्ञायुध)

" स्पयश्च कपालानिचाग्नि होत्रहवणीच शूर्पंच कृष्णाजिनंच शम्याचोल्ल
खलंच मुसलंचद्दषच्चोपल चैतानिवैदशयज्ञायुधानि " तै० सं० १. ६. ८. ३.
कपालेषु श्रपयति अग्निहोत्रहवए्याहवीं षिनिर्बंपति शूर्पेण विविनक्ति ।कृष्णा
जिनमधस्तांदुल्ल खलस्यावस्तृणाति शम्यां द्रषदुपदधाति उलूखल ।मुसलाभ्यां
हंति दृषदुपलाभ्यांपिनष्टि"

" A wooden sword, posherds, Aginhotra spoon, baskets black antelope's
skin, a cudgel, mortar, pestle, stone slab, muller are the ten sacrificial
weapons. He bakes a cake on potsherds ; he offers oblations with the
agnihottra spoons ; he winnows with the basket ; he spreads black deer's
skin under the mortar ; under the stone slab he places the cudgel;
he pounds with pestle and mortar ; he grinds with slab and muller."
Here in the above quoted passages, we see every instrument used in the
sacrifiee, is with an object in view.

The author proceeds to explain what he calls आरद्विन्याय. When
an object is described by its qualities which are mere
accidents, they will be treated as superfluous in the trans-
action ; as for instance "एकाहायिन्या अरुणया पिंगाख्या क्रीणाति' तै० सं० ६. १. ६. ७.
" He purchases with a year old cow of red colour and yellow eye.'
Here we have Ekahayani (a year old cow) qualified by red colour and
yellow eye. She is a means of purchasing soma ; it is the cow of one
year which forms the consideration of purchase but not her red colour
and yellow eye which are mere accidents accompanying her. They are
therefore not the conditions precedent to the act of purchase.

आरद्विन्याय

When an object in the singular number belongs to a class, what is
predicated of one applies to the class ; this principle is
called ग्रहैकत्व न्याय. As for instance, " दश्या पवित्रेण ग्रहं
सम्मार्ष्टि ". " He washes a cup with a fitering cloth." In a Soma
sacrifice, several cups are used , here washing is a predicate used with
reference to a cup belonging to the Soma sacrifice. A cup, therefore,
includes all cups of the Soma sacrifice. Man is mortal ; ' man ' here
means ' all men '.

ग्रहैकत्व न्याय

The predicate will not apply to an object of a different class ; when you predicate of a cup, you thereby do not include ' spoon ' and ' goblet ' under the term ' cup ' which is entirely different from them. When you predicate mortality of ' man ', you do not include ' goats ' and ' cows ' under the term ' man '.

Principle of meaning-lessness. A text of the Veda cannot be without a purpose ; if it does not apply to the principal but apply to one of its subsidiaries, it will be made applicable to it. It is based on the principle of ग्रानर्थंक्य or meaningless-ness. No Vedic text is meaningless, as for example, सप्तदश रत्निर्वाजपेयस्वरूपो भवति " " A sacrificial post in a Vâjapeya is of seventeen cubits," There is no sacrificial post in a Vâjapeya but there is a sacrificial post erected in the subordinate parts of the Vâjapeya. The text will, therefore, apply to the subordinate parts of the Vâjapeya to avoid meaninglessness.

Integrity of a sentence. When a sentence is one, its unity should not be broken up ; it is called the principle of वाक्यैकत्व and the breach of this rule is called वाक्यभेद. As for instance " ग्रभिक्रामंजुहोत्यभिजत्यै " T. S. II 6,2,4. " He offers an oblation for victory by going forward, " There are two actions contemplated, (1) one going forward (2) offering of an oblation ; under the rule, the sentence must be looked upon as a complex sentence in which the main action is offering of oblation ; and the subsidiary action which leads up to the offering of the oblation, is going forward. The sentence in the complex form will run thus " He after going forward offers an oblation " ; ' offers ' is a finite verb and ' going forward,' is an infinite verb expressed in the gerundial form.

Split of a sentence. On the other hand, when the sense of one part of a sentence is not clear and cannot be connected with another part of it by reason of an intervening clause, the unity of the sentence will be broken up and it will be treated as consisting of two coordinate sentences ; as for example, the description of the sacred thread comes after the recitation of the mantras for throwing sacred fuel in the fire. The author says that by virtue of the intervention, the principle enunciated above does not apply and the sentences will be treated as coordinate ones and the sacred thread will be worn throughout the sacrifice.

मिथोऽसंबंधन्याय When two or more subordinate acts constitute a principal act, the latter *inter se* are coordinate ; this principle is called मिथोऽ संबंध न्याय or mutual independence. As for instance, sacrificial vessels are necessary articles in an establishment of fire ;

the latter is a subordinate part of the full and new moon sacrifices. They both are therefore, subordinate parts of the new and full moon sacrifices but coordinate *inter se*. Amongst themselves, they are independent acts.

When a subordinate act has an inseparable part under a principal, बार्त्रघ्नीन्याय the subordinate inseparable part will be dependent on the subordinate which is directly under the principal, and will not be independent of it. As for instance, "वात्रघ्नी पूर्णमामेऽनुच्येते, वृधन्वती आमावस्यायाम्." "They (two) recite वार्त्रघ्नी verse on the full moon day and वृधन्वती verse on the new moon day." These verses are recited with the ghee offerings on the full moon and new moon days respectively, they are, therefore, the subordinate parts of Âjya offerings; the latter are in their turn subordinate to the Dars'apûrṇamâsayâgas. The principle of mutual independence enunciated above does not apply; the subordinate parts will depend upon the other subordinate part of which they are the satellites, it is called वार्त्रघ्नी principle or the principle of mutual relation- ship. It is contrary to the principle laid down above.

A sentence is complete when it does not depend upon another for the Complete sentence. completion of its sense; as, for instance, मुष्टीकरोति, वाचंयच्छति, दीक्षित भावेदयति, हस्तौ अवनेनिक्ते, उपलराजिं स्तृणाति " " He closes his fist, observes silence, explains to the initiated. He washes his hands and arranges a seat of grass." In the above example, we find different sentences complete in themselves not depending on each other for their sense though they are in close juxtaposition. They, therefore, denote several independent acts which are parts of a sacrifice.

Having discussed the mutual interdependence and mutual depen- Quartering of the cake. dence, the author says that the cutting of the cakes into four belongs to a sacrifice which is held in honour of Agni alone. The preceding discussion leads one to apply the text " आग्नेयंचतुर्धा करोति " (he divides the cake to be offered to Agni into four) to all sacrifices in which Agni happens to be joint with another, as ऐद्राग्न and अग्नीषोम sacrifices. The author says that the Taddhit form of Agni shows that the text is applicable only in the case when Agni is single.

PÂDA 2.

The author now proceeds to explain the applicabilitiy of the Vedic वर्हिन्याय mantras. Every Vedic mantra has its application. There is a Mantra " वर्हिं देवसदनं दामि " I cut thee O ! grass for the seat of God." It is recited at the time of cutting grass for a sacrifice. The word ' Varhi ' is used for grass in general and Kus'a in particular.

The former is the secondary sense and the latter is the primary sense. What is, therefore, the meaning of the word ' Varhi '? Should the mantra be recited on cutting every grass ? The author says that words should as a rule be used in the accepted or the primary sense. The word. वर्हि therefore, means the grass used in a sacrifice called कुश or दर्भ.

Sometimes the words in the mantras are used in the secondary sense, if the context so requires it. There is a mantra " निवेशनः संगमनो वसूनां " तै॰ सं॰ ४. २. ५. ४ ; about it, it is said ऐंद्र्या गार्हपत्यमभ्युपतिष्ठते " They worship the domestic fire with the verses pertaining to इन्द्र. The ऐंद्री verses are the verses " निवेशनः & etc. " in honour of Indra. In order to remove the inconsistency, the word Indra is used in the secondary sense and, therefore, means the Gârhapatya fire which is principal in the text.

The principle of the Gârhapatya applies to many cases. " इविष्कृदेहि (T. B. III. 2. 5. 8.) इति त्रिरवचनं आह्वयति ". " 'Come, O ! preparer of the offering ' beating thrice, he invites.' Which is principal here whether beating or inviting ? According to the Gârhapatya principle, inviting or calling on the sacrificer's wife to come, is principal and beating of the mortar with the pestle to indicate time for coming is subordinate. The mantra, therefore, applies at the time of invitation.

Application of गार्हपत्य principle.

" उत्तिष्ठन् अन्वाहार्यमिदग्नीन् बिहर " T. S., V. 3. 1. 2.

" Rising up, he says, O ! kindler of fire, carry fire." In the above passage *rising* is principal and carrying of fire is subordinate. The mantra, therefore, applies at the time of rising.

Similarly in the mantra "व्रतंकृणुतेति वर्चंविसर्जति " " Observe the vow " saying this, he breaks silence " *breaking silence* is principal and *observing the vow* is subordinate. So the mantra under the Gârhapatya principle will be read at the completion.

प्रस्तरम हरणन्याय

." सूक्तवाकेन प्रस्तरं प्रहरति " " He throws grass in the fire with सूक्तवाक ".

The grass when brought from the jungle and spread on the altar, is called Prastara. When the sacrifice is over, the grass so spread is no longer necessary but nothing belonging to the sacrifice is thrown away. The grass which is no longer required is ceremoniously thrown in the fire at the end of the ceremony with the recitation of the Sûktavâka verses which are given in the T. B. The throwing of this useless grass is called प्रतिपत्ति कर्म (final disposal). Now the question is, which is principal ? The प्रस्तर प्रहरण or throwing of grass in the fire, because the

सूक्तवाक being in the instrumental case is for the purpose of the प्रतिपत्ति कर्म. The throwing of grass serves two purposes that is the प्रतिपत्ति कर्म is performed and the grass is finally disposed of. This kind of serving two objects by one act is called प्रस्तर प्रहरणान्याय.

When it is said that the Sûktavâka should be recited, it does not mean the whole of it which goes under the name of Sûktavâka; but only those mantras which are pertinent should be recited.

सूक्तवाक.

The mantras that are recited from the Sûktavâka on the occasion of the full and new moon sacrifices are also called Sûktavâka. It is a figure of speech called Synecdoche.

याज्या and अनुवाक mantras are given at one place and the काम्येष्टि (the desire accomplishing sacrifice) is described at another place in the T. S. ; their connection can be determined by लिंग, क्रम and समाख्या.

Means of interpretation.

There are certain mantras which are called आग्नेय, ऐंद्र and वैष्णव they are to be determined by the समाख्या or classification made by the Riṣis. You cannot choose any mantra in which अग्नि. इंद्र or विष्णु occurs.

Anuvâka mantras are many; their applicability depnds upon the perpose and sense they denote. They are to be transferred forward and backward according to the circumstances. They are coordinate sentences they do not constitute one whole sentence.

Anuvâkas are in the nature of compound sentence.

When the mantras constitute one whole i.e., the sense of the one cannot be detached from another, they will be considered as one complex sentence.

Complex sentence.

When the mantras in honour of one deity are applied to another deity, they will be adapted by the principle of ûha to suit the deity. See the mantra quoted at p. 105.

Mantras are to be adapted to suit the deities.

The subject of ऊह naturally leads one to discuss the mantras in connection with the drinking of Soma juice. In an अग्निष्टोम sacrifice, there are several चमस cups full of Soma juice. The priests called मैत्रावरुण, ब्राह्मणाच्छंसी, पोत्र, नेष्टा and अग्नीध्र who are called hottrakâs help in offering and drinking Soma juice. The Soma juice is collected in the चमस cups. It is to be offered by pronouncing वषट् and अनुवषट् ; first Indra is invoked by hotâ by taking juice in a cup and by pro-

Principle of ऊह applies to अभ्युन्नीत cups.

nouncing Vaṣaṭ ; then the hottrakâs after taking fresh Soma juice in the cup in which there is residue left, offer it to different deities by pronouncing अनुवषट्. The juice thus taken second time is called अभ्युन्नीत.

अभ्युन्नीत.

The नैत्रावरण offers the juice to Mitra and Varuna after reciting मित्रं वयं हवामहे " ऋ० वे. १. २३. ४., 'we invoke Indra' then ब्राह्यणाच्छंसी to इंद्र after reciting "इंद्रं त्वा वृषभंवयं" ऋ. वे. ३. ४. १ "we invoke thee Indra, a bull" then पोता to मरुत after reciting " मरुतोवस्वहिषये " ऋ० वे० १. ८६ १. " Maruts in whose house," then नेष्टा invokes त्वष्टू and the gods' wives with " अग्नेपत्नी- रिह वह " ऋ० वे० १. २२. ९. " O Agni, bring the wives here." Then अग्नीध makes an offering to fire after reciting " उखानाय वशानाव " ऋ० वे० ४३. ११. " To the eater of a bull and the eater of a barren cow ". After the invocation of the deities, the soma juice is drunk by adapting the mantra in honour of Indra quoted at page 105. According to the principle of Ûha as laid down above, the names of different deities will be substituted in place of Indra but the view of the author is that the names of the different deities along with Indra will be recited by reason of the residue of the juice left in the cup originally offered to इन्द्र. This principle is called upalakṣaṇa because Indra is mentally associated with the deities that come after him.

उपलक्षण

The principle of upalakṣaṇa as enunciated above does not apply to the drinking of Soma juice in a पात्नीवत cup, because in it the juice is transferred from other vessels.

पात्नीवत is an exception.

The principle of उपलक्षण does not apply when any god is invoked in drinking in company with another god, the reason is that another god who accompanies the principal deity is subordinate to him.

The principle of उप- लक्षण does not apply.

वषट्कार is not a deity and the principle of उपलक्षण does not apply to it.

The general rule is that every oblation is accompanied by a mantra ; but where Indra is not invoked, drinking is done without any mantra ; but ' Etis'ayana's ' view is against it. When Soma is drunk from the Aindrâgna cup, no mantra is recited.

Recitation of mantra.

Every mantra that is recited has a metre but when mantras of different metres are recited while drinking Soma, it does not necessarily follow that no mantra is to be recited at all.

PÂDA 3.

The peculiar quality of a Veda which is its *differentia* governs the mantras contained in it; the peculiar quality of the Rigveda and Sâma Veda is that the mantras belonging to them are read aloud but the mantras in the Yajur Veda are read low. If a mantra from the Rig Veda or the Sâma Veda happens to be in the Yajur Veda, it will, therefore, be read low.

Peculiarities of the Veda govern the mantras in it.

If the ceremony to be performed belongs to the Yajur Veda and the verses recited are from the Sâma Veda, the verses will be read low; the Veda to which the ceremony belongs regulates the recitation of the mantras. As, for instance, अग्न्याधान is a ceremony belonging to the Yajur Veda but the verses in its performance are recited from the Sama Veda; they will under this rule be read low.

The Veda to which ceremoney belongs regulates the reading of a mantra.

The author then proceeds to explain श्रुति, लिंग, वाक्य, प्रकरण, क्रम and समाख्या; the one preceding prevails over the following. All these have been fully explained in the preceding Pages.

Modes of interpretation.

When any sentence or word is transferred forward or backward where it is appropriate, it is called उत्कर्ष or अपकर्ष, as for example, the transference of twelve Upasadas to the अहीन sacrifice; the transference of Pratipada mantras to कुलायबन्ध where their transference is fit and proper. The principle of Utkarṣa does not apply to the tail of an animal which is ordained to be offered in पत्नीसंयाज in the context of the दर्शपूर्णमासयाग. The principle of उत्कर्ष does not apply to संतर्दन *i.e.*, joining of the two stones for pounding the सोम and extracting the Soma juice from it; the text quoted at p. 118 applies to one of the Sansthâs in a ज्योतिष्टोम and the word दीर्घसोम means, the Soma twig, the knots of which are very strong or innumerable.

Principles of उत्कर्ष and अपकर्ष explained.

" In the first sacrifice, the प्रवर्ग्य ceremony is not to be performed.... ज्योतिष्टोम sacrifice is first of all the sacrifice." Does the prohibition as to the performance of प्रवर्ग्य relate to the ज्योतिष्टोम sacrifice? The author's view is that you are to interpret the whole text quoted at p. 120. It means that the प्रवर्ग्य ceremony is not to be performed when the first Sansthâ of the ज्योतिष्टोम *viz.*, अग्निष्टोम is performed.

Prohibition as to the performance of प्रवर्ग्य applies to the 1st संस्था in a ज्योतिष्टोम.

The offering of flour is ordained to be made to पूषा in the context of

Flour offering to पूषा in the चातुर्मास्य ceremony.

दर्श पूर्णमासयाग but no offering is made there. The चातुर्मास्य ceremony which is the modified form of the said Iṣṭis will have the offering to Pûsâ though it is mentioned in the context of the full and new moon sacrifices. The food of Pûsâ is flour because he is toothless ; hence in charu (boiled rice) offering, the flour of rice is boiled and offered. In पुरोडास (cake) offering there is already flour. The flour is offered to Pûsâ when he happens to be alone but not when he is a member of the dual deity.

In order to elucidate the above discussion, I may here describe

अग्निष्टोम described.

what Agniṣṭoma is. The Dars'apûrṇayâgas are the models of all Iṣṭis and the Agniṣṭoma is the model of all Soma sacrifices. The Dars'â and Pûrṇamâsayagas are also the models of the Agniṣṭoma. The former are simple sacrifices while the latter are complex ones. The Agniṣṭoma is the model of all the complex sacrifices.

The whole ground where it was performed was called Deva Yajana ;

Sacrificial ground.

there was an altar for the sacrifice called Uttara Vedi. A pandal was erected where different priests took their seat according to the place allotted to them and kept the fires burning. In the pandal, a branch of a fig tree

उत्तरवेदि.

was fixed into the ground. Outside the pandal, there were two Havir Dhâna carts ; in one there was Soma creeper and in the

हविर्धान.

other, there were materials for the purpose of the sacrifice.

प्राचीनवंश.

They were taken from the Prâchînavams'a in the west to the Uttaravedi in the East. In the North of these carts there was a place to keep the Soma. (See Fig. I. Frontispiece.) The Adhvaryu took his seat in the south east of the pandal, the Agnîdhra priest took his seat in the north east.

The Prâchînavams'a or the old altar was erected like an ordinary altar for the performance of the Dars'apûrṇamâsa Yâga in the west and the Uttaravedi as said above was to the east of the stand for the Havirahâna carts and the place for taking down the Soma creeper from the cart. To the east of the Uttaravedi, there was the sacrificial pillar called Yûpa topped up with Chasâla.

There were three fires in the extreme west; there was the Gârhapatya or domestic fire which was worshipped daily ; to the West was the Âhavanîya fire in which offerings were made on ceremonial occasions ; to

the south was the Dakṣinâgni to propitiate the Râkṣasas and the departed souls. A Dîkṣita or the initiated one had to
Appointment of the priests. invite the following priests for the performance of the
Agniṣṭoma *viz.*, ब्रह्मा, होता, मैत्रावरुण, अध्वर्यु, प्रस्तोता, उद्गाता, प्रतिहर्ता, प्रतिप्रस्थाता, नेष्टा, पोता, अच्छावाक्, अग्नीध्र, आत्रेय, सदस्य, व्रतप्रद, ग्रावस्तुत्, उन्नेता, शामिता and सुब्रह्मण्य. The sacrificer and his wife also took part in the Agniṣṭoma sacrifice. It was the
first stage.

After the priests' appointment, preparation of the ground and arrangement of the sacrificial utensils and the materials, the Yajamâna was
अमसुदीसा shaved and the nails of his wife were pared. They then
took their bath, which was called अण्सुदीसा. It was the
second stage.

Thirdly दीक्षणीयेष्टि was performed; Puroḍâs'â cakes were offered to Agni
दीक्षणीयेष्टि and Viṣṇu. The sacrificer is supposed to be reborn. He
was wrapped up in a deer's skin and his wife was clothed
with grass. He was bound to observe a vow of not telling lies, not speak-
ing much and of practising austerities. Fourthly the sacrificer had to
procure means of performing the sacrifice, as for instance, gold, silver, cloth
and cattle.

Fifthly प्रायणीयेष्टि was performed. It consisted of the offering of ghee
प्रायणीयेष्टि and boiled rice in the fire ; four gods were worshipped
पथ्यांस्वस्ति, अग्नि, सोम and सविता in the वाज्यामंत्रs from
Rg. V. X. 63. 15 and 1. 189. 1.

The sixth stage is पदचर्या ; a cow with which Soma was purchaased was
पदचर्या. made to walk and the यजमान followed her. At the seventh
step she went away and a line was drawn with a wooden
sword on the three footsteps and ghee was poured on the line with the
recitation of a mantra.

Seventhly, Soma was purchased ceremoniously and then it was brought
आति थ्येष्टि as a guest of respectable position ; an आतिथ्यहोम was
performed with the mantras.

Eightly, the Tanûnapta ceremony in which both the priests and the
तन्नप्त Yajmâna solemnly undertook to assist one another in the
performance of the sacrifice, was performeed.

Then, ninthly, the sacrificer sprinkled water on the Soma twigs to keep
आप्यावन them wet and fresh ; this ceremony was called आप्यावन
After this the 10th stage was reached, all the priests
निन्हव folded their hands in respect and made an obeisance to
heaven and earth. It was called निन्हव.

Then, eleventhly, the Pravargya ceremony was performed, provided
प्रवर्ग्य it was not the first performance. Two pegs were driven into the ground ; a cow and a sheep with their
young ones were tied. Two altars in which fires were kindled were
महावीर constructed. An earthen vessel called महावीर consisting
of three bowls piled upon one another contained the
milk of the cow and the sheep mentioned above was heated.
Then the milk oblations were made in the Gârhapatya fire of the
Prâchinavedi twice a day.

उपसद After this followed the twelve upasad homas ;
this was the 12th stage in the Agniṣṭoma.

All these ceremonies up to this stage were performed in the Prâchina-
प्राचीन वंश vaṁs'a. It consisted of the गार्हपत्य, आहवनीय and दक्षिणाग्नि
fires in the extreme west. To the east of the Prâchîna-
vaṁs'a, there was constructed the उत्तरवेदि. It was called Vedikaraṇa
वेदि करण and was the 13th stage in the sacrifice.

To the east of the uttaravedi, there was a sacrificial post where an
यूप animal was tied and killed. A ceremony was performed upon the animal which was then tied to the post
and killed. Its flesh was offered to the fire and was also partaken of
by the priests. अग्निषोम, सवनीय and अनुबंध्य animals were killed and
Three kinds of sacri- offered in an order. There was a special place
ficial animals. for extraction of Soma juice. It was called
uparava. Water was sprinkled upon the Soma
उपरव twigs and a large quantity of Soma juice was
Extraction of सोम] extracted ; jars were filled up with it. It was
then offered to fire. It was called Grahaprachâra.
ग्रहप्रचार The Soma juice was then drunk from the same cup
by the priests in a systematic order by singing
समाख्या songs. It was called Samâkhyâ. It was the
fourteenth stage in the Agniṣṭoma.

After this, the balls of rice were offered to the ancestors who were
पितृयज्ञ remembered. It was the 15th stage in the Agniṣṭoma.
The last stage was the उदयनीयेष्टि oblation, it resembled the प्रायणीयेष्टि
उदयनीयेष्टि. and the यज्ञs in it were in the reverse order. It
is also called उदवसानीय. This is only bird's eye
view of the सोमयाग which has been described in detail in chapters VII
to XI of Kâtyâyana Śrauta Sútra. Mr. Kuṇṭe is of opinion that it was an
emblem of the departure of the ancient Âryans from Central Asia their
home, to the Panjâb where they settled. It is very probable.

PÂDA 4.

This pâda opens with the sacred thread and an important discussion about the interpretation of a Vedic text is raised.

यज्ञोप वीत explained.

It is necessary to explain what a sacred thread is. A single fine thread is taken; it is plied with two other fine threads and made into one. Such three-fold threads are taken equal to the size of man's hand stretching full length from the shoulder to the pit formed by the thumb with the index finger There is a knot at the extremity ; it is called Brahmagranthi. After the Upanayana ceremony is performed, it is always worn by a twice-born hanging from the left shoulder to the right side under the right arm pit. When attending the call of nature, the sacred thread is put on the right ear by encircling it round the head so that it might not be spoiled while performing ablutions. The wearing

Kuṣṭi.

of the sacred thread resembles the tying of the girdle round the waist (Kuṣṭi) amongst the Pârsis.

There is a text in the Adhvaryukânda of the T. S. quoted at p. 124 with its translation. It is in connection with the context of the new and full moon sacrifices.

Why is उपवीत fashion of wearing the thread is preferred ?

The context (प्रकरण) as explained in the preceding pâda shows that the sacred thread is to be worn in a peculiar fashion when certain ceremonies are to tb performed; but the text shows that the description as to the different modes of wearing the sacred thread is by way of Arthavâda (supplement) to the Vidhi contained in the concluding part of the text. The text must prevail over the context and the custom of wearing the sacred thread in the Upavîta fashion is, therefore, in consonance with the Vedic text.

The same principle of interpretation applies to the text relating to the division of the directions and the differen-

The same principle of interpretation applies to other texts.

texts quoted at p. 127. They need not be re peated here as they are fully explained there. Next we come to the text which prohibits tell-ing lies and which occurs in the context of the दर्शपूर्णभासयाग " नानृतंवदेत् " " Do not tell lies ". Here it will not be amiss, if I explain the ' क्रतुधर्म and मनुष्य धर्म ' terms used in the Mîmânsâ.

Distinction between क्रतुधर्म and मनुष्यधर्म explained.

The Kratudharma rules are those, the obser-vance of which is binding during the perform-ance of a sacrifice ; while the Manuṣyadharma rules are the rules which are always to be observed by a man during his life; they may be rules of consci-ence i.e., moral precepts or social rules. . To the latter class the term *quasi* law of the modern legal terminology may be applied. The former may be compared to the positive rules of law. It is the duty of a man not to tell lies in his life, it is a rule of conscience : but no law court will punish him for acting contrary. But when he tells a lie in a law court after the administration of an oath, he shall be liable to be punished. Similarly the text quoted in the beginning, is from the context of the Dars'apûrṇamâsayâga. It is a Vidhi rule to be observed strictly during the performance of the sacrifice and the breach of it entails a penalty in the shape of a penance. Keeping the above distinction in view, the author

Instances of the same.

accumulates instances of action belonging to the ethical and liturgical codes as for example the rule as to yawning is liturgical while not assaulting a Brâhmaṇa is moral and social. Not talking with a woman in her menses or not taking food touched by her are rules belonging to man's conduct in life. So also wearing gold ornaments is a social rule. Offering of oblations in connection with victory or sovereignty, performance of अश्वमेधियज्येष्टि or वार्षवेष्टि as a penance and offering of oblations to Soma and Indra on vomiting Soma juice in a sacrifice by the sacrificer are all liturgical.

The author then proceeds to describe the offering in connection with

Offering of पुरोडाश cake.

the Proḍâs'a cakes. They are divided into two, to facilitate the offering to the fire. They are thus offered in parts and the remaining portions that fall from the cakes are offered to Sviṣṭakrit, forming what is called Pratipatti Karma in the Mîmânsâ. The residue of the cakes are distributed amongst the priests and the sacrificer as presents.

The distinction that is drawn between मनुष्यधर्म and ऋतुधर्म does not necessarily lead one to hold that the rules of the former class are binding

What are मनुष्यधर्म and ऋतुधर्म precepts. ?

only in common life and while those of the latter class are binding only when one is performing a sacrifice. If that were so, it would lead to much confusion.

The मनुष्यधर्म consists of the social and moral rules which bind a man always during his ordinary course of life but the ऋतुधर्म are those rules which are binding while one undertakes to perform a sacrifice and the breach of which entails a sin removable by the performance of a penance. If a rule is social or moral, it does not necessarily follow, that it cannot be liturgical ; and *vice versa*.

I may here note that Mr. Kuṇṭe in his learned summary has drawn

Mr. Kuṇṭe criticised.

much upon his imagination in depicting the ancient Aryan society. There is no foundation for him to suppose that the controversy raised in the Adhikaraṇas relates to the real controversy between the followers of Buddhism and Vedism. He has been perhaps misled by Kumârila in whose time the controversy between the two schools became very keen and real. Jaimini's Mîmânsâ is anterior to the rise of Buddhism.

The nature of the sûtras given in the appendix.

There are some sûtras given in the appendix by me ; they are considered spurious and therefore find no place in the authorised edition of the Mîmânsâ.

PÂDA 5.

What are remaining rites ?

We have seen in the preceding Adhikaraṇa that a पुरोडाश cake after its division into two parts was offered to अग्नि ; the residue was given to the priests for food and offered to स्विष्टकृत्. They constitute what are called remaining rites ; the portion that was given to the ब्रह्मा priest was called प्राशित्र and the portions given to other priests were called इडा. Lastly

प्राशित्र भक्षण, इडाभक्षण and स्विष्टकृत् explained.

the portion was offered to स्विष्टकृत्. Now this naturally leads one to enquire whether such division applies to the ghee contained in the vessel called ध्रुवाज्या. The author says that as the ghee is for the whole

The remaining rites are not performed by reason of no residue.

sacrifice, there is no residue left and therefore no performance of the remaining rites with it. Similarly, in the साकंप्रस्थाय्य, there being no residue left in the ध्रुवा vessel, the remaining rites were not performed.

In the सूत्रामणि sacrifice where cups full of milk and wine, were drunk, no residue was left ; so no remaining rites consisting of प्राशित्रभक्षण, इडाभक्षण and स्विष्टकृत् were performed.

In सर्वपृष्ठ they are performed.

In सर्वपृष्ठ where a cake was made, the remaining rites were performed only once but not with each oblation.

Drinking twice with इन्द्रवायव cups.

In a ज्योतिष्टोम sacrifice while Soma is drunk, there happen to be two cups consecrated to Indra and Vâyu ; as *Soma* is offered twice, so there will be residue twice : accordingly there will be drinking twice.

Drinking of residue of Soma in a ज्योतिष्टोम.

As said above, Soma juice was profusely extracted in a ज्योतिष्टोम sacrifice ; it was purified by recitation of *mantras*. It was then filled in several cups and offered to the fire with the याज्या मंत्रs The residue was then drunk as appears from the text quoted at p. 146.

The persons entitled to drink residue.

Having established that the residue of the Soma juice was drunk, the next question to be determined is the person or persons entitled to drink it. The चमसी priests are entitled to drink the residue of Soma juice. चमस is a cup in which Soma was kept for drinking ; होता, ब्रह्मा, मैत्रावरुण, ब्राह्मणाच्छंसी and अग्नीध्र are called चमसी.

चमसी.

उद्गातृ group entitled to drink.

All the priests of the उद्गातृ (singer) group are entitled to drink ; because they sing Vedic psalms in the sacrifice. The ग्रावस्तुत् was entitled to drink from हारियोजन cup only. All the priests who perform Homa and extract Soma are entitled to drink Soma. It was drunk after pronouncing Vaṣaṭ. The याज्यामंत्र were recited when the Soma juice was offered to the fire. The pronounciation of Vaṣaṭ entitled one to take the first sip from the चमस cup. It was Hotâ who pronounced the Vaṣaṭ and was, therefore, entitled to drink first. He also reads याज्या mantras but that did not entitle him to the first drink, because in his absence, the sacrificer used to recite याज्या.

ग्रावस्तुत् entitled to drink from हारियोजन.

Who is entitled to a first drink ?

Invitation in the form ' उपहूत उपहूयस्व ' ' you who are invited, invite '. The reply was also given in the form ' उपहूत ' ' invited.' On this, the priests used to drink the Soma from the same cup.

Invitation.

होता and यजमान entitled to the sacrificial food.

Both the Hotâ and sacrificer were entitled to the sacrificial food as they used to recite the Yâjyâs.

There was a mixture called फलचमस ; it was prepared by taking young sprouts of an Udambar tree, pounding them and mixing them with curd. It was a substitute for an offering to the fire and was also drunk like Soma juice.

फलचमस explained.

There was a ceremony called दशपेय in connection with राजसूय sacrifice. It was a substitute for a सोमयाग. There were hundred Brâhmaṇas and ten cups of Soma juice; each ten carried one cup in procession to the seat and then the juice was drunk ceremoniously. Though राजसूय was a sacrifice performed exclusively by a Kṣattriya king, yet the procession consisted of Brâhmaṇas alone,

दशपेय.

PÂDA 6.

There are three kinds of Vedic texts (1) अनारम्भ विधि scattered texts which belong to no context ; (2) प्रकृतिवाक्य, texts laying down the procedure of a model sacrifice (3) बोधकवाक्य, texts showing the relationship between the model and modified sacrifices.

There is a Vedic text यस्य खादि रःस्नुवोा भवति छंदसामेवर सेना वदति यरसा अस्य आहुतयेा भवंति……यस्यपर्णमयी जुहू भंवति नपापश्लोकंश्रुणोति" " He whose ladle is made of खादिर wood offers the oblation with the juice of the Veda ; his offerings become full of juice……one whose जुहू is made of पर्ण wood does not hear evil news. " The above quoted text belongs to no particular context and is in the nature of अनारम्भविधि, a general statement. *Prima facie* such texts ought to apply to the context of all the sacrifices in general but our author having discussed the opposite view, has laid down as a rule that अनारम्भ texts apply to the model sacrifice only.

अनारम्भ विधि applies to the model sacrifice.

The distinction is like that of a general and a particular statement. The अनारम्भविधिs are like the general statements belonging to no particular context. If there were no rule of the मीमांसा the general statement will apply to all. Accordingly, the author has restricted the application of the अनारम्भविधि to the model sacrifice.

General statement explained.

When there is a text already applicable to the model sacrifice and there is also an अभ्यनार विधि, the latter will in this state of conflict, apply to the modified sacrifice ; as for instance there is a text laying down fifteen Sâmadhenî verses in the model sacrifice and there is an अनारम्भविधि which enjoins seventeen Sâmadhenî verses. According to the general rule laid down above, the अनारम्भविधि will apply to the model sacrifice ; according to one text there are 15 सामधेनी verses and according to the other there are 17 सामधेनी verses in the model sacrifice ; in this state of conflict, the general rule will be relaxed and the अनारम्भविधि relating to the seventeen Sâmadhenî verses will apply to the modified sacrifice.

In a conflict, अनारम्भ विधि applies to the modified sacrifice.

The special rule will not apply when there is a reason to deviate from the text applicable to the model sacrifice. " चमसेन अपः प्रणयेत् । गोदोहनेन पशुकामस्य प्रणयेत्." " Carry water with the spoon, ; one desirous of cattle should carry water with the गोदोहन vessel." The texts are read in connec-

When there is a special reason both texts will apply to the model sacrifice.

tion with the दर्श पूर्णमासयाग. There is apparently a conflict between the two texts, but there is a reason given why the water should be carried in a गोदोहन vessel : it is a desire to possess large number of cattle. So both the texts will apply in the model sacrifice. In this view, the first text contains a general statement and the last contains a particular statement applicable in the particular circumstances.

From the context It appears that the अग्न्याधान is for the performance of a पवमानेष्टि but in reality the पवमानेष्टि is performed for keeping the sacred fire fresh; if there were no अग्न्याधान, there would be no पवमानेष्टि; the former is prior to the latter. The latter is, therefore, subservient to the former.

पवमानेष्टि is for अग्न्याधान.

The अग्न्याधान will be connected with the model sacrifice under the general rule laid down above but as it is a preliminary act in a sacrifice, it therefore applies to all sacrifices.

अग्न्याधान applies to all the sacrifices.

The पवमानेष्टि related to the model sacrifice as cause and effect, is performed in the unconsecrated fire.

पवमानेष्टि performed in an unconsecrated fire.

The sacrificial animals are of three kinds (1) अग्निषोमीय (2) सवनीय and (3) अनुबंध्य. They are described in the context of अग्निष्टोम संस्था of the ज्योतिष्टोम ; the पशुविधिs, *viz.*, preparatory ceremonies such as carrying the animal to the sacrificial ground,

In the case of पशुविधि, the sequence prevails over the context.

tying it to a peg, suffocating it to death and dissecting it are described in the context of the सवनीय animal.

According to the principle laid down above, the पशुविधिs will apply to the सवनीय animal ; but on the contrary the अग्निषोमीय animal is killed on the day called औपवसथ्याह (a day before the extraction of Soma juice) and the सवनीय animal is killed on the सुत्याह (the day on which Soma juice is extracted.) Though the context is stronger than the sequence, yet here the sequence will prevail over the context being useless and not applicable.

There are certain ceremonies performed upon a cow before she is milked ; she is driven to the forest for grazing, with a branch of a tree and praised. According to the sequence relied on above, the ceremonies are to be performed only at the time of milking her in the evening but

Ceremonies in connection with milking a cow should be performed twice a day.

not while milking her in the morning. Because the ceremonies are described in one context, they will apply to both the milkings which are indispensable for the preparation of curd.

Washing of the cups in each सवन.

Similarly the washing of the cups of Soma juice should be done in each *savana* namely, प्रात:सवन, माध्यंदिन सवन and सायंसवन.

The description of a bridle applies to all the sacrificial animals.

Though by the context, the description of a bridle applies to the अग्नीषोमीय animal, yet as the Vedic sentence makes it applicable to all the sacrificial animals, the sentence prevails over the context. A horse cannot be carried to the post of slaughter without a rope or a brid'e. It, therefore, stands to reason that the description of a bridle should apply to the rope of every sacrificial animal.

Washing etc., apply to the अंशु and अदाभ्य.

The Aṃs'u and Adâbhya cups are described in connection with the upasad which is distantly connected with the Jyotiṣṭoma. The washing of the cups is mentioned in the context of the Jyotiṣṭoma; but by the force of the Vâkya the washing etc., will be performed on the Aṃs'u and Adâbhya though distantly connected with the Jyotiṣṭoma. The general statement will prevail over the particular statement contained in the Prakaraṇa.

Ceremonies in connection with चित्रिणी apply to all the bricks used in an अग्निचयन.

Similarly the ceremonies described in connection with वज्रिणी and विचित्रिणी in a different context apply to other bricks which are used along with them in the Agnichayana ceremony. The Vâkya prevails over the context.

Soma ceremonies should not be performed on the फलचमस.

Ceremonies of the principal should be performed upon its substitute.

The ceremonies which are performed upon *Soma* should not be performed upon a फलचमस being a special preparation in the special case of a drink prepared for a Kṣattriya or a Vais'ya. The Soma juice is exclusively drunk by a ब्राह्मण. But the ceremonies shall be performed on the substitute whether directly mentioned or not, because the latter represents the principal for all intents and purposes. The case of Soma and फलचमल is different; the former is the model of the latter; they, therefore, stand in the relationship of a model and a modified sacrifice.

Minor oblations of the ज्योतिष्टोम also apply to its modifications.

Whatever minor ceremonies are performed in the ज्योतिष्टोम shall also be performed on its modifications; they are अग्निष्टोम, अत्यग्निष्टोम, उक्थ्य, षोडशी. अतिराम आप्तोर्याम and वाजपेय. They are of समानविधान in the language of मीमांसा *i.e.*, what is laid down in connection with the model sacrifice will apply to the modified sacrifice by the चोदक text. The ज्योतिष्टोम is the नित्यकर्म or a duty which should be performed. The modified sacrifices are the काम्यकर्म or causal; they are performed with a certain object in view.

It will be better if I explain here the nature of the modified sacrifices which are called संस्था. The word Saṃsthâ means a stop. In big sacrifices Stotras or verses from the Veda are read and an arbitrary stop is made to mark the completion of a Stotra. It corresponds with the *sipara* of the Quran which is finished within 30 nights of the Ramzan by reading one *para* a night.

संस्था explained.

The Agniṣṭoma is both a model and modified sacrifice. When it is performed with a certain object in view, it is a modified sacrifice. The model sacrifice is indispensable and the modified sacrifice is optional. It has twelve Stotras. The last one is called अग्निष्टोम, hence the name of the sacrifice.

अग्निष्टोम.

The उक्थ्य संस्था consists of the whole अग्निष्टोम sacrifice with three more stotras in addition to the twelve stotras of the अग्निष्टोम and on the completion of the 15th stostra, the 16th stotra is commenced which forms the षोडशी संस्था.

उक्थ्य संस्था

षोडशी.

After the performance of the षोडशी, twelve stotras are recited at night three times and the स्तोत्र called आश्विन is recited last. This constitutes अतिरात्र.

अतिरात्र.

According to some, these are the real modified forms and the three others mentioned above are included in these four Saṃsthâs.

The अग्निष्टोम, उक्थ्य and षोडशी स्तोत्रs being repeated along with the अग्निष्टोम sacrifice, constitute अत्यग्निष्टोम sacrifice.

अत्यग्निष्टोम.

When after the performance of the षोडशी sacrifice वाजपेय स्तोत्र is recited, it is called वाजपेय sacrifice.

वाजपेय.

When the whole अतिरात्र sacrifice is performed and in addition to the stotras recited three times, there is a recitation of three stotras for the fourth time, it is called आप्तोर्याम.

आप्तोर्याम.

From the above analysis, it is clear that the संस्थाs are only the modifications of the ज्योतिष्टोम; the minor oblations that are performed in a ज्योतिष्टोम shall necessarily be performed in the modified sacrifice as well.

From the above summary, we see how the author has explained a general and a particular sentence and their connection by means of a चोदक text. चोदक

चोदक texts explained.

text is that which connects a general sentence with a particular sentence
It is either विशिष्ट or अतिदेश. A विशिष्ट text makes an original statement
and supplies information necessary for its application. An original
statement may prescribe an act which may be obligatory or optional.
The former is नित्य, the latter is नैमित्तिक.

Division of the चोदक texts. अतिदेश lays down that a particular act or
sacrifice should be performed like another act
or sacrifice ; the former is विकृति and the latter is
प्रकृति.

A *chodaka* text is, therefore, indispensable for determining the model
and modified sacrifices, and the relationship between the parts and their
whole and ; it is helpful in determining which actions are parts of a whole
and what action is a whole in relation to its parts. The following table
will explain fully.

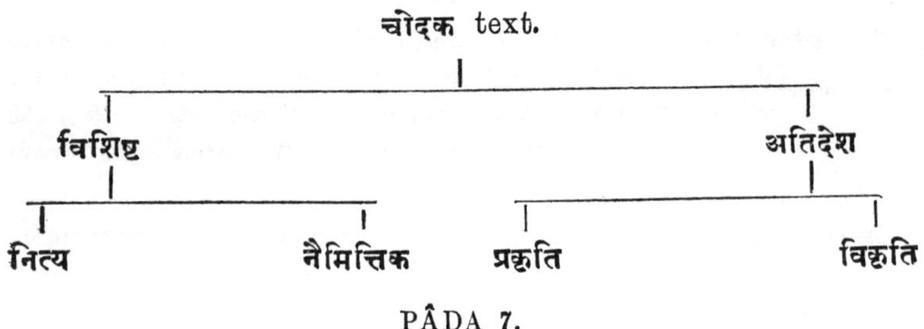

PÂDA 7.

Now we come to the Angas. They are of two kinds आराडुपकारक
अंग. and सन्निपत्योपकारक. They have been fully explained
at p. 170 and also previously in the introduction. They
are like division and sub-division.

The author lays down a principle which corresponds with the well-
Dictum de omni et nullo. known Maxim of Aristotle in logic *viz.*, *dictum
de omni et nullo*. As for instance, the purificatory
ceremonies of the materials are described in the
context (प्रकरण) of दर्श पूर्णमासयाग s by a वाक्य (sentence), the details described in connection with the दर्श पूर्णमासयाग s
will apply to their parts. The purificatory
ceremonies have been performed on दर्भ
grass in the दर्शपूर्णमासयाग ; पिण्डपितृयाग is its
subsidiary part, so there will be no necessity
of performing the purificatory ceremony on
it again.

**The ceremonies perform-
ed on a material in a
principal enures for
the benefit of all its
parts.**

In a sacrifice, there are the activity or effort of the यजमान, the result that accrues to him and the subsidiary actions that lead to the accrual of the result.

Purificatory operation on a sacrificer.

As the sacrificer is the recipient of the reward of his action he has to undertake certain operations preparatory to make him a fit person to receive the reward. It is for the benefit of the principal act.

On the other hand, the altar, and touching of पूर्णमासी and अमावस्या offerings with Chatuhotri and Panchahotri mantras are for the benefit of the principal through its divisions and subdivisions; they are, therefore, सन्निपत्योपकारक in the language of the Mîmânsâ, while the Dîkṣâ and Dakṣiṇâ are directly for the benefit of the whole sacrifice and are, therefore, Ârâdupakâraka.

The Vedi is not an anga (part) of a sacrificial post (यूप); it is a particular space marked out; so also the Havirdhâna is a place where Soma juice is extracted and where

Places.

the Havirdhâna cart stands. A sacrificer is principal because he reaps the fruit of a sacrifice ; he, therefore, offers the main oblation, and the priests engaged by him perform the subsidiary actions.

Priests.

There are 16 Ṛitviks or priests as given at p. 180. The Chamasâdhvaryus are ten in number and they have been already described previously in the introduction. A S'amitâ and an Upaga priest are not separate ; an ordinary priest does the duty prescribed for a S'amitâ or an Upaga. While on the other hand, a vendor of Soma is a separate priest.

A Ṛitvik is a priest who performs a sacrifice in a season, the term is applicable to a sacrificer and the sixteen priests mentioned above. The term Ṛitvik is not a case of

ऋत्विक्.

अवयुत्ववाद but that of a परिसंख्या. For the difference between अवयुत्ववाद and परिसंख्या see p. 178. In a word, the term Ṛitvik is not used in its general sense but in its restricted meaning.

The sixteen priests mentioned at p. 180 and the sacrificer make up 17 Ṛitviks. Their functions and duties are different ; one cannot perform the duty of another. Their duties

17 Ṛitviks.

are separately fixed ; but the function laid down by a Vedic text sometimes overrides that which appears from the etymology of the word.

A Maitrâvaruṇa's duty is to repeat the पुरोनुवाक्य ; an Adhvarya who makes an oblation from Chamasâ cup is Chamasâdhvaryu. If the sacrificer and the Adhvaryu are unable to use the Chamasa cups, the Chamasâdhvaryus are engaged by the priests.

Duties of a मैत्रावरुण चमसाध्वयुँ.

When a sacrifice is described under a particular Samâkhyâ (classification, it does not thereby necessarily follow that the sacrifices to is be performed by the priest after whom the Samâkhyâ is given; as for instance, the S'yenayâga is described under the heading (Samâkhyâ) of Audgâtra and the Vâjapeya is described under the heading (S'amâkhyâ) of Âdhvaryava. From the heading it would therefore, follow that Syenayâga is to be performed by an Udgâtri and Vâjapeya by an Adhvaryu, but it is not so. A direct text about the procedure is the guide in the first instance; secondly, the principal and its subsidiary parts are performed, under a Chodakâ text. In the absence of the direct and Chodaka texts the Samâkhyâ will govern the procedure.

A Samâkhyâ does not necessarily determine functions of a priest.

From the above discussion, the author has clearly shown the difference between a principal and its parts; what benefits the principal directly is the Ârâdupakâraka and what benefits its parts, thus benefits the principal itself indirectly is the Sannipatyopakâraka. He has given illustrations of each class.

Summary of the whole Pâda.

PĀDA 8.

Keeping the distinction of the principal and subordinate as explained in the preceding Adhikaraṇa it necessarily follows that the appointment of Ritviks is vested in a sacrificer but if there is a direct text, an Adhvaryu can also appoint a Ritvik. As a sacrificer is the principal person in the sacrifice by reason of reaping its fruit, the purificatory ceremonies are to be performed upon him.

Appointment of a ऋत्विक् vests in the sacrificer.

Purificatory ceremonies are to be performed on the sacrificer.

Similarly austerities are to be performed by the sacrificer but if there is a direct text, a Ritvik shall have to undergo a vów.

Austerities

The priests are to put on red turbans and gold necklaces under a direct text.

Dress of a priest.

Desire accomplishing acts (Kâmyakarmas) are connected with the sacrificer, because it is he who performs a sacrifice with a certain object in view; but if there is a direct Vedic text, a priest can have also his desire fulfilled.

Desire accomplishing acts.

The mantras are of two kinds, (1) करण मंत्र (2) and अकर्म करण मंत्र; the former class of mantras regulates the procedure of a sacrificial operation, while the latter is chanted in the course of a sacrificial operation. The latter class as the आयुदी and the उपस्थान मंत्रs though read in a chapter on ऋत्विक, is connected with the sacrificer and therefore belongs to him.

अकर्म करण मंत्र.

There are mantras which are read in the अध्वयु and यजमान कांडs ; they are to be repeated by both the sacrificer and Adhvaryu.

The mantras twice repeated in two Kâṇḍas.

A literate Yajamâna is to repeat the mantras himself.

The duties are not determined by the Kâṇḍas in which they are described ; as for instance, washing of the sacrificial utensils is mentioned in the Yajamânakâṇḍa but it is to be performed by a priest who is specially engaged for the purpose.

Sacrificial work to be performed by the priests.

When a Hotâ priest is officiating for an Adhvaryu, then another priest performs the duty of the former.

Locum tenens.

An Adhvaryu is the general manager of the sacrifice ; he passes orders : they are executed by an Agnîdha.

Adhvaryu is a general manager.

A priest while chanting the Karaṇa mantra recites ममाग्ने-वर्चो विह्वेश्वस्तु " T. S., IV. 14. 1. " O ! fire let there be my splendour in the offerings." Though the priest uses *my splendour*, yet thereby he means his client's, splendour ; he represents his clients for all intents and purposes. It happens every day in the British law court ; a lawyer uses the same expression which would be appropriate in the mouth of his client. When an army is victorious every individual from the general down to the soldier in the army thinks it his own achievement. The principle is called वर्चोन्याय in the language of the Mîmânsâ.

वर्चोन्याय.

The reward of the principal act accrues to the sacrificer and the subordinate acts are performed for the successful completion of a sacrifice by the priests. The fruit of the subsidiary acts in the shape of the successful termination therefore accrues to the priests.

The reward of the Karaṇa-mantra for the successful completion accrues to the priets.

The purificatory ceremonies performed on the materials ensures for the
benefit of the constituent parts primarily and for the benefit of the principal secondarily.

The purificatory ceremony performed on the materials subserves
the purpose of the constituent
parts and thereby that of the
principal.

The Apûrva applies to
the model sacrifice.

The principle of Apûrva or the extraordinary applies to model sacrifice ;
if it were to apply to both the model and the
modified sacrifices, there would be then two
extraordinary principles which is absurd.

In a conflict direct text
prevails.

Where there is a direct statement about the application of a text it
will apply there but it cannot be made appli-
cable where its application is not mentioned.
In a sacrifice, the grass brought from the
jungle is sacrificially operated upon before it is used ; there is also a
bundle of grass kept in reserve which is not so operated upon : it is called
the परिभोजनीय. It is stated by a Vedic text that an altar should be
covered with the purified grass but there is no provision for covering the
vessel containing ghee with grass. In this state of conflict it is laid
down that the altar shall be covered with the purified grass and the पवित्र
and विधृति, the grass placed under and above the ghee vessel should be
from the परिभोजनीय grass.

The purificatory ceremony
is not necessary on the
Indravâyu vessel in
which a slice of
Purodâs'a cake
is placed.

A portion of a Purodâs'a cake is placed in the Indravâyu vessel
which is not sacrificially operated upon ;
it is the Purodâs'a upon which ceremonies
are performed. Though the piece of the
Purodâs'a cake is consecrated it is placed
in the vessel upon which there is no necessity of performing any consecration ceremony.

Low reading pertains to
the principal.

Low pronouncing of mantras pertains
to the principal in a Kâmyeṣṭi because it is
the principal that leads to the object in
view.

Constituent parts of
S'yenayâga should be
performed with ghee.

Old stored up butter in a leather bag is used in the performance of
a S'yenayâga under the principle of sequence
in lieu of Soma ; but it is not sufficient and
so Soma is absolutely necessary. Under this
state of affairs the stored up ghee is used in
the constituent parts of the S'yenayâga. Agnyâdhâna being in another
context is not a constituent part of S'yenayâga though it is a preliminary

act. All the constituent parts without an exception should be performed with ghee.

सवनीय cakes made of flesh in शाक्वानामयन.

There is a sacrifice called the Sâkyânâmayana which lasts for 36 years; in it the Savaniya cakes are made of flesh instead of rice flour as is usually done.

Mr. Kuṇṭe, the learned editor of the षड्दर्शन चिंतनिका says that अंगिरसामयन and शाक्वानामयन are the emblems of the migration of the Angiras and S'âkya races into India. He is further of opinion that the traces of the ancient colonization by the Âryan and Angiras races in southern country are still found amongst the present Brâhmaṇs who call themselves Ayyars (आर्य) and Aiyangars (आर्यांगिरस). It is a very plausible theory.

CHAPTER IV.
PÂDA 1.

पुरुषार्थ and क्रत्वर्थ explained.

The author proceeds to explain the Puruṣâtha and the Kratvartha fully dealt with in the preceding pages of the introduction. Accordingly what secures a man's object to which he is naturally prompted is called the Puruṣârtha and that which secures the object of a sacrifice is the Kratvartha. Accordingly the ten sacrificial weapons enumerated at p. 202 are for the objects of a sacrifice, because from the use which is mentioned in that connection, it appears that they are with the object of the sacrifice; while the penances which deliver one from sins are for the benefit of a man.

It will not be out of place, if I mention the ten sacrificial weapons mentioned at p. 202 of the book. They are (1) स्फ्य wooden spade or sword : (2) कपाल potsherd (3) ऋग्निहोत्र हवणी sacrificial dish (4) शूर्प winnowing basket (5) कृष्णाजिन black antelope's skin (6) शम्बा cudgel or pin (7) उलूखल mortar (8) मुसल pestle (9) दृषद् stone slab or lower part of the grinding stone (10) उपल muller or upper part of the grinding stone.

(1) We are not in a position to determine the shape of the wooden sword or spade; we know from the text quoted at p. 202 from the तैत्तरीय संहिता that it was used in digging an altar. A book called दर्शपूर्णमासप्रकाश has recently been brought out by the Ânandârama authorities at Poona showing figures of the sacrificial weapons. (See figure, of Vol. I.)

(2) कपाल or potsherd has been fully described in the preceding pages. (See figures 2 in the दर्शपूर्णमास प्रकाश Vol I.)

(3) अग्निहोत्रहवणी is described by Jhâ at p. 268 of the Prabhâkara School of the Mîmânsâ. "It is made of *vikankata* wood 15 inches long with one end shaped either like the lip of the elephant or the beak of the swan or the tail of the crow, with a hollow 8, 5 or 4 *anguls* deep respectively; the rest being kept as handle ; this is used in making the Agnihotra offerings." (See दर्शपूर्ण प्रकाश vol. 1 for its description and figure No. 3.)

(4) शूर्प or winnowing basket as is current in these days is made of twigs, for removing the husk mixed with corn. It is a common article of use and is still called by this name. It cannot be said with certainty whether the शूर्प used by the ancient Aryans has undergone a change but I believe it is the same. (See item No. 4 in दर्श पूर्णमास प्रकाश Vol I.)

(5) कृष्णाजिन black deer's skin was used under a mortar when any grain was pounded in it by a pestle to remove the husk from it (Ibid item No. 5.)

(6, उलूखल has been translated by the word mortar. The उलूखल or commonly known as ऊखल or ऊखली is made of stone and fixed in the earth. In it the grains are placed for pounding. It is a common article of daily use in an Indian household or in agricultural villages. The mortar which is used for pounding medicine is also called उलूखल or shortly खल. It is described by Dr. Girindra Nath Muhopadhyaya in the surgical instruments of the Hindus vol. 1 p. 318. See also Plate No. LXXXI figures 1 and 2 in Vol. II. (Ibid, item No. 7.)

(7) मुसल pestle. It is made of wood for the purpose of pounding rice or other corn to remove the husk from the grain. It is big and long ; but in pounding medicine it is small and is also called अयोग्र. See the diagram in Dr. Mukerji's Surgical instruments of the Hindus Vol. II Plate LXXXI figures 1 and 2. (Ibid, item No. 8.)

(8) दृषद् is a stone slab according to Kuṇṭe but it is the lower part of a grinding stone according to Keith. (Ibid, figure No. 9.)

(9) उपल is a muller according to Kuṇṭe and the upper part of a grinding stone according to Keith. (Ibid, figure No. 10.)

(10) यभयार is a cudgel according to Kunte for the support of the stone slab and pin according to Keith. (Ibid, item No. 6.)

As to the numbers 8, 9 and 10. See the figures 4 and 5 in the plate LXXXI in the surgical instruments of the Hindus in Vol. IIs and their description at p. 327 of Vol. I of Dr. Grindra Nath Mukerji,

I agree with Kuṇṭe in holding that in ancient India when sacrifice were common and the be-all and end-all of the Hindu life was the performance of the sacrifices, the complex machinery of the grinding stones was not known. There is no doubt that in Mahavagga VI. 3.2, the grinding stone is referred to thereby showing that in the time when Buddhism flourished in India, grinding mill was known. In the Sanchi Topes, however, we find the stone slab and muller. See Cunningham's Bhilsa Topes at p. 206. All these facts show that the stone slab and muller were used in preparing flour for which we have 'पिष्टि' in Sanserit. It is still called *pitthi* in vernacular. Any grain or pulse is first put in water; when it is sufficiently wet, it is pounded by a muller on a stone slab the latter being raised at the top by means of a wooden cudgel. This process of pounding or grinding is still performed in India in the case of pulses.

Corn is converted into flour by means of grinding stones. They vary in different parts of the country. In the east the lower stone is fixed in the ground by means of an iron pin or *kili* and the upper stone moves round it on the lower stone. There is a hole in the upper stone in which there is wood fixed on the pin. The corn which is to be ground is put into this apperture and the upper stone is moved by the handle which is fixed in it. See figure 4 in the plate LXXXI of Dr. Mukerji's Surgical instruments of the Hindus. In the western part of India, the stones are placed on clay-made structure which is like a ditch round the stones. In this ditch-like structure flour is collected. I do not for a moment contend that the grinding stones were not known in ancient India ; what I say is that the stone slab and muller appear to me to be more primitive by reason of their simplicity than the more complex machinary of a grinding mill. Be that as it may, I have explained both sides of the case.

<table>
<tr><td>पर्वेकत्वन्याय</td><td>A number in a noun is very important and conveys the oneness, duality or plurality of the materials. When a singular number is used, it means one only but does not include many. This principle is called पर्वे कतव न्याय.</td></tr>
<tr><td>Gender.</td><td>So also a gender in a noun is also very important. Masculine gender does not therefore, include feminine or neuter or vice versa.</td></tr>
<tr><td>Principal and subordinate extraordinary principles explained.</td><td>The Apûrva has been explained in the preceding pages of the introduction. The principal act secures it, which is called the main Apûrva. The subsidiary parts of an act help in securing it : every one of them conduces to the main Apûrva.</td></tr>
</table>

They produce visible effects and also the minor Apûrvas leading up to the principal Apûrva. Take for instance the Prayâjas ; they are minor parts in a sacrifice but they produce some invisible effect in addition to the visible effect.

वैषम्य and साम्य explained. When in the performance of an act, two effects are produced, one of which is directly connected with the principal object and the other is not, it is a case of disparity (वैषम्य) ; but if two effects thus produced are directly connected with the principal it is then a case of parity (साम्य). As for instance, when curd is put in the heated milk, the latter is converted into curd and a watery substance of blue colour called Vâji (whey). The former is directly connected with the आभिक्षा dish but the latter is not. It is a case of disparity (वैषम्य). The holding of a staff by the Maitrâvaruṇa priest and the sacrificer, being connected with the main object is an example of parity (साम्य.)

वाजिन्वाय.

प्रयोजक and अप्रयोजक explained. In the above illustration of the Vaiṣamya we see that two substances are produced, the one is essential प्रयोजक and the other is non-essential (अप्रयोजक). The former constitutes a dish called the Âmikṣâ and the latter is useless. It is called वाजिन्वाय.

Illustration of the purchase of सोम. There are many other illustrations of प्रयोजक and अप्रयोजक. A Soma is purchased with a cow of one year ; before the bargain is struck, she is made to walk seven steps. The seventh step is like the fall of the hammer in an auction sale. Here the bargain or purchase of Soma is (प्रयोजक) essential and the walking of the cow is incidental (अप्रयोजक.)

Potsherd. The potsherds are used for baking sacrificial cakes ; but before the rice flour is kneaded into paste, the husk from the rice is removed by winnowing it with the potsherds. The chief use of a potsherd is for baking of the cakes ; it is प्रयोजक. The winnowing of the rice with it is incidental अप्रयोजक.

Animal. In an animal which is killed for a sacrifice, the viscera and its flesh are प्रयोजक and blood and fæcal matter are अप्रयोजक.

Sacrificial cake. The sacrificial cake which is offered to fire is principal (प्रयोजक) while slices cut off from it for a Sviṣṭakrit offering are incidental अप्रयोजक.

No ghee is required for sprinkling the omentum. In a Vâjapeya sacrifice some animals are killed ; in the morning all the parts meant for offering are sprinkled with ghee ; this process is called the Abhighâraṇâ. In the noon, only *omentum* is offered ; because it is once sprinkled over with ghee in the morning, there is, therefore, no necessity of the Abhighârañâ in the noon. No ghee is therefore reserved for the sprinkling in noon and no vessel is, therefore, required for keeping it. Further no vessel is required for keepiug a part of ghee if there be any, it is therefore अप्रयोजक.

There are ghee oblations in the beginning and at the end of a sacrifice, called प्रयाज and अनुयाज. They are five in number ; the 1st is called समित्, the second is तनूनपात, the third is इडा, the fourth is बर्हि and the 5th is स्वाहाकार. The ghee for sacrificial offering is kept in a big vessel from which it is taken sufficient for both sorts of oblations by means of a wooden spoon called उपभृत्. From it the ghee is carried by means of a जुहू a sacrificial spoon once for the first three offerings. Carrying of ghee from the wooden spoon to the sacrificial spoon for the 4th offering is called समानयन. It would follow from the view taken above in the case of अभिघारणा that समानयन is अप्रयोजक, but it is not so ; it is on the contrary प्रयोजक.

समानयन is प्रयोजक.

From the above discussion it follows as a corollary that the ghee taken in जुहू is only for प्रयाज offering and that taken in the उपभृत् is for both. In this view, the ghee contained in उपभृत् is sufficient for the oblations in both the प्रयाज and अनुयाज. It will be much better to explain the various texts in this connection. "चतुगृर्हीतंवा एतदद्भुत तस्य आचारेणा धार्यत्रिरित: प्राचीनं प्रयाजान् यजति समानयते चतुगृर्हीततवाव." " It became taken four times ; having sprinkled in downpour, he makes an oblation of three प्रयाज towards the east : he carries it for the 4th offering (taking)." According to this text, the five प्रयाज offerings are considered to be made up of four offerings ; three prior to समानयन and two after समानयन which constitute one for the purpose of the text.

Ghee in जुहू for प्रयाज only.

Texts explained.

"चतुगृर्हीतं जुहोति " तै॰ संं॰ ५. १. १. ११.

" He makes offerings taken four times." It is an अनारभ्यविधि and is applicable to all sacrifices.

"चतुगृर्हीतानि आज्यानि भवंति । नह्यत्र अनुयाजान् यक्ष्यन् भवति" ।

The ghee is enough for taking four times ; but with it, the अनुयाज oblation cannot be offered.

"अष्टा वुपभृति" तै॰ ब्रा॰ ३. ३. ५. ५.

" (He takes) " eight times in an उपभृत्." Had there been no such text, there would have been a necessity for the second vessel for other four offerings ; lt is in order to prohibit the necessity of the second vessel that the word eight is used. It means that ghee sufficient for eight offerings should be taken in the उपभृत् vessel. In this view, the 'eight ' is अप्रयोजक.

PÂDA 2.

The author accumulates other examples to explain the प्रयोजक, अप्रयोजक,
साम्य and वैषम्य. He takes up the case of a
sacrificial post. I may explain here what a युप
is. A tree selected for the construction of a युप
must be of such girth that it can be clasped within the arms of a man
and must not be smaller than a span. Five cubits from the tree are
to be cut in length from the upper side and 4 fingers in length from
the front with the following mantra " अच्छिन्नोऽताव : सुबीर : " तै॰ सं॰ १.३.५.१
" Thou art uncut, wealth and a good warrior ". The first portion cut is
made into a sacrificial post and the other portion which is 4 fingers in length
is perforated with holes and mounted on the sacrificial post. Leaving a
cubit of the tree at the bottom, the remaining portion is cut from it
and chiselled into four or eight faces but of these chips the first piece
that falls is called स्वरु and three others are to serve as props to अरणि at
the time of producing fire. From what we have seen from the description given above, about the construction of a युप and a स्वरु it is clear
that the former is प्रयोजक and the latter is अप्रयोजक. A tree is felled for the
construction of a युप but not for getting the chip called स्वरु. It is a case
of वैषम्य.

Construction of a युप explained.

In connection with the new and full moon sacrifices, it is said " प्राचीं
माहरेत्." " Let him bring east." There the
term ' प्राची ' does not mean eastern direction,
because it is said in connection with the driving
off the calves with a branch of a tree at the time of milking a cow. It,
therefore, means a branch of a tree to fit in the circumstances.

प्राची means a branch of a tree.

A branch is cut off from a tree ; the upper part of it serves the
purpose of driving off the calves and the lower portion is used in arranging the potsherds. The former
is called शाखा and the latter is called उपवेष. Where there is no necessity
of driving off the calves, no branch is cut off and no उपवेष is separately
prepared. From this, we see that the branch is principal and the tree
is cut for procuring a branch but not for making an उपवेष.* The former
is प्रयोजक and the latter is अप्रयोजक ; it is, therefore, a case of disparity
(वैषम्य.)

उपवेष is अप्रयोजक.

---

* उपवेष is explained at p. 850 fully. As to the diagram see No. 26
of first volume of the दर्शपूर्णमासप्रकाश recently brought out in the
Ânandâs'rama series.

The principal act which is an object in view is called अर्थकर्म, and
when an act is completed and the thing used up
is finally disposed of, it is called प्रतिपत्तिकर्म.
As for instance the branch of a tree used
for driving off the calves is the अर्थकर्म; and when it is no longer
required in a sacrifice, it is burnt in the fire : this is called प्रतिपत्तिकर्म.
Burning of Darbhâ grass after it is used up in the sacrifice constitutes its
प्रतिपत्तिकर्म.

अर्थकर्म and प्रतिपत्तिकर्म explained.

Pranîtâpa is the pure and sacrificially
operated upon water brought for the purpose
of a sacrifice. It is mixed with the rice flour
in preparing the sacrificial cake ; it is called
Samyávana. Subsequently the water is thrown
in the interior of an altar ; it is called
Ninayana. From this explanation of the terms, it is apparent that निनयन
is प्रतिपत्तिकर्म.

प्रणीताप water.

संयवन explained.

निनयन is प्रतिपत्ति कर्म.

On the contrary the holding of the staff by the Maitravaruna after
it has been held by the sacrificer is an Artha-
karma because the Maitrâvaruna priest performs subsequent sacrificial acts with it.
Passing over the staff to the Maitrâvaruna priest is, therefore, not a
Pratipattikarma.

Holding of the मैत्रावरुण staff is अर्थकर्म.

There is a ceremony called कुष्ठाविषाणप्रासन ; in it a horn of a black
antelope is used in scratching the body during
the performance of a sacrifice. When it is
no longer required, it is thrown into a pit
called चात्वाल. The former is अर्थकर्म and the latter is प्रतिपत्ति कर्म.

कुष्ठा विषाण प्रासन explained.

When the Soma sacrifice is over, the sacrificer and his wife with the
priest go to a bathing place where the priest
throws off all the sacrificial materials used up
in the water. Going to the Avabhritha (bath) is, therefore, a Pratipattikarma.

अवभृथ is a प्रतिपत्तिकर्म.

From the above discussion about the अर्थकर्म and प्रतिपत्तिकर्म, a
reader will fully understand the difference
between the two ; the former is principal and
is productive of an invisible effect while the latter constitutes the final
disposal which is visible.

End of the discourse.

Next the author proceeds to explain उत्पत्ति विधि and नियम. When
an organic act is directed to be performed,
it is called उत्पत्ति विधि and the qualities of

नियम explained.

the materials described there constitute नियमविधि, because general description of the materials is vague but the particular statement of the quality of a sacrificial material being restrictive in nature is Niyama. In this view the Vedic text which prescribes time, place and agent of the performance of a sacrifice is by way of a restrictive rule (Niyama). Similarly the rule as to the purificatory ceremonies on the materials is a Niyama.

In a Yâga there are materials, god and performance of a ce remony.

याग and होम defined. The text which inculcates the performance of a ceremony is characterised by any of the verbal forms of $\sqrt{yaj}$; but when the text which directs the performance of the ceremony is characterised by any of the verbal forms of $\sqrt{hu}$ in addition to relinquishment, the Yâga is called Homa.

In a Yâga, the materials offered are relinquished in favour of a deity and if the relinquished materials are consigned to a fire, it becomes Homa. In a gift (दान) the ownership is transferred to another and is denoted by any of the forms of डुदाञ्_ $\sqrt{Du\ Dân}$.

Their difference.

Gift.

According to Kâtyâyana, a Yâga is performed in a standing posture with the accompaniment of Yâjyâ and Puronuvâkya ending in Vaṣaṭ while a *homa* is performed in a sitting posture similarly but with Svâhâ at the end.

कात्यायन's view.

वर्हि of the आतिथ्येष्टि used in उपसद and अग्नीषोमीय The Varhi grass which has been brought for an अग्नीषोमीय shall be used for the उपसद and अग्नीषोमीय as they are not specially described. The grass brought for the purpose of a sacrifice lasts for ¦the use of every action performed during its continuance.

PÂDA 3.

भावना and its three constituents *viz.*, साध्य, साधन and इतिकर्तव्यता have already been explained. The nature of the last two has been dealt with in the preceding two Pâdas. The nature of the साध्य or fruit is explained in the present Pâda. There is a text " वस्य पर्णमयी जुहू भवति न पापं श्लोकं शृणोति " " He whose जुहू is made of पर्ण wood does not hear bad news " There is no relationship of cause and effect between a Juhû made of Parṇa wood and hearing no bad news. It does uot necessarily follow that one who uses Parṇa ladle should not hear bad news. There is no Vyâpti or invariable concommittance as a logician would say. What is the nature of the text ? It is by way of an Arthavâda and therefore Kratvartha.

अर्थवाद nature of reward.

Subordinate nature of the नैमित्तक sacrifice.

There are two kinds of sacrifices called Nitya (permanent) and Naimittika (occasional). The former is permanent because it is always performed while the latter being performed on a certain occasion is modified and, therefore, impermanent or non-essential. As for instance, it is said " चमसेनापः प्रणयेत् " in the model sacrifice (let him carry water with a spoon), then it is said " " चुन्मयेन प्रतिष्ठाकामस्य प्रणयेत् " " Let him carry it with an earthen vessel, if desirous of honour." We see that a vessel of clay is used for carryi ng water on the occasion of the performance of a sacrifice with the object of honour. It is an occasional act and, therefore, impermanent.

The same substance can be used in the नित्य and नैलिचिक sacrifices.

A substance can be used both in the permanent and occasional sacrifices but the texts governing them will be independent i.e., they will constitute two coordinate sentences. As for instance " दध्ना जुहोति " " He makes an oblation with curd" " दध्नेद्रिय का मस्य जुहुयात् " " Let one who is desirous of the strength of the organs, offer curd ". In these texts we see that there are two independent sentences and the same substance is used in the Nitya and Kâmya sacrifices.

Subsidiary nature of the purificatory rites.

The purificatory ceremonies performed on the materials being for the purpose of the sacrifice are subsidiary.

विश्वजित् न्याय explained.

When in a Vedic text, an act is prescribed, but no fruit is mentioned the presumption is that a fruit accrues from the performance of the act prescribed by the Veda. There is a further presumption that only one fruit accrues. Take for example " विश्वजिता यजेत " Let him perform a Vis'vajit. Under the rules laid down above, you can presume that some fruit will accrue from the performance of a Vis'vajit which is enjoined by the above quoted Vedic text. The highest fruit that one can obtain is heaven ; it, therefore, follows that one secures heaven by the performance of a Vis'vajit. It is called Vis'vajit principle.

रात्रिसत्रन्याय explained.

When the fruit is mentioned in the original text or in the subordinate parts, there is no such presumption which arises under the Vis'vajit principle. If the fruit is mentioned in the Vidhivâkya, it is by way of Arthavâda and if it is by way of Arthavâda of any part, it is really in praise of the principal. This constitutes Râtrisattranyâya.

When a Kâmya sacrifice is performed, you cannot presume the attainment of heaven in addition to the accomplishment of the desire for which the sacrifice is performed in the absence of a text to the contrary. As for instance, " योऽब्रह्मवर्चसकामः स्वार्द तस्मा एतं सौर्यं चरं निर्वपेत् " तै० संं० २. ३. २. ३. If one desires Brahmaṇik glory, let the boiled rice be offered to the sun for his sake." Here the text is clear ; if the desire is for the Brahmaṇik glory, the boiled rice is to be offered to the sun god. You cannot, therefore, make any presumption for the attainment of heaven under the Vis'vajit principle in addition to securing the object mentioned directly in the text.

In a काम्येष्टि, *the attainment of the desire is the only fruit.*

When a text refers to the accomplishment of all desires by means of a sacrifice, it refers to the main act, it should be performed on the occasion of each desire to be accomplished. The desires are not fulfilled all at once on the completion of the act ; they are fulfilled consecutively ; each act performed in succession fulfils each desire. This is called दर्शंपूर्णमासन्याय.

दर्शंपूर्णमासन्याय.

When a certain fruit of a sacrifice is not reaped in the present life, the presumption is that it will be obtained in the life hereafter. It is called योगसिद्धिन्याय.

योगसिद्धिन्याय

The author now proceeds to explain the difference between an Angavidhi and Kâlavidhi. When a text lays down the performance of a subsidiary part after the performance of the main act, it is called Angavidhi, but when it lays down the performance of two independent acts one after the other it is in the nature of Kâlavidhi. As for instance Sautrâmaṇi is a constituent part of the Agnichayan ; Vaimridha is a constituent part of the full moon sacrifice. In the case of the latter, the doubt arises by reason of the text " संस्थाप्यपौर्णमासीं वैमृधमनुनिर्वंपति " having made the offering of the full moon sacrifice, he performs the Vaimridha sacrifice." occuring in the context of the new and full moon sacrifices. It is an axiomatic truth under the Mîmânsâ that a sentence prevails over the context and the Vaimridha is, therefore, not a constituent part of both but only of the full moon sacrifice.

अङ्गविधि and कालविधि explained.

On the other hand the text " अग्निभारुतादूर्ध्वंमनुयाजैश्चरंति." " They perform Anuyâja after the recitation of the Agnimâruta ". Agnimâruta is a part of a Soma sacrifice, and Anuyâja is a part of an animal sacrifice ; each of them is independent of the other. So the above quoted text lays down the sequence of time.

When there is a doubt as to whether a text is an Angavidhi or a Kâlavidhi it will be presumed to be a Kâlavidhi. As for example "दर्शपूर्णमासाविष्ट्वा सोमेन यजते" He perfoms Soma sacrifice after the new and full moon sacrifices "; as in the original, no details are mentioned, it does not, therefore, appear that one is the part of the other. So the presumption is that it is a Kâlavidhi.

When there is doubt as to the nature of a text it will be presumed to be a कालविधि.

As a rule the fruit of an action accrues to the person who performs it ; but when a son is born to a person, he performs a Vais'vânara sacrifice ten days after the birth. No fruit is mentioned ; the presumption is that it accrues to the son, since he is not different from his father under the text "आत्मावैपुत्रः " " A son is certainly one's self."

जातेष्टिन्यायं.

The subordinate parts are performed at their own time but not with their principal. We have seen that सौत्रामणि is a part of the Agnichayana. The Sautrâmani having Iṣṭis as its model shall be performed on the new and full moon days one day after the performance of Agnichayana and carrying of Ukhâ. Vrihaspatisava is the part of Vâjapeya. "वाजपेयेनेष्ट्वा बृहस्पतिसवेन यजेत" After performing the Vâjapeya, let him perform Vrihaspati Sava. Vrihaspati Sava being a modified form of the Jyotiṣṭoma shall be performed in spring, but the Vâjapeya is to be performed in autumn ; so the Vrihaspatisava shall be performed on the new or full moon day of spring as usual after the performance of Vâjapeya.

PĀDA 4.

In the Râjasûya or coronation sacrifice, there are minor acts such as animal sacrifice, Soma sacrifice, gambling, narration of old stories and Darvihoma (ghee oblations). They do not produce any visible result ; they are, therefore, subsidiary acts of their principal Râjasûya. Gambling and other acts occur under the context of the Abhiṣechanîya which is a subsidiary part of the Râjasûya, but that denotes the sequence i. e., the time when gambling etc., are to be performed, while on the other hand the oblation of Soma juice is offered at the time of Upasats and is also their part and the text about the offer of the cups is by way of restatement and does not violate the principle of ekavâkyata. Âmanahoma is subsidiary to Saṅgrahini because the former does not produce any **fruit**

राजसूय and its subsidiary acts.

Soma cups are subsidiary to Upasats.

आमनहोम.

LXXXII.

Those acts which do not produce any effect are subordinate to the principal. The author now proceeds to show the difference between the Nitya and Naimittika acts by examples. Dadhigraha is a ceremony in which curd is offered to fire to appease the gods when any mistake is committed in the performance of a sacrifice. It, therefore, follows that when no mistake is committed, no Dadhigraha ceremony will be performed. From the description of the ceremony given above, it is apparent that its performance is casual and is not permanent.

दधिग्रह is नैमित्तिक.

A person who performs Agnichayana has to carry the Ukhâ fire for a year. It is a small iron grate mounted upon a sling and is tied to the sacrificer's neck by six or twelve strings. The fire placed in it is called Ukhya. If a sacrificer for some reason is incapable of carrying the Ukhya fire for a year, he has to make Vais'vânara offerings. The latter are, therefore, casual or occasional but not permanent.

वैश्वानर offerings are occasional.

In an Agnichayana ceremony, a Chiti which is a place made of various kinds of bricks in the form of a bird on a ground of two spans levelled by a plough is constructed; such five Chitis are first made in which fire is established. The sixth one is also constructed to meet the emergency; if there is an error or omission in the performance of an Agnichayana, the sixth Chiti sacrifice is resorted to. Though the Ṣaṭchiti is mentioned amongst the permanent things, yet it is occasional as appears from the description given above.

षट्‌चिति sacrifice is occasional.

Piṇḍapitri Yajña is an independent act; it is not a part of the new moon sacrifice though it is performed on the new moon day.

पिंडसुपितृयज्ञ is an independent act.

A rope which is used in an animal sacrifice is not a part of the animal but of the sacrificial post round which it is tied to make it firm. It is mentioned in connection with the sacrificial animal.

A rope is a part of the sacrificial post.

We have seen how Svaru is constructed; it is the first chip that falls from the tree felled for the construction of a sacrificial post. It is used in annointing eleven animals with butter, called परश्वेकादशिनी.

स्वरु is a part of an animal sacrifice.

After the completion of the sacrifice the Svaru is thrown into the fire and burnt instead of the sacrificial post. The throwing of the Svaru into fire is called निष्क्रयवाद or the ransom of the sacrificial post. Now the question is whether the Svaru is *sine qua non* of the sacrificial post or of the animal. From the description given above it is clear that it is a part of the sacrifice of the animal which is annointed by it with ghee.

The author now proceeds to explain the Anga and Angî. The अङ्ग and अङ्गी explained. Anga is the constituent part of the Angî the principal ; it is Itikartavyatâ. It does not produce any fruit independently. As for example आग्नेय, अग्नीषोमीय, उपांशुयाज, ऐंद्राग्न, साम्नाय. आघार, आज्यभाग, प्रयाज, अनुयाज, पत्नीसंयाज समिष्टयजु and स्विष्टकृत् constitute the new and full moon sacrifices. They are the constituent parts of their principal, दर्शपूर्णमासयाग.

There are also two terms Pradhâna and Guṇa. The Pradhâna is प्रधान and गुण explained principal ; when it is known, its qualities are described by the Guṇ which is subordinate. A principal is known by its subordinate quality called Guṇa. It does not exist independently of its principal ; it produces a fruit. It is correlative and therefore depends upon its principal. It is, therefore, called a subordinate part.

The author proceeds to explain the difference between a constituent Difference between the constituent and subordinate parts. part and subordinate part. They are both subordinate to the principal. The constituent parts constitute the sacrifice ; it does not exist apart from the constituent parts of which it is made up. It corresponds to the Ayutasiddha of Samavâya in the Vais'eṣika School of philosophy. Many such constituent parts go to make up one organic whole called the principal act. They do not produce any fruit independently. The subordinate part (Guṇa) is a correlative of the principal ; it describes the quality of the principal. You know the principal from the subordinate part ; It produces a fruit independently. It may also be a constituent part (Anga) but an Anga cannot be a Guṇa.

Keeping the above distinction in mind the Âgneya etc., mentioned above are the constituent parts of the दर्शपूर्ण मासयाग ; while the दीक्षणीया and प्रायणीया are the subordinate parts of a ज्योतिष्टोम and are also its Anga. The Anga has a larger circle than Guṇa.

There is a text which says ज्योतिष्टोमेन स्वर्गकामो यजेत। कतमानि तानिज्योतींषि। य एतस्य स्तोमा इति। त्रिवृत् Subordinate parts of a ज्योतिष्टोम. ज्योतिष्टोम पंचदश सप्तदश एक विंशः एतानिवाव तानिज्योतींषि यएतस्य स्तोमाः।" "One who desires heaven shall perform Jyotiṣṭoma How many are its lights which are the *stomas* ? They are त्रिवृत्, पंचदश, सप्तदश, एकविंश. These are verily the lights which are its Stomas." So we see that the Stomas (psalms) are like the lights and describe the Jyotiṣṭoma and explain why it is so called. So they are subordinate ; being subordinate, they are also its constituent parts.

Stoma is a particular tune in which a verse of the Rigveda is sung.

Stoma and its variations explained. When three verses of the Rigveda are sung three times they constitute त्रिवृत स्तोम. When the same are sung in the direct and inverse order fifteen times, seventeen times and twenty-one times, they constitute पंचदश, सप्तदश and एकविंश स्तोमs.

CHAPTER V.
PÂDA 1.

The author has described the organic act with its subordinate or consti-

Karma explained. tuent parts in the preceding chapter. An act can be said to be completed when all its details and minor parts are performed in a systematic way. The question that naturally arises is, in what order or sequence should the subordinate acts be performed ? The present chapter deals with the order. It

Division of क्रम. is of six kinds ; consisting of श्रुतिक्रम, अर्थक्रम, पाठक्रम, स्थानक्रम, मुख्यक्रम and प्रवृत्तिक्रम. They are described in the preceding pages of the intrdouction ; here I can only refer to them cursorily. The श्रुतिक्रम is determined by the Vedic text and has therefore, priority over other Kramas. The अर्थक्रम is the order determined by the object in view ; as for example, he kills an animal and brings a sword ; but the accomplishment of the object in view requires the bringing of the sword first in order to kill the animal. The पाठक्रम depends upon the reading in the Vedas ; the reading in the mantra prevails over that in the Brâhmaṇa. The स्थानक्रम is the sequence according to the location ; the following example will explain it properly.

In a ज्योतिष्टोम three animals are killed अग्नीषोमीय on the औपवसथ्य day, the सवनीय on the सूत्याह and the अनुवंध्य after the sacrificial bath. In the सादस्य which is the modified form of the ज्योतिष्टोम all three animals are sacrificed on the सूत्याह. What will be the order there ? As सूत्याह is the day of a सवनीय animal, it will come first and the other will come in their order. There the order of the model sacrifice is not adhered to but the association of सूत्याह has reversed the order.

The मुख्यक्रम is the order of the subordinate parts depending upon that of the principal. The प्रवृत्तिक्रम is the order to which you will have

to stick and which you first chose according to your first impulse ; as for example, you have to perform certain ceremonies on eleven horses ; you perform one ceremony on the eleven horses one by one in an order of your own choice. You will have to perform the second ceremony on the remaining horses in the same order.

From the above analysis, there is no difference apparently between a

Difference between श्रुति-क्रम and पाठक्रम.

श्रुतिक्रम and the पाठक्रम. The difference between them is that in श्रुतिपाठ, the sequence is determined by one sentence or number of sentences and is generally denoted by अथ, अधुना etc., while in a पाठक्रम, the order is inferred from a number of sentences which, therefore determine it. The example of the former is at p. 179 which lays down the order in clear and direct terms.

समिधोयजति । तनूनपात यजति । इडोयजति । वर्हिर्यजति । स्वाहाकारं यजति । तै॰ सं॰ २.६.१.१ "He offers Samidh ; he offers Tanûnapâta ; he offers Iḍa ; he offers Varhi ; he offers Svâhâkâra " In the above text, the five offerings that are made in a Prayâja are mentioned but their order is not mentioned *directly*. The order in which they are read, shall be the order of their performance.

A Chodaka text is to be preferred to the Vidhâyaka text as to order

A चोदक text prevails over the विधायक text.

in a sacrifice. A Chodaka text lays down that a modified sacrifice is to be performed according to the model sacrifice, while a Vidhâyaka text makes it obligatory to perform the modified sacrifice. The former lays down the form of a sacrifice and the latter makes its performance a duty.

About the constituent parts. If there is a conflict in पाठक्रम and

पाठक्रम prevails over मुख्यक्रम.

मुख्यक्रम, the former prevails because it is supported by the sentences. As for instance, in the new and full moon sacrifices, the gods Agni, Viṣṇu and the twin gods Agniṣoma are propitiated with the Puroḍâs'a consecrated to Agni, clarified butter and the Puroḍâs'a cake consecrated to the twin gods respectively. There are different sacrificial operations made upon them ; if the order laid down in the principal is to be adhered to, the operation must be performed upon the clarified butter first and then on the cakes. This is not adhered to and the order mentioned in the text will be followed as "निर्वपाम्यग्नीषोमाभ्यां" तै॰ सं॰ १.१.४.२. I make an offering to अग्नीषोमः. "शुक्रम सिड्यीति रसितेजोऽसि " तै॰ सं॰ १.१.१०.३. "Thou art strength, thou art light and thou art splendour ". The first text refers to the offering of Havi and the last to the clarified butter.

When there is a conflict between a मंत्रपाठ and ब्राह्मणपाठ, the former prevails because the mantra is Abhidhâyaka *i.e.*, it gives a form to a sacrifice while the Brâhmaṇa is only Vidhâyaka *i.e.* it prescribes what act is to be performed. The former is Antaranga, the internal part of the sacrifice and the latter is vahiranga, the external part of it.

मंत्रपाठ has precedence over the ब्राह्मणपाठ.

There is a Sâkamedha sacrifice the model of which is दर्शपूर्णमासयाग. The latter are performed in two days; so it will follow that the Sâkamedha will also take the same time but there is a direct text under which all the ceremonies namely आग्नीकब्बतेष्टि, सांतपनीयेष्टि, गृहमेधीयेष्टि are hurried up and completed on the first day. This is called साकमेधीय न्याय.

साकमेधीय न्याय.

Having described the order in which the minor ceremonies are performed, the author says that the order is sometimes changed. The first becomes last and the last becomes first. When the details are performed not at their due time but before their time, it is called उत्कर्ष (transference forward); when they are postponed and performed after their due time it is called अपकर्ष (transference backward). When any ceremony is transferred forward, its accompaniments are also transferred along with it; as for instance when the Anuyâja is transferred forwards *i.e.*, performed before its due time, the सूक्तवाक and शंयुवाक which follow it are also transferred along with it, because the Anuyâja happens to be in their beginning. This transferrence is called तदादिन्याय.

अपकर्ष and उत्कर्ष explained.

तदादि explained.

When the ceremony is transferred backward *i.e.*, postponed, its accompaniments that precede it are also transferred along with it; as for instance when Prayâja is postponed, the Âghâra and Sâmadhenî which precede it are also postponed because it happens to be in their end. This principle in called तदन्तन्याय.

तदंतन्याय explained.

In the course of उत्कर्ष or अपकर्ष, only necessary accompaniments are transferred forward or backward; as for instance in the transferrence of a sacrificial post, that consecration and ornamentation of Puroḍâs'a cake are not transferred : they will be performed in their due course.

The accompaniments trnsferred must be necessary.

An incidental act (प्रासंगिक) is also not transferred. As for instance, पिष्टिलेप the remnants of the flour stuck to a slab and फलीकरण the particles of rice are offered to the fire after Anuyâja offering; when

An incidental act is not transferred.

the Anuyâja offering is transferred forward they are not transferred under the नदादिन्याय because they are incidental

When an act is itself an Apûrva or a model in itself there is no trans-

No transferrence in the model sacrifice.

ferrence ; as for example in connection with the new and full moon sacrifices covering of the Purodâs'a cake with ashes and then the construction of the altar are described ; but under the text " पूर्वेद्यु रमावस्या यांवेदिं करोति " " (He constructs an altar a day preceding the new moon day.") the covering of the Purodâs'a cake with the ashes will not be transferred forward, because the new moon day sacrifice is not a modified sacrifice but a model in itself.

An act which is essential in itself i.e., not connected with another

An essential act shall not be transferred forward or backward.

and for which time is fixed by a Vedic text, cannot be transferred forward or backward. As for instance in Sâkamedha which is one of the constituent parts of Châturmâsya, Sântâpanîya is performed in the noon and the Agnihottra is performed in the evening ; if for some reason or other Sântâpanîyeṣṭi is delayed and is performed in the evening, the performance of the Agnihottra is not transferred because it is an essential act and its time is fixed by the Vedic text. There is no harm if both of them are performed together.

When an act is to be performed subsequent to a particular act under

If there is a connection between two acts, one will be adjourned with the other.

a text, the former will be adjourned if the latter is delayed for some accidental cause because both of them are connected with each other. As for instance there are three Soma cups called Ukthya offered and subsequently the Ṣodas'î song is sung ; if for some reason or other the performance of the Ukthya is delayed the Ṣodas'î which follows it under the Vedic text. " तंपतांचं उक्थ्येभ्यो विगृह्णाति " (He takes it after उक्थ्य.") is necessarily delayed.

Châturmâsya is a name of a sacrifice ; it does not mean a sacrifice

Châturmâsya ceremony explained-

lasting for four months. It is Nâmadheya in the language of the Mîmânsâ. (See Karka's commentary on Kâtyâyana Śrauta Sûtra V. I. 6. It consists of वैश्वदेव, वरुण प्रघास, साकमेध, शुनासीरीय the constituent parts.

Before Vais'vadeva, a sacrifice called Vais'vânara to secure rains was performed. After this a sacrifice to अग्नि, सोम. सविता, सरस्वती, पूषा, मरुद्गण, विश्वेदेवा, द्यावापृथ्वी was performed. It is called Vais'vadeva sacrifice.

After this, the sacrificer and his wife in order to expiate their sins offered clarified butter to the god Varuṇa to be delivered from His meshes, for their sins.

Then it was followed by Sâkamedha consisting of आनीकवसेतेरिष्ट, संतापनीयेष्टि, वृष्मेयीयेष्टि, क्रीडनीयेष्टि महाहवि, महापितृयज्ञ, प्रसिद्धेरिष्ट. This sacrifice was celebrated by the gods to get victory on the Titans. The minor ceremonies which were performed within two days constitute its constituent parts. Ânîkavateṣṭi was performed in the forenoon of the first day ; the Santâpanîyeṣṭi was performed in the noon and Gṛihamedhiyeṣṭi in the afternoon.

The other ceremonies were performed on the next day ; the Krîḍanîyeṣṭi was performed in honour of seven Maruts with seven potsherd cakes. Then followed Mahâhavi in honour of Mahendra and Vis'vakarmâ. Mahâpitṛiyajña performed to proptiate the departed souls of the ancestors. The last ceremony was the Prasiddheṣṭi ; before its celebration, Tryambaka Yajña was performed. In it one more cake in addition to the number of the cakes according to the number of the members of the sacrificer's family was offered to Rudra. These cakes were baked on one potsherd and there were as many rice balls. The sacrificer and his family marched to the square of the villiage which is now called *chaupal* with a fire brand, Palâs'a leaves and water. They drew a line and placing the firebrand in it kindled the fire to whlch they offered the bits of the cakes covered with पलाश leaves. They threw the last leaf on the hole made by rats ; the remaining cakes were distributed amongst the people gathered. Two Puroḍâs'a cakes were given to the sacrificer. They then patted their laps and circumbulated round the fire. They went to the north where they tossed up their cakes and caught them on falling and going round the fire they stood to the north. The men of the village came there and gazed towards the north. A maiden desirous of a bridegroom came to the north and iuvoked Rudra. Then she patted her left lap and went round the fire three times tossing up and catching the Puroḍâs'a, cake. The members of the family gave the Puroḍâs'a cakes to the sacrificer ; he passed them on to his wife. The latter passed it on to her daughter who handed over to the Adhvaryu who tied them with a string and placed them on a dry branch of a tree. The people who assembled there also worshipped Rudra. It was a Tryambakeṣṭi ; after the completion, the sacrificer and his family returned to their dwelling house and offered boiled rice to Aditi. This is called Prasiddheṣṭi. Śunâsîrîya which is the last part of the Châturmâsya was performed last in which Indra or Śunâsîra was worshipped.

by offering of cakes baked on twelve potsherds and milk to Vâyu. A cake baked on one potsherd was offered to the sun god and the fee was one plough-share yoked with six oxen or bullocks. If the model was the Sûryayâga, then the fee consisted of a white horse ; in the absence of a horse, a cow was given as its fee. See Kâtyâyana Śrautasûtra, Chapter V.

Mr. Kuṇṭe thinks that the marriage by Svayaṃvara was the relic of the ancient Prasiddheṣṭi in which the young girls selected their bridegrooms.

PÂDA 2.

The author proceeds to explain पदार्थानुसमय and कांडानुसमय. If different ceremonies are performed at a time upon a number of objects arranged in a serial number, the order of the object is called कांडानुसमय. When

पदार्थानुसमय and कांडानु-समय explained.

the different objects have the ceremonies performed one after the other, the order in which the ceremonies will be performed is called पदार्थानुसमय. As for example, in a Vâjapeya several animals are to be sacrificially acted upon ; a ceremony should be performed on all the animals at a time and then other ceremonies in the same order ; but in an अश्वप्रतिग्रहेष्टि where several sacrificial cakes are to be sacrificially operated upon, all the ceremonies should be performed at a time till all the Puraḍâs'a cakes are exhausted. The former is the example of पदार्थानुसमय and the latter is that of the कांडानुसमय. In the former, several ceremonies are performed upon an object till the ceremonies are exhausted ; in it the ceremonies play an important part. In the latter, several objects are sacrificially operated one after the other till all the different sacrificial operations are completed ; in it the objects play an important part.

In the case of handfuls of grass, potsherds etc., the principle of कांडानुसमय applies because their parts cannot be broken ; as for instance, " he offers four handfuls "; it means an offering at a time, but not one handful at one time, the second at another time and so on.

Parts of a whole cannot be broken up and the principle of कांडानुसमय applies.

When a principal act is to be performed, it shall be performed till all its parts are exhausted ; as for example, when an oblation is to be offered to a god, all the sacrificial acts will be performed upon it before it is offered to the god under कांडानुसमय

Principal act shall be performed with its constituent parts.

principle.   Similarly, several sacrificial operations such as annointing, erecting, measuring and tying a string round a sacrificial post will be performed under the कांडानुसभय principle.

The Niruddhapas'ubandha is a model of all animal sacrifices. It
consists of offerings to a deity called दैवत, to स्विष्ट कृत called सौविष्टकृत and the sacrificial food to the priest called इड. These offerings are called Avadâna. The Vâjapeya is the modified sacrifice in which seventeen animals

When flesh of animals is offered in a Vâja-peya-the principle of कांडानुसमय applies.

are killed. In the present case, the offering of the flesh of all the animals will be first made to the deity, then to the Sviṣṭakṛit and subsequently the remainder shall be distributed amongst the priests as food under the पदार्थानुक्रम principle, because this method wil lnot break up the homogeneity of the act.

In a Râjasûya ceremony, there is a नानाबीजेष्टि in which a variety of seeds is required to be pounded under a Tantra principle which shall be dealt with later on in chapter XI and which is connected with पदार्थानुक्रम. One set of pestle and mortar is sufficient for pounding them all, it is not necessary that there should be diffe ent pestles and mortars for each variety.   When there is a real necessity, differ-

If there is necessity there will be different vessels.

ent vessels will be required ; as for instance, in a Jyotiṣṭoma sacrifice, an Agniṣomîya animal is killed and parts of it are offered to a fire. At that time Prayâja and Annyâja offerings are made : the Prayâja offering consists of clarified butter and the Anuyâja offering of a mixture of clarified butter and curd called Praṣdajya. As there are two different materials required, so there will necessarily be two vessels for them.

When a ceremony is transferred from a model sacrifice to the modified sacrifice under a Chodaka text it will have precedence over minor ceremonies, as for instance, in a Nakṣatreṣṭi there are the principal oblation and the minor Upahomas. The Nariṣṭa

A ceremony transferred from the model sacri-fice will have pre-ference to the minor ceremonies of the modified sacrifice.

homas are transferred there from the model sacrifice under a Chodaka text. What will be the order ? According to the principle laid down above after the principal oblation, the Nariṣṭa homas will be performed before the Upahomas.

Upon this subject, there is a difference of opinion between two great Mîmânsakas ; the view of Âtreya is that the continuity of the modified sacrifice should not

Difference of opinion.

be broken up by the intervention of the Narishṭahoma, but on the other hand, Bâdarâyaṇa the other eminent Mîmâmsaka holds the Nârishṭahoma to be principal and it should, therefore, have preference over the Upahomas.

When there is a direct authority in the Veda, as to a particular order, it will be strictly adhered to under the principle called Śrutikrama; as for instance, in a Râjasuya, gambling is prescribed first and then a sacrificial bath : this order will be strictly followed and the dictum of Bâdarâyana will not apply.

Exceptions to Bâdarayaṇa's dictum.

When there is a Pâṭhakrama in the Veda, the dictum of Bâdarâyaṇa does not apply ; as for instance, the Agnichayana is the molified sacrifice of a Jyotiṣṭoma in which Dîkṣaṇîyâ is performed. But in an Agnishayana sacrifice, Sâvitrahomas are performed, altars of bricks are erected, parts of an animal are offered and Ukhâ is worn round the neck of a sacrificer. According to Bâdarâyaṇa the Dîkṣaṇîyâ will have precedence ; but under the order given in the Taittarîya Saṃhitâ, Sâvittri Homas will have precedence.

In the absence of a Pâṭhakrama, the order of the model sacrifice will prevail ; as first Dîkṣaṇîyâ, second wearing flat piece of gold in the neck to protect it from the heat of Ukhâ fire and lastly carrying the Ukhâ tied up with string in the neck of the sacrificer in the modified sacrifice in accordance with the order in the model sacrifice.

In the absence of a Pâṭhakrama, the order the model sacrifice prevails.

Mr. Kuṇṭe traces the wearing of the Linga by the Lingâyats in Southern India to wearing the gold Rukma and carrying Ukhâ. It has a resemblance no doubt but cannot be said to have originated from wearing the gold plate and carring Ukhâ fire only on the ground of similarity.

PÂDA 3.

Before entering upon the analysis of this Pâda, it is necessary to describe the Vedic music. The Jyotiṣṭoma is the model of all the Soma sacrifices. They are of three kinds एकाह, अहीन and सत्र. Ekâha lasts for one day ; in it soma juice is extracted three times in a day ; once in the morning called प्रातः सवन, once in the noon called माध्यं दिन सवन and once in the evening called सायंसवन. There is, therefore, eno

system of Soma extraction in एकाह; if it lasts for more than two nights, and not less than eleven nights, it is called Ahîna. If it extends beyond twelve days, it is called a Sattra.

Each Savana was accompanied by music; the music in the morning Savana was in वहिष्पवमान tune; the noon Savana was in माध्यंदिनपवमान and the evening Savana was in आर्भवपवमान. There are other tunes such as रथंतर, वामदेव, वैरूप्य, वैराज वृहत्पृष्ठ, नौधवपृष्ठ, त्रैयोक, यौधाजय, रौरव, कालेय, श्वावाश्व, आंधीगव, अभिवर्त, वृहद्रथंतर etc.

Vedic tunes.

A verse from the Rigveda was adapted to music. A song in praise of a deity is called Staubh; it is also called Sâma. The former conveys the idea of the praise of a god and the latter is the tune of the song. A Sâma consisting of three verses from the Rigveda is called a Tricha. The first of a Tricha is called Stottrîya, the second is called Anurûpa and the third is called Paryâsa.

Difference between a Staubha and Sâma.

तृच explained.

When a number of Trichas is sung together, they constitute a Stoma. Any insignificant word thrown in the course of singing to complete time is called Stobha.

स्तोम.

स्तोभ

Stoma is divided into Paryâya, each of which consists of a Tricha. In the first Paryâya, the first verse of the first Tricha is sung once, the second verse thrice and the last one once, thus making up five verses. In the second Paryâya, the first verse of the second Tricha is sung thrice, the second and third verses once only. In the third Paryâya, the first and second verses of the third Tricha are sung once only and the third verse is sung thrice. Thus we see that the nine verses of which the three Trichas consist are sung fifteen times and constitute पंचदश स्तोम. In the same way, we have सप्तदशस्तोम, etc.

पंचदश and सप्तदशस्तोमs explained.

When the musical tunes, Bṛhat and Rathantara are varied a little, they, form a पृष्ठ. The Pṛiṣṭas are रथंतर, वृहत, वैरूप, वैराज यज्ञक्रत, रैवत. The Sâmas of different tunes constitute the above said Priṣṭas. The last part of Sâma is called Nidhana.

पृष्ठ

निधन

It is needless to mention here the terms, योनि, उत्तरा and प्रगथन explained in the commentary thoroughly (see at pp. 540 and 542). When one प्रगाथ is mixed with another and tuned, a musical mode called अभिवर्त is formed

योनि, उत्तरा and प्रगथन

The Vedic musicians divided the musical air into three parts ; the first

प्रस्ताव, उद्गीथ and प्रतिहार explained.

was called प्रस्ताव and was sung in a low key; in the second which was called उद्गीथ, the voice was raised and the style was changed. In the third called प्रतिहार the style was again changed. The priests who sang them were, therefore, respectively called प्रस्तोता, उद्गाता and प्रतिहर्ता.

There are seven musical notes called षड्ज, ऋषभ, गांधार, मध्यम, पंचम, धैवत and निषाद which are represented by सरगमपधन shortly. The Svara accent consists of उदात्त, अनुदात्त and स्वरित. The first is high tune, the second is low tune and the third is a mixed one. The अनुदात्त and स्वरित are represented by the lines below and above the letters in the Veda. When there is no perpendicular or horizontal line on the head or at the bottom of a letter it is to be accentuated as udátta; the perpendicular line over the head of a letter, represents Svarit and the horizontal line at the bottom of a letter indicates anudâtta. The following s'loka from the Yajñavalkya S'ikṣâ explains the musical notes and accents.

उच्चैर्निषादगांधारौ नीचावृषभधैवतौ ।

शेषास्तुस्वरिताज्ञेयाः षड्जपंचम मध्यमाः ॥

The Gândhâra and Niṣâda are of the acute (उदात्त) tune ; the ऋषभ and धैवत are of low tune (अनुदात्त) ; the rest namely षड्ज, पञ्चम and मध्यम are of middle tune (स्वरित).

The present Pâda treats of the anomalous orders for which no fixed rule can be laid down.

What do eleven Prayâja offerings mean ?

When it is said " he offers eleven Prayâja offerings, " it means five Prayâja offerings, five Anuyâja offerings and one offering in the end.

In an Agnichayana sacrifice there are six days ; there are in reality three Upasads which are to be made six by repetition.

दंडकलित and स्वस्थानविवृद्धि explained.

How are they to be repeated ? There are two methods. If you perform the three Upasads in the consecutive order and complete them on the third and commence performing them again from the fourth day, and complete them on the sixth day, this kind of repetition is called दंडकलित but if you perform the first Upasad on the first two days, the second Upasad on the 3rd and 4th days and the last Upasad on the 5th and 6th days, this kind of repetition is called स्वस्थानविवृद्धि. Both kinds of repetition are fully explained at p.p. 754 and 755. Here in the present case the repetition is on the स्वस्थानवृद्धि principle.

There are verses of the Ṛigveda called समिध्यमानवती repeated at the time of and kindling the fire and the others called सनिद्धवती repeated after the fire has been kindled.

There are धाय्या verses of general and particular kinds. The particular

Where should धाय्या be read ?

Dhâyyâs mentioned in the Vedas are to be read in the middle of समिध्यमानवती and सनिद्धवती and the general Dhâyâs which are mentioned in Panini III. 1. 129 are to be read at their end.

In a Jyotiṣṭoma there are three Pavamâna songs at three different

Additional *rik* verses are sung after पर्यास in a बहिष्पवमान.

times as explained in the preceding pages. In the modified form of the sacrifice some additional verses are added by modifying Bahiṣpavamâna song. According to the *dictum* of Bâdarâyaṇa laid down above, these additional Ṛik verses come after Paryâsa. Reliance is placed on the following text :—

"स्तोत्रियानुरूरौतृवौ भवतः । वृषएवंत स्तृत्राभवंति । तृत्र उत्तमः पर्यासः" ।

" A Tricha consists of Stoṭṭriya and Anurûpa ; in it there are, verses which have a word Vṛiṣam. The last one is Paryâsa ".

When the additional Sâma verses are introduced in भाध्यंदिनपवमान or

Exception in the case of साम verses.

आर्भवपवमान, the above rule is relaxed and they are sung along with the गायत्री, बृहती and अनुष्टुप् metres under a direct Vedic text.

Here it is proper to describe the construction of an altar from Eggel-

Construction of an altar.

ings Śatapatta Brâhmaṇa (Vol. IV. pp. 1-2, S. B. E.) "It is constructed in the shape of a bird, the body of which is a square usually of four men's length as shown in Fig 2 (Frontispiece). The ground of the square having been ploughed, watered and sown with seeds of all kinds of herbs, a square mound the so-called Uttara Vedi measuring a Yuga on each side is thrown up in the middle of the body and the whole of the latter then made level with it. In the centre of the body thus raised where the two spines—connecting the middle of each of the four sides of the square with that of the opposite side—meet, the priest puts down a lotus leaf and threeon the gold plate (symbol of the sun) which the sacrificer wore round his neck during the time of initiation. On this plate, he then lays a small gold figure of a man (representing अग्नि, प्रजापति and यजमान) so as to lie on his back with the head towards the east and beside him he places two offering spoons one on each side filled with ghee and sour curds respectively. Upon the man he then places a brick called Svayamâtriṇṇâ of which there are three in the altar, *viz.*, in the centre of the first, third and fifth layers supposed to represent the earth, air and sky respectively and by their holes to allow the sacrificer (in effigy) to breathe and ultimately to pass through on his way to the eternal abodes. On the Svayamâtriṇṇâ, he lays Durvâ grass—with the root lying on the brick and the twigs hanging down—meant to represent vegetation on earth and good for the sacrificer. Thereupon he puts down in the east of the central brick on the spine a Dviyajus brick, in front of that on both sides of the spine two Retaḥsich bricks then in front of them one Vis'vajyotiḥ, then two Ṛitavyâ; and finally Âsâdhâ representing the sacrificer's consort. These bricks each of which is a pada square occupy nearly one third of the line from the centre to the middle of the front side of the body of the altar. South and north of the Âsâdhâ leaving the space of two bricks he places a live tortoise, facing the gold man and a wooden mortar and pestle respectively. On the mortar he places the Ukhâ or fire pan filled with sand milk and thereon the heads of the five victims after chips of gold have been thrust into their mouths, nostrils eyes and ears. At each of the four ends of the two spines he then puts down five Apasyâ bricks, the middle one lying on the spine itself with two on each side of it. The last set of the five bricks, those laid down at the north (or left) end of the cross spine are also called Chhandasya by the Brâhmaṇa. He now proceeds to lay down the Prâṇabhrit meant to represent the orifices of the vital airs in five sets of ten bricks each. The first four sets are placed on the four diagonals connecting the centre with the four corners of the body of the altar beginning from the corner (? or according to some optionally from the centre) in the order, S. E., N. W., S. W., N. E., the fifth set being laid down round the central brick at the distance (or on the range) of the Retaḥsich bricks."

See the Fig 4 (Frontispiece); it is a help to understand the above.

The central part of the first layer is shown in the said figure. The letter *P* represents Prâṇabhrit bricks which are ten in number. The letter *S* in the centre represents Svaymâtriṇṇa brick. *R*. represents Retaḥsich bricks; *V* represents Vis'vajyoti; then we have two Ṛitavyâ bricks and lastly Àsâdhâ; *DV*. represent Dviyajus brick.

From the IV. figure we clearly see that the Svayamâtriṇṇâ brick is in the centre; the Dviyajus brick is just close to it. Round them we find two Retaḥsich bricks and ten Prâṇabhrit bricks arranged in a circular rim. The Vis'vajyoti is outside the bigger circle. Then to the east of the Vis'vajyoti two Ritavyâ bricks are arranged and then to the east of them, we have Âsâdhâ.

Then two Lokamprinâ bricks are laid in the south east corner. These bricks are for the purpose of filling up spaces. The body of the altar requires in the first layer 1028 Lokamprinâ bricks of three different kinds *viz.*, one pada, half pada and quarter pada occuping together a space of 321 square padas while 98 Yajusmatî bricks fill up 79 square padas. In the wings there are 309 Lokamprinâ bricks on each side occuping a space of 79 square padas. The total number of the bricks in the wings therefore comes to 618. In the tail there are 283 bricks altogether occupying 110 padas. The total number comes to 1929 as shown in the table below :—

The number of the bricks.

1028	Lokamprinâs	in the body.
309	,,	in 1st wing
309	,,	in the 2nd wing
283	,,	in the tail
1929	...	Total.
21		
1950	...	Total.

Add to this 21 bricks of the Gârhapayta fire. }

We see that 1950 Lokamprinâ bricks are in the 1st layer. The total number of these bricks in four layers comes to $1,950 \times 4 = 7800$ Lokamprnâs.

In the fifth layer there are 972 Lokamprinâs more than in any other layer. The number in the 5th layer stands as below.

1950	Lokamprinâs	
972	Additional ditto.	
78	Yajusmatîs	
3000	...	Total.
7800		
10800	...	Total.

By adding the number of the bricks in the four layers. }

See Eggeling Part IV. P. 22. [Central part of the 2nd layer (Fig 5 Frontispiece.)

The bricks are Âs'vinî represented by â, Vaisvadavî by *V*, Prâna-bhrit, by *P* and Apasyâ by a.

On the eastern side, you will find आश्रवनी, वैश्वदेवी, प्राणभृत and अपस्वा of the first group; you will find the same half bricks of 2nd group in the extreme south ; then the 3rd group in the west and the fourth group in the north and the fifth group of half bricks just above the 2nd group in the south.

The two Ṛitavyâs of the second layer are placed immediately above the Ṛitavyâ of the first layer leaving the intermediate space vacant.

We have then 19 Vayasyâ bricks, four in the east at the end of the spine and five in the other directions round the other three points of the spine. Thus the total number of the Vayasyâ bricks comes to 19 only. The diagram ultimately comes to the Fig. 6 (frontispiece).

Third layer. The central part of the third layer is shown in Fig. 6 (frontispiece.)

In the figure, the Svayamâtriṇṇâ is represented by S, Dviyajuṣes are represented by D, Vis'vajyoti is represented by V and Ṛitavyâs by Rit.

See Fig. 7, (frontispiece) for the central part of the 4th layer.

The Sṛiṣtis are seventeen in number ; 9 of them are to : the south of the spine running from the west to the east and eight are to the north of it. In the north we have four bricks and five in the south, two of them being half pada. In the eastern and western planks we have two bricks of square pada one after the other on the spine running from the west to the east ; both of them are flanked in the north and south by one half pada bricks.

The two Ṛitavyâ bricks are represented by Rit and are situated on the spine in th eeast exactly on the Ṛitavyâ of the; lower layer. For the central part of the fifth layer, see Fig. 8. (Frontispiece.)

The fifth layer is the last one in the altar and represents heaven. In the figure, we see that there are 21 Stomabhâga bricks represented by St. In the southern semi-circle there are 15 Stomabhagas and 14 in the northern semi-circle. There are two half bricks in the southern semi-circle one just in the east to the south of the cross-spine and another in the extreme south towards the east of the cross-spine. We further see that there are eight Stomabhâyas in the eastern quadrant and seven in the western one of the southern semi-circle.

We have the two Ṛitavyâ bricks just on the radius of the inner circle; one to the north and the other to the south represented by Rit. To the north of the northern Ṛitavyâ we have half-sized Nâkasad and one half Paṅchachuḍâ making up one mixed brick represented by $N.P.$ We have four more mixed bricks one in the north, the other in the west and two together in the south. To the east of the Ṛitavyâ we have a

Vis'vajyoti represented by *V*. We find the Chhandasyâ bricks, namely, Anuṣṭup, Gâyattrî and Triṣṭubh represented by *a*, *g* and *t* in the diagram.

The remaining space in the centre is filled up by 8 Gârhapatya bricks and above them we have eight Punas'chiti bricks shown by patching in the sketch. The vacant spaces are filled up by Lokampriṇâ bricks and loose soil on it. Then finally above them are laid one named Svayammâtriṇṇâ in the centre and the other called Vikaraṇî to the north of it. See Eggeling's Ś. B. part IV, p. 78.

The cups and bricks are subordinate parts of a sacrifice.

Having digressed so far, let us now proceed with the subject under consideration. The cups are the subordinate parts of the sacrifice and the bricks are similarly its subordinate parts.

ब्राह्मणवती bricks.

There are ब्राह्मणवती bricks called चित्रणी and वज्रिणी, in the middle layer after Lokampriṇâ.

Order in an अग्निहोत्र.

The order in an Agnihottra is (1) establishment of fire (2) penance and (3) पवमानेष्टि.

An अग्निचित्'s vow is a पुरुषार्थ.

An Agnichit has to observe certain vows, as for example अग्निश्चिद्वर्षति नधावेत् । नस्त्रियमुपेयात् । तस्मादग्निचिता पश्चिणोनश्चि-तव्याः:" " An Agnichit should not run in the rains ; he should not cohabit with a woman: he should not therefore partake of birds' flesh ". These vows are to be observed by him when he has already performed an Agnichayana sacrifice.

When is a Dîkṣita initiated ?

A Dîkṣita carries a staff, ties a girdle round his waist and puts on a deer's skin. When should it be done ? When he is initiated by the performance of Dîkṣaṇiyeṣṭi, he becomes entitled to carry the staff, tie the girdle and wear the deer's skin.

No order in a Kâmeyṣṭi.

In a Kâmyeṣṭi sacrifice, there is no order because there is no order in the human desires; they arise at any time. The Pâṭhakrama in the Vedic text is only with a view to teach accentuation.

Priority of a Jyotiṣṭoma.

When such expressions as ' यएतेनेष्ट्वा ' (who by sacrificing it) are used, they show the priority of that particular sacrifice over the others. It is said in connection with a Jyotiṣṭoma that it is the best of all ; if one performs any other sacrifice without performing it, the performance of the other sacrifices is useless. This indicates the priority of a Jyotiṣṭoma over the other sacrifices.

Jyotiṣṭoma is the model sacrifice of all the sacrifices.

In the description of a Jyotiṣṭoma in the preceding pages we have seen that there are seven Samsthâs which have different names. They are the modified forms of a Jyotiṣṭoma. In this connection it is much better to explain Âpatti and Vihâra.

Âpatti and Vihâra explained.

In a sacrifice, there is one fire from which other fires are taken; this taking of the fire is called Agnivihâra: the transference of the details from the model sacrifice to the modified sacrifice is called Dharmavihâra. These sacrifices which are derived from the Jyotiṣṭoma have one essential quality in common with the Jyotiṣṭoma. It is called Âpatti or Vyâpti. The Vihâra and Âpatti are the characteristics of the dependent but not of the independent sacrifice.

अग्निष्टोम is the model of एक स्तोमक and अनेक स्तोमक.

There are sacrifices in which one Stoma is sung and there are others in which more than one are sung; the former is called Ekastomaka and the latter is called Anekastomaka. The model of all these sacrifices is Agniṣṭoma.

PÂDA IV.

श्रुतिक्रम predominates.

अर्थक्रम prevails over पाठक्रम.

When there is a conflict amongst the श्रुतिक्रम, अर्थक्रम and पाठक्रम, the श्रुतिक्रम will have a preference; when there is conflict between अर्थक्रम and पाठक्रम, the former will prevail.

मुख्यक्रम prevails over प्रवृत्तिक्रम.

When there is a conflict between the मुख्यक्रम and प्रवृत्तिक्रम, the मुख्यक्रम has preference. As for instance, in the दर्शपूर्ण-मास, curd (संन्नाय्य) is first prepared and पुरोडाश is also prepared, but पुरोडाश offering will be made before the curd according to the order of the principal, and the ceremonies such as cutting it into pieces, anointing it with ghee and placing it shall be first performed.

In आनंतर्य practice सोमयाग is performed and in व्यवधान, इष्टिs are performed before the establishment of fire.

Now we have to see the order of इष्टि and सोम after अग्न्याधान. There are two practices, called आनंतर्य and व्यवधान, Under the former practice of immediateness, after the अग्न्याधान, the सोमयाग is performed and subsequently the इष्टिs are performed; but under the practice of व्यवधान (intervention) the Iṣṭis are performed after

C.

Agnyâdhâna and lastly the Somayâga is performed. Both the practices are valid ; if the object is to perform the *Somayâga*, the practice of immediateness is followed, and in such a case no season or time is necessary for the establishment of fire ; but if the object is other, then Somayâga should be performed in the end and the season or time of the performance will be that of the establishment of fire.

Optional practice in the case of a Brhâmaṇa.

A Brâhmaṇa can adopt either आनंतर्य्य or व्यवधान practice. If he adopts the former, in that case he will make all the offerings of the full moon on the पूर्णमासी day, excepting the last which shall be made after the performance of the Somayâga; in the Ânantarya case, the order, will therefore, be (1) अग्न्याधान, (2) पूर्णमास offerings with the exception of the last (3) सोमयाग (4) last offering of the पूर्णमासयाग. The last offering consists of a Purodâs'a cake to Agni and Soma, the dual deities.

The time of the modified sacrifice.

The time of the modified sacrifice is the same as that of the model sacrifice but it is to be completed within one day. The model sacrifice, however takes two days for its completion.

सन्नाय and पुरोडाश offering after सोमयाग.

The cows are milked in the previous evening in the new and full moon sacrifices. This milk is stored up and kept at night. The cows are again milked in the morning of the following day. The evening milk that has been reserved, is mixed with the morning milk. This mixture is called Sannâya. (See at p p. 297 and 357). The Sannâya offering is made on the new moon day after the performance of the Somayâga. Similarly Purodâs'a is offered on the full moon day to Agni and Soma after the performance of the Somayâga because the Iṣṭis are performed after it (Soma).

The modifications of Soma are performed after the Iṣṭis.

The modifications of Soma such as ekâha and gauh. etc. which last for one day are performed after the Dars'a-pûrṇamâsayâga according to this Ânantarya practice. The order in them will be as follows : (1) Agnyâdhâna (2) Somayâga (3) Iṣṭis (4) Soma modifications. This is the order in the modified sacrifice.

अग्न्याधान.

As in this Pâda, Agnyâdhâna of two kinds-namely, one before the Iṣṭis and the other before the Somayâga-is mentioned, it is better to get an idea of an Agnyâdhâna (establishment of fire) It is a name of a sacrifice (कर्मनामधेय). In the beginning there is a कुष्मांडहोम' It lasts either three days or six days or twenty-four days. About 59 offerings of ghee are made to different deities excepting the sun to whom boiled rice is offered. A sacrificer has to observe a vow of celibacy and abstain from animal food. After the sacrificer has his head shaved and nails cut, he commences Kuṣmâṇḍa homa on a new moon or a full moon day. Fifty-nine mantras from the Veda are recited and different offerigs are made to the fire.

कुष्माएडहोम.

It is followed by Gaṇahoma which is performed in a fire taken from Gârhapatya hearth. The sacrificer makes ghee offerings called Âghâra and Âjyabhâga in the fire. Boiled rice is offered to the sun. One hundred and three offerings are made with the repetition of the Vedic Mantras.

गणहोम.

Minor oblations are also made to the fire with the mystic syllables भूः, भुवः स्वः; then Sviṣṭakṛit follows. A vessel of water is taken by the sacrificer and placed to the south-west of his house. He sees his reflection repeating the Vedic mantras. After throwing away the water the sacrificer enters his house without casting a glance behind.

Minor oblations.

After finishing it, the Brâhmaṇas are fed with milk and gold is given as their fee. Subsequently, the Agnyâdhâna is commenced in the spring. Before the ceremony is commenced, Naṇdi Śrâddha is performed ; on the same night, Udaka Śânti is performed. The place where it is performed is besmeared with cow dung and husked or unhusked rice is thrown under the vessel of water placed there. The altar is marked out with the Darbhâ grass wh'ch is thrown into the north of the altar. Another branch of Darbhâ is spread towards the north of the altar with the ends of the grass towards the east. Upon this grass a vessel called Prokṣaṇî full of water, a vessel of bell metal and thread are placed. The Prokṣaṇî is then removed to the altar. It is covered with the Darbhâ grass ; the water from it is poured into the bell metal vessel and sprinkled from it on the sacrificer and his wife with recitation of the Vedic mantras accompanied with the monosyllable ʻom' by the four Brâhmaṇas appointed for the purpose. They are paid according to their posture. A Brâhmaṇa in the east gets gold; the one standing in the south gets silver ; the others in the west and north get bell metal and cloth. When different materials are not available, gold alone is distributed amongst the priests. The whole ceremony is finished during the night and in the morning, the Vedic mantras suited to the morning are sung and water is sipped by and sprinkled on the sacrificer and his wife. The sacrificer then sits to the north and his wife to the south; the priests be-

उदकयांति.

प्रोक्षणी vessel.

side the sacrificer sit in a line with the faces towards the fire. The sacrificer and his wife then make a Sankalpa (mental vow) to perform the Agnyâdhâna.

Sankalpa.

After this, ब्रह्मा, होता, अध्वर्यु, उद्गाता, अग्नीध्र and सदस्य are formally appointed and are given reception by a feast called Madhuparka. After this, kuṇḍas and Vedis are prepared.

मधुपर्क

The vessels used are स्रुच्, अग्निहोत्रहवनी, जुहू. उपभृत and ध्रुवा. They are of the form of the lip of an elephant, or of the mouth of a swan or of the tail of a crow.

Sacrificial vessels.

They are all ladles; the bowls of the ladles are of the above forms. When the bowl is in the form of an elephant's lips, it is about eight *angulas* in breadth and when it is in the form of a swan's mouth or of a crow's tail, it is about five *angulas* in width. The handles vary from a span to two cubits in length.

अग्निहोत्रहवनी and ध्रुवा are made of the वैकंतत (*Flacourtia Sapida*) wood ; the जुहू is made of the पलाश (Butea Froudosa) wood; the उपभृत is made of the पिप्पल (*Ficus religiosa*) wood; the स्रुवा is made of the wood of *acacia catechu*. The धृष्टि and मेक्षण are ladles with flat bowls a span in length; they are made of the पिप्पल (Ficus religiosa) wood.

A mortar is made of *Butea froudosa* about six angulas in depth and mounted on a pedestal of six fingers in height.

Sacrificial instruments.

A pestle is made of the wood of *acacia catechu*. An oblong vessel called प्राश्नित्रहरण is also made of *acacia catechu* in the shape of a cow's ear. A स्फ्या (wooden sword) and a शाम्या (cudgel) is also made of the *acacia catechu* wood. इडापात्र, दारुपात्र and प्रणीतापात्र are made of the wood of the *Pipal* tree. A string made of *munj* grass consisting of three knots is tied round the waist of the sacrificer's wife. Potsherds are also prepared and their ends are sharpened in order to fit in with one another.

The sacrificer goes out to the jungle in search of wood from a *pipal* tree on which there has grown up शमी tree. He prepares the lower अरणी and upper अरणी from the *Pipal* tree of the above description.

अरणी

A sacrificial site is selected by the priests ; the ground for the sacrifice is dug up and the earth removed. Sand, saline soil, earth from the holes of rats, from an anthill, from the depth of a river, and that dug up by a wild boar, a leaf of lotus, nodules of unburnt lime-stones and six pieces of gold are brought in and placed upon the altar.

Sacrlficial place.

A rite called नैपितृयज्ञ is performed. It is so called because a straw
of the Darbhâ grass is held behind the ears
नैपितृयज्ञ
of a sacrificer and is cut constituting the act
of gift of a cow, in the course of the oblations to the departed soul.
The oblations to the *manes* are of the clarified butter or of the boiled rice-
balls. The clarified butter is offered to the fire and the rice balls are offered
to the Pitṛis. The sacrificer then plays dice with his children.

When in the evening, the sun's rays touch the top of the trees, an
oblation called सर्वौषधिहोम is performed. Sesamum, lentil, unhusked rice,
barley, particles of rice, wheat, panicle, wild sesamum, *kangni* seed, wild
grain, wild barley and the bamboo seeds are mixed and washed. The
Adhvaryu, Brahmâ, the sacrificer and his wife covered in clothes, march
towards the fire. They place the sacrificial utensils before them and make
offerings of ghee called Âghâra and Âjyabhâga. Afterwards they offer
the seeds and grains mixed as above to the fire.

Next follows the Brahmaudana ceremony. Fire from the ordinary
hearth is transfered to the Gârhapatya fire-
ब्रह्मौदन ceremony.
place. The sacrificial vessels are arranged
on the altar ; a hide of a bay bullock is spread and the rice to
be boiled is taken upon it. It is pounded and boiled. In the rice
thus prepared, a hollow is made and ghee is poured in there ; offerings
are made to Brahmâ from this rice. The priests recite the verses in praise
of the sacrificer who gives three morsels of rice to each of them and *oxen*
as their fee.

Then follows the fire-producing ceremony. The sacrificer holds Araṇî in
his hand and recites the Vedic mantras. He is
अग्निमंथन ceremony.
kept awake at night ; when the greater portion
of the night has passed, the priests begin to produce fire by rubing the
Araṇis together. The Adhvaryu enjoins upon the sacrificer not to
tell lies and points out a black goat. The sacrificer remains silent.
Ordinary fire is brought in, some fuel is thrown in and it is stirred up
and kindled. The churning process by means of Araṇîs continues ;
the sacrificer rubs first ; the hotâ recites mantras and the udgâtâ sings.
When fire is produced, the Adhvaryu and the sacrificer recite the verses
in praise of the fire and carry it to the Gârhapatya hearth with the
accompaniment of Sâma in the Rathantara tune. The sacrificer touches
the Gârhapatya hearth and /places gold pieces to the north ; pieces of
silver are given to an ignorant Brahmaṇa.

The fire from the Gârhapatya hearth is taken to the Dakṣiṇâgni hearth

with the accompaniment of music and distribution of Dakṣiṇa (fee) consis·
ting of silver to an ignorant Brahmaṇa. When the sun has risen, the
sacrificial fire is placed in the Gârhapatya hearth. A horse, an ox, a goat,
a ram, or a *kamaṇḍ,ilu* in the absence of one another in the above order
is bathed and made to stand near the Gârhapatya hearth.

The sacrificer takes the fire from the Gârhapatya hearth to the
Âhavanya with the accompaniment of the Vâmadeva song chanted
by the udgâtâ priest (see the plan I of the frontispiece). The
sacrificial vessels are held in hand by some one else and a horse
is presented to the Adhvaryu and the Brahmâ priest each. In the
Âhavanîya hearth, sand, saline earth and other things mentioned above
are placed and the fire carried from the Gârhapatya hearth is placed there
amidst the Sâmas known as Bṛihat, Vâravantîya and S'yaita sung by the
Udgâtâ priest. This constitutes the establishment of fire. The sacrificer touches it and recites the verses with the Adhvaryu priest in praise
of the fire. Oblation of sacrificial fuel is made to all the three fires.
This is the consummation of Agnyâdhâna and is expressed by an oblation of the clarified butter called Pûrṇâhuti. The priests pronounce the
benedictions on the sacrificer.

A Pavamâneṣṭi which consists of minor oblations is subsequently
performed. Its principal deities are अग्नि, पवमान, पावक, शुचि, इंद्राग्नी and
अदिति. The Puroḍâs'a cakes and boiled rice are offered. The model of
the पवमानेष्टि is दर्शपूर्णमासयाग. The Yâjyâs and Anuvâkas are recited
by the Hotâ priest. A pillow is given to the Agnîdha, a horse to the
Brahmâ, a cow to the Hotâ, an ox to the Adhvaryu and gold and cloth
to the Udgâtâ priest.

The order which we have described in the preceding pages is as
follows. (१) अग्न्याधान (२) पवमानेष्टि (३) अग्निहोत्र (४) दर्शपूर्णमासयाग (६) सत्र (५)
सोम. This order is liable to changes according to the emergency of the
case. (See Kuṇṭe's षड्दर्शन चिंतनिका.)

CHAPTER VI.
PÂDA 1.

<table>
<tr><td>Right to sacrifice.</td><td>The present chapter treats of ' rights ' to perform a sacrifice and thereby indirectly ' rights ' to property. The Smṛiti writers have deduced from the</td></tr>
</table>

right to perform a sacrifice the law of inheritance.

According to the Mîmâmsâ school of philosophy, no act is possible
without a motive. It is useless to discuss
the component factors of an act which have
been very fully discussed in the preceding pages. An act performed
without a motive is an act of a lunatic. The motive or object in view
may be either visible or invisible.

Motive.

What is the object of a sacrifice? It is to secure heaven; it is said
‘ स्वर्गे कामोयजेत ’ ‘ let one desirous of heaven
perform a sacrifice.’ Here an agent is the per-
former; the heaven is the object and the sacrifice is a means to obtain it.
We have therefore three factors; the actor, the object and the act.

Object of sacrifice.

Any person who is possessed of the desire to secure heaven is entitled
to perform a sacrifice. No person can be said
to be without such desire. Every human being
possessing capacity, has a desire to secure
heaven. The animals or birds cannot have such desire or capacity.

*Who is entitled to per-
form the sacrifice?*

The Vedic text which confers the right to perform a sacrifice has the
agent in the masculine gender. It can be
argued with plausible reasons that a female is
excluded from performing a sacrifice. Aitisayana
a great Mîmâmsaka is of opinion that a female
is not entitled to perform it, because she has no independent property but
Jaimini following the view of Bâdarâyana concedes the right to the
females as well for the following reasons.

*A woman's independent
right to perform a
sacrifice recognised.*

(1) The gender used is not very important, because some gender
must have been used in the Vedic text; the masculine gender includes
feminine gender as is the case in the modern legal literature.

(2) A female is also possessed of the desire to secure heaven.

(3) She is an equal owner with her husband in the property; she is
not a saleable commodity.

(4) The goddesses with their husbands have equal shares in the
offerings in the sacrifice.

It follows as a corollary from the above discussion that a wife is
equally entitled with her husband to perform
a sacrifice with him. Our author relies on
the Vedic text quoted at P. 304 in support of
his view.

*Husband and wife can
both perform a sacri-
fice.*

One person is only entitled to perform Agnyâdhâna; where in the

One person is entitled to perform अग्न्याधान.

text, the words "क्षौमेवसानौ" "two clothed in silk" are used, they contemplate the husband and wife who are one body for the performance of all religious ond temporal duties.

A woman is not equal by reason of her sex with man in many things and possesses many disqualifications; she can perform all those acts which are specially mentioned for her to perform ; as for example,

What are the disqualifications of a female ?

she is equally entitled to observe a vow of celibacy, to have her head shorn or nails pared.

The most important question for determination is whether a Śûdra is entitled to perform a sacrifice. A Śûdra is not entitled to wear a sacred thread ; he is therefore, not entitled to study the Vedas.

Śûdra is not entitled to perform a sacrifice.

Without the study of the Vedas, he is not entitled to perform the sacrifice. Further there is a Vedic text under which only the three higher castes are entitled to establish fire ; from this fact, it appears that a *S'adra* is not given the privilege of performing the sacrifice.

Poverty and deprivation of sense organs are no disqualifications provided the latter is not permanent, natural and incurable. Incurable and natural deprivation of the senses are, also in this view disqualifications in cases of inheritance.

Poverty is no bar ; but deprivation of limbs is a bar if it is incurable.

It is customary to repeat the family clan, Gottra and the Pravaras i.e. the different members of the Gottra. They are one, two, three and five. Any person who has not three Pravaras is not entitled to perform a sacrifice. It is unnecessary to mention that under the principle of Avayatyuvâda as

A person having not three Pravaras is not entitled to perform a sacrifice.

explained in the preceding pages, the higher number includes the lower number.

A Rathakâra who belongs to a mixed class is entitled to perform a sacrifice under a special text "वर्षासु रथकार आदधीत." " A Rathakâra shall perform Agnyâdhâna in the rainy seasons." The term Rathakâra is used in a conventional sense

Rathakâra is entitled to perform a sacrifice.

The word रथकार explained.

(योगरूढि) and means a particular mixed class "माहिष्येण करणयांतु रथकार: प्रजायते" Yâjñavalkya Smṛiti I·95. " By a (man of the) Mâhiṣya class on a (woman of the)

Karaṇa class is begotten Rathakâra (S. B. H , XXI. p : 200.) He also says in I·92.

वैश्या शूद्रयो स्त्नुराजन्यान्मा हिष्योग्रौ सुतौस्तृ गै ।
वैश्यात्तुकरणशूद्रयां विन्नास्वेषविधिस्मृन ॥

" The sons begot ten on a Vais'ya and a Śûdra woman by a Kṣattriya are called Mâhiṣya and Ugra respectively ; by a Vais'ya on a Śûdra woman, a Karaṇa : this law is propounded with regard to married women. " (S. B. H., XXI. p : 190.)

This is in Aṇulomâ marriage. From the above extracts, we find that रथकार न्याय expeained. a Rathakâra is of mixed caste ; it does not necessarily follow that he carries on the business of chariot-making. It is an accident. A twice-born by carrying on the trade of chariot-making does not become a Rathakâra. The term Rathakâra is used here in its conventional sense. Where a word is used in a conventional sense but not in its derivative sense by reason of the convention being stronger than the derivation, it is called रथकार न्याय.

A noble in the community of Niṣâda, a non-Aryan tribe is entitled to perform a sacrifice called Rudrayâga. The term A निषादस्त्रपति is entit-led to perform रुद्रयाग. Niṣâda is used for a mixed breed from a Brâhmaṇa father and a S'ûdra woman in an Anulomâ system of marriage.

विप्रान्मूर्द्धांवसिक्तोहि क्षत्रियायां विशः स्त्रियां ।
अम्बष्ठः शूद्रयांनिषादो जातः पाररवोऽपिबा ॥

Yâjñavalkya I. 91.

" By Brâhmaṇa in a Kṣatriya woman is produced merely a Mûrdhâva Who is a निषाद sikta ; in a Vais'ya woman an Ambaṣṭha ; and in a S'ûdra woman, a Niṣâda or a Pârar'ava even." (S. B. H., XXI. p. 189.)

The text which confers a right of performing a Rudrayâg runs thus "बास्तुमध्येरौद्रं चरं निर्वेपेसत्ररुद्रः प्रजा शमयेत्······एतबानिषादस्त्रपर्तियाजयेत. " " Let him offer boiled rice consecrated to Rudra in the dwelling house where Rudra pacifies the family......let him cause a निषादस्त्रपति to perform a sacrifice with it. "

What is the meaning of the term 'निषादस्त्रपति.' There are two com-pounds in this word ; कर्मधारय or, तत्पुरुष. It निषादस्त्रपतिन्याय explained. therefore, means ' a निषाद who is noble ' or 'a nobleman of the निषाद caste. The former is preferable ; in this view कर्मधारय prevails over the तत्पुरुष समास. It is called निषादस्त्रपतिन्याय.

PÂDA 2.

In a sacrificial session, there are many sacrificers varying from seven-

Fruit in a sacrificial session.

teen to twenty-four. "सप्तदशावरारत्रचतुर्विंशतिपरमाः सत्रमासीरन्" How is the fruit of the Sattra to be distributed ? Each and everyone reaps the entire fruit of it. There is no impossibility in it; as for example, one animal is perceived by a large gathering of people. When we say, ' burn the town ' it means each and every house in the town.

In this connection, it is better to explain विरुद्धचिह्नद्वय. In a sentence,

विरुद्धचिह्नद्वय explained.

we have a subject and a predicate ; the former is known and the latter is unknown : this is one contradictory. The subject being known, any statement about it is a restatement. the predicate being unknown, it makes an original statement : this is the second contradictory. The subject in relation to the predicate is principal and the predicate is subordinate; this is the third contradictory.

In the Dars'apûrṇamâsayâgas, there is one sacrificer, and there is only

One alone is entitled to perform दर्शपूर्णमासयाग.

one main fruit ; the incidental fruits that may accrue are not different from the main fruit i.e. the attainment of heaven.

The acts are either religious or profane. Every act has three stages

Two kinds of acts.

(1) Commencement (2) Continuance (3) Completion. When a Vedic act is once commenced, it must be completed whether the fruit thereof has accrued or not ; the

A religious act must be completed.

completion of the act is itself a fruit. Its completion generates an extraordinary principle called Apûrva in the performer. If a religious act which has been commenced is left incomplete, the society

It is distinguished from the wordly act.

will condemn the performer. A wordly act on the other hand, does not necessarily require completion because there is no code of procedure ; it does not produce an Apûrva.

The author then proceeds to explain the difference between Pratiṣedha

प्रतिषेध & पर्युदास explained.

Paryudâsa. It has already been explained in the preceding pages. If the negative in the text is connected with the predicate, it is Pratiṣedha and prohibits the actual commission of the act. It it is connected with the subject, the mental commission of it is prohibited. It is called Paryudâsa.

The Kalañja Nyâya is the actual prohibition of an act. 'न कलंजभक्षयेत्'

कलंज न्याय explained.

'one should not eat flesh stuck with a poisonous arrow.' The actual eating of Kalañja is prohibited. When a man is told not to see the rising sun, there is no commission of the act ; it is only a mental resolution ; as soon as one resolves not to see the rising sun, he refrains from seeing it. It is a vow (व्रत). In this view, the actual performance of an act constitutes a Yâga and mental forbearance or commission is a Vrata.

Difference between a याग and व्रत.

A person has to observe good manner during his life ; it consists of respect to his preceptor and the elders ; he must make an obeisance to his elders and must rise when they approach. At what period should he observe the social etiquette ? The reply of our author is that one should commence observing good manners and behaving properly according to the rules of the society after his Upanayana ceremony has been performed.

Âchâra explained.

He is also required to perform Agnihottra twice a day and also on ceremonial occasions during his life till his death. " यावज्जीवमग्नि होत्रं जुहोति " ." Let him perform Agnihottra as long as he lives ". The text does not mean that you are to perform Agnihottra at every time in your life giving up all the worldly acts. What it really means is that one is to perform Agnihottra at the fixed time mentioned at p. 323. It does not contemplate giving up all wordly acts. This is called अग्निहोत्रन्याय.

अग्निहोत्रन्याय explained.

The Agnihottra is, therefore, to be repeated every day at the stated time according to the view which we take, during one's lifetime. The non-performance thereof entails the loss of heavenly bliss. Similarly, good manners should always be observed towards the elders and superiors.

Performance of अग्निहोत्र. and observance of good manners are insisted on.

When any sacrificial vessel is broken or when its content is spilt, you are to perform an expiatory libation on every such occasion.

Expiatory ceremony.

A twice-born is under a three-fold debt from his birth under the well known text of the Taittarîya Sanhitâ quoted at p. 325. They are (१) देवऋण (२) पितृऋण and (३) ऋषि ऋण. The first debt is paid off by performance of a sacrifice ; the second is discharged by begetting children and continuing the race and the third is paid off by entering the preceptor's house, leading a life of celibacy and studying the Vedas from him.

A twice born has to discharge three debts.

PÂDA 3.

There are two kinds of sacrifices ; (१) नित्य and (२) काम्य. In a sacri-

Difference between a नित्य and काम्यकर्म.

fice there are two parts one principal and the other subordinate. In a नित्यकर्म (permanent rite) the principal part is indispensable; the subordinate parts may be omitted but in a काम्य कर्म (desire accomplishing rite) all the details must also be performed. The reason is obvious. A Nityakarma is essential and permanent ; the non-performance of it entails a sin ; but a Kâmyakarma is performed with a certain desire which cannot be fulfilled if any detail is omitted.

An act is not changed by a change of material ; as for instance

An act is not changed by a change of a material.

the act of throwing is not changed by the change of material thrown. You may throw a stone or brick ; the act of throwing remains the same.

Accordingly, when the original material is lost or is not available,

Substitute.

another material may be substituted in its place in the नित्य and नैमित्तिक कर्मs. " यदि सोमं विंदेत पूतीकानभिषुणयात् " 'If Soma is not available, one shall extract juice of a Pûtikâ ". There will be a substitute in the case of a Nitya-karma either commenced or to be commenced when the original material is spoilt or lost but in the Naimittika-karma, the substitute will be used only in the case when the act is commenced and the emergency arises.

There will be no substitute for a deity, fire, mantra and act because

No substitute in certain cases.

they constitute the special parts of a sacrifice. You cannot substitute a deity in place of another, because that will change the nature of the sacrifice. The same principle holds good in the case of the fire, mantra and act.

Similarly, the master cannot be substituted because the fruit accrues to him. No one can therefore be substituted for him.

Forbdden material cannot be a substitute.

The material substituted should not be a forbidden material. अवधिया वैवरका: कोद्रवा: । अवधियावैमाषा: " " Wild Kodru cereal is unfit for a sacrifice ; the beans are unfit for a sacrifice ".

In a sacrificial session there is a large number of sacrificers, varying

A substiute can be appointed in a Sattra for a sacrificer.

from seventeen to twenty-four. If any one dies another *locum tenens* may be appointed. We have seen that there cannot be a substitute in a sacrifice for a master but in the

सत्रन्याय *explained.*

Right of the locum *tenens.*

case of a sacrificial session, there is an exception. It is called Sattra Nyâya.

The *locum tenens* to all intents and purposes steps into the shoes of the dead or absent master save the fruit of the sacrifice which accrues to the original master.

A substituted material should be of the same class as the original.

A substituted material used for an original material should be of the same species; it must resemble the original material. When there is an option in two or more materials and the option is once made, but subsequently the material selected is lost, you cannot make a choice of another optional material but you will have to select the material of the same class which bears resemblance to the original material lost or spoilt.

A prescribed material by a text should be used as substitute.

Where a Vedic text enjoins a substitute in the absence of the original material, it shall be used as substitute; as for example, Putîkâ is prescribed by the Veda as substitute for Soma.

The second substitute in place of the first substitute lost must resemble the original.

When the original material used is lost or otherwise made useless and the substitute used in its place is also made useless, the second substitute which will be used shall resemble the original but not the first substituted thing though it may have been sanctioned by the Veda. As for instance Pûtîkâ is a substitute for Soma; both of them are lost; the third substance used must resemble Soma.

The original material when found out after loss should be used provided the sacrifice is not commenced with the substitute.

When the original material is lost and the sacrificer while searching the substitute finds out the original material the latter shall be used; but if the act is commenced with the substitute and subsequently the original material is found out, the act must be continued with the substituted material.

The original material is preferred, even if it is not fit to have purificatory ceremony performed.

The original material though not fit to have a purificatory ceremony performed on it is preferable to the substitute even if it is sufficient to have the purificatory ceremony performed on it; but when the original is not fit for the object for which it is required, the substitute may be used provided it is fit for the object; as for instance, Khadira wood which is strong enough for a sacrificial post for fastening a strong and restive animal to it, is preferable to Kadira wood which is weak though sanctioned by the Veda. In such a case, fulfilment of purpose is the guide. In the Sûtra the word Seṣa is used. A constituent part of a sacrifice is called Anga but Śeṣa is that which subserves the purpose of a sacrifice though it may not be its constituent part. As for example, a man has several parts of his body; he can exist alone with them; but the society and the environments which subserve his purpose and are essential ingredients without which he cannot be what he is, are not his constituent parts. The first relationship with his body is called Angângibhâva and the last is called Śeṣas'eṣîbhâva. The man is Angî and Śeṣî both, but his bodily parts and the surroundings are Anga and Śeṣa respectively.

Marginal note: But if the original material is not fit for the object required, the substitute if fit is preferable. शेषशेषीभाव distinguished from अंगांगिभाव.

The original material is always to be preferred even though it is not sufficient to perform the subordinate parts of a sacrifice provided it is sufficient for the performance of the principal part. As for example, Vrîhi is not sufficient for the Sviṣṭakṛit, Iḍâ and Prâs'ittra but only for the principal offering and Nîvâra which is a substitute for Vrîhi is sufficient for all. Here Vrîhi though insufficient is preferable to Nîvâra and the subordinate parts may be omitted.

Marginal note: The original material though not sufficient for the subordinate parts is preferable if sufficient for the principal.

PÂDA 4.

In Dars'apurṇamâsayâga the main offering consists of two portions of a Puroḍâs'a cake cut into three parts. The first and the middle parts of the Puroḍâs'a cake constitute the principal offering to the deity and the remainder is reserved for the Sviṣṭakṛit offering, Iḍâ and Prâs'ittra foods. If the two portions of the cake are destroyed or otherwise made unfit for the offering, another cake should be prepared and the third portion cannot be used for the main offering; but when the third portion is destroyed, no other cake shall be prepared for the Sviṣṭakṛit as it is only a Pratipattikarma; the offering shall be made from the residue of the destroyed cake if there be any.

Marginal note: On the destruction of the main offering another पुरोडाश cake should be prepared but not on the loss of स्विष्टकृत offering.

As we have seen above in the Dars'apûrṇamâsayâga, there are Iḍâ and Prâs'ittra foods. The text in their connection is "यजमानपंचमा इडांभक्षयंति" "The four Ṛitviks and the sacrificer who is the fifth eat Iḍâ." By means of Parisankhyâ, it may be deduced as a corollary that of a Prâs'ittra food, all others are entitled to partake, excepting the Ṛitviks but our author says that it is a Vidhi. The reason is that the sacrificer being not a worker like the Ṛitviks, he is given the right to partake of the Iḍa along with the Ṛitvik. In this view the sacrificial food-whether Iḍâ or Prâs'ittra—is to be eaten by the Ṛitviks including the sacrificer ; others are not entitled to it.

The officiating priests are entitled to the sacrificial food.

When a sacrificial vessel is partially or totally destroyed, an expiatory ceremony in the form of a penance is performed to ward off any evil that may befall ; when on the other hand, a Puroḍâs'a cake is partially burnt, it may be used and no expiatory ceremony is performed but when it is totally burnt an expiatory ceremony is indispensable. It is called Kṣâmeṣṭi Nyâya.

An expiatory ceremony on the partial or total breakage of a sacrificial vessel.

सामेष्टिन्याय explained; expiatory rite on the total destruction of a cake.

There is a text in connection with the full and new noon sacrifices to the effect that one whose *two offerings* are spoilt, should make an offering of five dishes full of boiled rice to the god Indra. In order to understand the text, it is necessary to explain the Sannâya offering in connection with the full and new moon sacrifices. In the evening, the cows are milked and the milk is stored up in a vessel. In the evening of the full moon or new moon day that follows, the cows are again milked and this milk is also mixed with the evening milk that was stored up. Two offerings are prepared from this milk which is called Sannâya ; one is made in the morning and the other is made in the evening of the full moon or new moon day. If by chance one of the offerings or both offerings are spoiled, what should be done ? The above quoted text provides an offering of five dishes full of boiled rice to Indra as expiation in case both the offerings are spoiled. How are we to interpret the term ' two offerings ' in the text, whether collectively or severally ?

सन्नाय explained.

There are two terms in connection with the mode of interpretation. प्रत्येकंवाक्य परिसमाप्ति is a sentence in which the word is used in the distributive sense as for instance, ' Feed John, Peter and Samuel.' The sentence means that each is to be fed separately. समुदाये वाक्य परिसमाप्ति

प्रत्येकं वाक्य परिसमाप्ति explained.

is a sentence in which a word is used in a collective sense ; as for example, 'Let this village be fined 100 Rs.' here the word village is used in the collective sense. It is very well explained by Kumârila in the following couplet.

शरीरेानिग्रहेायन्त्रत्रप्रत्येकमिन्न ना । हिरण्यादान दंडस्तुसमुदाये समाप्यते ॥

Where the punishment inflicted is bodily restraint, it is always dis-

गर्गेयतद'इन्याय explained.   tributively awarded but where the punishment
is a fine consisting of gold, it is collectively
awarded (in the absence of any term to the contrary.) The latter is called गर्गेयतदंडन्याद. See p. 315.

Keeping this distinction in view, let us take the above text and see whether the term 'two offerings' is used in the distributive or collective sense. The author says that it is used in the distributive sense. Accordingly, five dishes of boiled rice should be offered to Indra on every occasion when Sannâya is spoiled. It also stands to reason.

There is another text " हविर्धनिेग्रावभिरभिषुत्याहवनीयेहुत्वा प्रत्यंचं परेत्य
Application of   सदातिभज्ञात् भत्वयंति " "In a place where *Soma*
गर्गेयतदंडन्याद.   is kept *having extracted its juice and having
made an offering in the Ahavanîya fire*, they
partake of the food on returning." Are both acts mentioned in the text *viz.*, extraction of juice and the offering in the fire, necessary to make one entitled to the food ? Here the principle of गर्गेयतदंड applies and accordingly only those who extract the Soma juice and make the offering are entitled to the food.

There is another text "वस्वोभावनुगतावग्नी अभिनिम्बोचेतवस्य वाभ्युदियात्
Another illustration of   पुनराधेयमेवतस्य प्रायश्चित्ति:" "One whose *both*
गर्गेयतदंड न्याद.   *fires* are extinguished and the sun rises, his
penance consists in the re-establishment of
fire." In what sense is the term *both fires* used in the above text ? The term ' both fires ' refers to the गार्हपत्य and आहवनीय fire. They are produced at one and the same time; so the extinction referred to in the text is the extinction of both of them collectively. The principle of गर्गेयतदंड न्याद applies ; and the पुनराधान is to be performed on the extinction of both the fires collectively.

Nature of the expiatory   What is the nature of the expiatory cere-
ceremony.   mony which consists of five dishes of boiled
rice to Indra ? It is an independent but not
a substituted rite and is a part of the new moon sacrifice.

<table>
<tr><td>विश्वजित् sacrifice in expiation.</td><td>When a man who has made up his mind to perform a Sattra and subsequently gives it up, shall have to undergo an expiatory ceremony by performing a Vis'vajit sacrifice. The reason is that one by</td></tr>
</table>

making a vow becomes indebted to the gods ; he can discharge the debt by performing the Vis'vajit.

There is another text which requires an interpretation " बर्हिषावैपौर्ण भासे व्रतं उपयंति वत्सेनामावस्यायां" " They break the fast with the *grass* on the full moon day and with the *calf* on the new moon day." What is the meaning of calf ? Does it mean veal ? No ; it cannot mean flesh because the corresponding word ' grass ' makes it absurd. The terms therefore, mean the time when the Darbha grass is brought on the full moon day and the time when the calves are driven off with a branch of a tree at the time of milking the cows on the new moon day. Such instances are found in every language as Godhûli (dusk).

" The curfew tolls the knell of parting day ;

The lowing herd winds slowly o'er the lea ;

The ploughman homeward plods his weary way ;

And leaves the world to darkness and to me."

[Gray's elegy.]

We have seen in the preceding pages that Sannâya offering is also made by one who has made a Soma sacrifice on the new moon day. He has to milk the cows, prepare Sannâya oblations and to take

<table>
<tr><td>How the वत्सापकरण came to mean the time for meal.</td><td>meals after milking the cows. There are others who make no Sannâya oblations and there are no cows milked, nor are the calves driven off. It matters very little whether</td></tr>
</table>

the calves are driven off or not but the Vatsâpakarṇa came to denote the time of taking food from the fact of driving off the calves at the time of milking the cows.

There is a text in connection with the Dars'apûrṇamâsa Yâgas ;

<table>
<tr><td>प्रस्तरप्रहरण means the time of final disposal.</td><td>" सह्याखवा प्रस्तरंप्रहरति " ' He throws grass with the branch in the fire ". How are we to interpret it, as there is no branch or poker</td></tr>
</table>

where there is no Sannâya oblation ? According to the principle laid down above, it indicates the time of the final disposal in a sacrifice irrespective of the branch or poker. If they are there, they may be also consigned to the fire as an act constituting final disposal thereof.

PÂDA 5.

Abhyudayeṣṭi is a small sacrifice consisting of the three kinds of rice

अभ्युदयेष्टि described.

offerings to Agni, Indra and Viṣṇu. The rice is divided into three portions, the Purodâs'a cake of the rice of the middle class, baked on eight pans is offered to Agni ; the grossest rice boiled in curd called Âtañchana set apart specially for the purpose, is offered to Indra and minutest rice boiled in water is offered to Viṣṇu. This sacrifice is the Naimittika ceremony. If a sacrificer under a mistaken belief of a new moon day performs a Dars'ayâga, and during its progress the moon rises he shall have to pay

Its nature.

the penalty by performing the Abhyudayeṣṭi. It is not an independent rite ; it is a part of the Dars'ayâga and is performed when a mistake is committed in ascertaining the correct date. The materials are already present in the Dars'ayâga ; there is a change of deities ; the offerings are directed to the other deities.

An Upâns'uyâga is performed on the full moon night and the ghee

उपांशुवाग in an अभ्युदयेष्टि described.

offerings are made to Viṣṇu in a low tone. In a Dars'ayâga, when Abyudayeṣṭi is performed Upâns'uyâga is also performed. The deity of Upâns'uyâga, *viz*, Viṣṇu is changed and three other deities in his place come in as said above.

In the text quoted at

Consecration of material is not a condition precedent.

p. 355 in connection with the Abhyudayeṣṭi, it is said, ' if the moon rises when he has already consecrated the offering '; does it mean that one has to perform an Abhudayeṣṭi, only when the materials are consecrated ? It does not mean that ; the cause of the performance of an Abhyudeṣṭi is the mistake of the date ; the consecration of the materials is not a precedent condition. Whether the materials are consecrated or not, an Abhyudayeṣṭi should be performed if the moon rises on the supposed wrong date of Amâvasyâ. The Dars'ayâga is commenced on the 30th day of a month i. e. on the Amâvasyâ during the day time ; the sacrificer goes to the jungle and brings the Durbhâ grass and the Samit (sacrificial fuel.) He then formally makes a vow (Sankalpa) to make offerings to the gods. This is called Anvâdâna. The moon rises at night ; if she rises, then the Abhyudayeṣṭi is performed. The word Nirupt (consecrated) in the text includes every act connected with the consecration.

When the materials are not consecrated, the offerings are made to the deities of the अभ्युदयेष्टि.

When the materials are not consecrated, the offerings are made to the deities of the model sacrifice according to Âs'marathya but according to Âlekhana they are made to the deities of the modified sacrifice i. e. the Abhyudayeṣṭi. Jaiminî adopts the latter view.

What is the procedure in a case of the moon rising after consecration of a portion of the materials.

When a portion of the materials is consecrated to the deity of the Dars'ayâga and the moon rises, the remaining portion which is not yet consecrated cannot be consecrated to the deity of the Dars'ayâga nor can it be consecrated to the deity of the Abhyudayeṣṭi as it has not yet commenced; it shall be offered silently without mentioning the name of any deity.

अभ्युदयेष्टि is to be performed by a सन्मायी and non सन्मायी as well.

We have explained what Sannâya is in the preceding pages. On the Amâvasyâ night cows are milked, the milk is put in a vessel and heated: a little curd is put in it and the whole is converted into curd. On the morning of the Pratipada of the bright half, the cows are milked and the milk is put into a separate vessel. At the time of the offering, both the milk and curd are placed in separate vessels. Two sacrificial spoons are used; the curd is first put into a Śruvâ and from it, it is transferred to a Śruchâ. The Śruvâ is then filled up with milk which is also transferred to the Śruchâ. This mixture of milk and curd is offered to the Âhavanîya fire. This oblation is called Sannâya and the milk or curd is also called Sannâya. We have seen in the preceding pages that a person who performs a Soma Yâga has to make an oblation of Sannâya. Now the question arises, whether the Abhyudayeṣṭi is to be performed by a Sannâyî alone. The reply of our author is that it is to be performed by a Sannâyî and a non-Sannâyî both.

A विश्वजित् is to be performed when the determination to perform a सत्र is given up.

We have also seen in the preceding pages that if persons having engaged in performing a Sattra, give it up, they have to perform a Vis'vajit sacrifice as a penalty. The question is when should it be performed? Should it be performed after the Soma having been purchased and then no Sattra performed? The reply of our author is that it should be performed as an expiatory ceremony even when you have made up a determination to perform it and then give it up. The purchase of Soma is not material for its performance.

In a नवाचमवन, an initiation ceremony is performed four days before the full moon of the माघ.

As a rule an initiation ceremony lasts for twelve days in a Jyotiṣṭoma sacrifice. The Dîkṣâ ceremony in a Gavâmayana should be performed four days before the full moon of the Mâgha so that Soma may be purchased on the eighth day of the dark half of the same month.

Daily duties are suspended during the continuance of a sacrifice.

When a person is engaged in a sacrifice, say a Jyotiṣṭoma his daily duties such as Agnihottra etc,, are stopped; after the sacrificial bath, they are to be performed. Sometimes during the continuance of a big sacrifice certain ceremonies are prolonged or put off; the sacrificial bath (Avabhritha) is necessarily put off. The Agnihottra and other daily duties will be suspended till the sacrificial bath is not performed. A Dîkṣita remains initiated till the sacrifice is over.

प्रतिहोम as an expiatory ceremony for the suspension of a ज्योतिष्टोम.

When the continuance of the performance of a Jyotiṣṭoma is put off for some uncontrollable circumstances, a Pratihoma consisting of as many oblations as the days for which the ceremony was deferred is performed to remove the sin of the sacrificer arising from the non-performance of the daily duties.

Daily duties are suspended till the उदवसानीय after the sacrificial bath.

There is an Udavasânîya ceremony performed after the sacrificial bath which completes the sacrifice to all intents and purposes. If the Udavasânîya is deferred for some reason or another, the sacrificer need not perform the daily duties in the interval.

Time of the performance of a प्रतिहोम.

A Pratihoma is performed in the evening in a Jyotiṣṭoma, because the sacrificial bath which completes it to all intents and purposes is resorted to in the evening; but in a Ṣoḍas'î which is finished in the morning at night, the Pratihoma is performed in the morning.

कृत्वा चिन्ता न्याय explained.

Here it is necessary to explain the term Kritvâchintâ which is used by Śavara in commenting upon the Sûttra 43. It consists in assuming the contrary proposition of the aphorism as correct and then arriving at a conclusion on such assumption. It is very often used by the commentators.

When an expiatory ceremony is performed on the breakage of a sacrificial vessel as described in the preceding pages, it is a part of the Dars'apûrṇamâsayâga, as the text in connection with that occurs in the context of the Dars'apûrṇamâsayâga. ' भिन्नेजुहोति, स्किन्नेजुहोति ' He performs a *homa* on breaking, he performs a *homa* on spilling.'

An expiatory ceremony on the breaking of a vessel is a part of the new and full moon sacrifices.

So the texts do not apply to the Jyotiṣṭoma and the Agnihottra sacrifices.

The author proceeds to explain the term Vyâpanna. Anything contaminated and not fit for eating by a human being is Vyâpanna. It includes food in which a dead insect or hair is found. Such a contaminated food should not be eaten but should be thrown in water.

व्यापन्न explained.

In a Jyotiṣṭoma sacrifice, Vahispavamâna air is sung. The priests walk out of the sacrificial ground and there they sing the Vedic songs. While going out of the sacrificial ground. first the Prastotâ goes out ; then the Udgâta holding the tucked up clothes behind the Prastotâ follows him ; lastly the Pratihartâ holding up the tucked up clothes behind the Udgâtâ goes out of the sacrificirl ground. The proceession of the singing priests continues in the above order from the sacrificial ground to some place outside of it. If by chance, they let go the tucked up clothes in the procession it is called Kachchhavimochana. There are two priests—the Udgâtâ and the Pratihartâ,—who hold the tucked up clothes in their hands. The Prastotâ has no one to precede him, so he does not hold the tucked up clothes, in his hand. There are four possible accidents ; (1) the Udgâtâ alone may lose the hold of the tucked up clothes ; (2) the Pratihartâ alone may lose the Kachhcha (3) They may simultaneously lose the hold (4) They may successively lose hold of it.

कच्छविमोचन explained.

Four possible mishaps.

The general proposition is that a penalty shall have to be paid whether they lose the hold of the tucked up clothes singly or together. If Udgâtâ lets go the tucked up clothes of the Prastotâ, the sacrificer may either conclude the sacrifice without payment of a fee or may recommence the sacrifice on the payment of the same fee ; (2) if the Pratihartâ lets go his hold of clothes, the sacrificer shall pay his entire wealth in the same sacrifice : (3) if both of them let go the hold of the clothes simultaneously there is an option for the sacrificer to choose either of the above alternatives, either he may pay the fee or not or pay the whole wealth (4) If the

Four kinds of penalties.

priests lose hold of the tucked up clothes one after the other, first the Pratihartâ and then the Udgâtâ, then there is no penance in the case of the Pratihartâ, but in the case of the Udgâtâ, the sacrificer shall have to pay the whole fee to the Udgâtâ. We have seen above that the Pratihartâ also gets the whole wealth on losing the hold singly.

There is a Soma sacrifice in which Soma juice is extracted. Soma Sutya is a word used for an oblation of Soma juice; it consists of different operations such as bringing in the Soma creeper, preparing it for extraction, extracting its juice, putting the juice in the cups, offering it to the gods and drinking it. In an Ekâha there is only such Somasutya but in an Ahargaṇa where a sacrifice lasts for days and which is called Ahîna, there are as many Somastuyâs as there are days. If by chance, there is Kachchhavimochana in any of these Sutyâs, all the Sutyâs shall not be repeated; it is only the one in which the Kachchhavimochana takes place, that alone shall be repeated.

सोमसुत्या explained.

What is to be done when कच्छविमोचन takes place in any of the सुत्या० ?

If a sacrifice that lasts for more than twelve days, it is both an Ahîna sacrifice and a Sattra. The latter is a sacrificial session lasting for 12 days or more than twelve days. The Gavâmayâna which is referred to here, is a Sattra which lasts for a year or ten months. It is optional. Literally the word means the revolution of the sun or earth according to the *heliocentric* or *geocentric* view, because the word 'go' means a cow, sun or earth. In the Nighaṇṭu which is the Vedic dictionary, the word 'Go' is read amongst the synonyms of the earth. The diurnal and annual motions of the earth were known to the ancient Aryans. Aryabhatta, the well known astronomer knew at least diurnal motion of the earth; he says

गवामयन explained.

meaning of गवामयन.

भवग्रहोऽस्थिरोभूरेवावृत्याद्घृत्य प्रातिदैवसिकौ ।
उदयास्तमयौ संपादयति गृहनक्षत्राणां । इति ॥

" The constellation of the stars is stationary (with reference to the earth); while the earth by moving on its axis causes the rising and setting of the stars."

He again says.

अनुलोमगतिनौंस्थ पश्यत्यचलंविलोमगंयद्वत् ।
अचलानिभांतितद्वत् स पश्चिमगानि लंकायामिति ॥

" Just as one one sitting in a boat sees everything immoveable going to the contrary direction, so does one see everything immoveable going to the west in Lanka."

From these passages, it is clear that there were astronomers in ancient India who accepted the *heliocentric* view. Gavâmayana which is an annual sacrifice shows that the ancient Aryaus knew the annual motion of the earth. They also knew the precession of equinoxes to an exact point.

The Gavâmayana commences from the 8th of the black half of Mâgha which is called Ekâṣṭakâ when the sun is said to turn from the south in the Zodiac sign of *capricornus* towards the equator. The Viṣuvân will, therefore, take place on the 8th day of the dark half of Śrâvaṇa. The Gavâmayana is a Soma sacrifice and in an annual Gavâmayana there

प्रायणीय and चतुर्विंश described.

are 360 Sutyâs, one Sutyâ being performed every day. See at P. 753. The initiatory ceremony in it, is called Atirâttrasoma sacrifice or Prâyaṇîya Atirâttrasoma sacrifice and is performed on the first day. On the second day another modified Soma sacrifice is performed which is called Ârambhaṇîya Chaturvims'a Ukthya. Then we have six days following them taken up in performing six Soma sacrifices; they are really three

अभिप्लव, explained.

called Jyotiḥ, Gauḥ and Âyuḥ; but as they are repeated in an inverted order, *viz.*, Gauḥ, Âyuḥ and Jyotiḥ, they are called Abhiplavas; because they last for six days, they are also called Ṣaḍaha. They are repeated four times and

षडहपृष्ठ explained.

so we have 26 days already. Then follows Ṣaḍahapriṣṭa; it is a sacrifice in which a musical mode called Priṣṭa is sung. We have already explained what Brihat and Rathantara are. The musical mode which is sung in a higher key is called Brihat and the one which is sung in a lower key is called Rathantara. The musical mode which is based upon these in a particular way is called Priṣṭa. Stottra is a musical mode and is distinguished from Śasttra which is a recitation of a prose composition. A Stottra is also called Stoma. A षडहपृष्ठ consists of त्रिवृत्, स्तोम, पंचदशस्तोम, सप्तदशस्तोम, एकविंश स्तोम, त्रिणवस्तोम, and त्रयस्त्रिंशस्तोम. All these have been explained before. The six days of Ṣaḍaha are completed by singing of these six Stomas and performance of the six Sutyâs, thus bringing the first month consisting of 32 days to an end.

Similarly with the exclusion of the first two days of the first month, the same ceremonies are performed in the second, third, fourth and fifth months. A month consists of thirty days. In the sixth month there are three Ṣaḍah Abhiplavas lasting for 18 days, then the Priṣṭyaha of six days, one Abhijit of one day and lastly three Svara Sâmas of one day each. The Abhijit and Svara Sâma are the modified Soma sacrifices. Thus the total of the sixth month comes to twenty-eight days; adding the first two days of the 1st month, the total of the days of the six months comes to 180 days.

The Viṣuvân sacrifice which is performed on the completion of the six months shows that it was on the occasion of the summer solstice when the sun commenced to move from the north to the south in the Zodiac sign of cancer. All ceremonies in this period were therefore performed in the reverse order. After the Viṣuvân ceremony, three days were taken up in the performance of three Svara Sâmas. The fourth day was taken up in the performance of the Vis'vajit sacrifice. Pṛiṣṭya Ṣaḍaha was performed for six days, the order of the Pṛiṣṭas was reversed ; अयस्त्रिंश, त्रिणव, एकविंश, सप्तदश, पंचदश and त्रिवृत् were sung in the above order. In this way ten days were finished ; then three Abhiplavas of six days each were performed thus bringing the total days of the 7th month to twenty-eight days.

विषुवात् and post—विषुवात् ceremonies described.

In the eighth, ninth, tenth, eleventh months, a Pṛiṣṭya of six days is performed, the songs being sung in the reverse order as in the 7th month. Then follow four Abhiplavas of six days each thus making the total of 30 days of each month. Similarly in the 12th month the order with some modification is reversed. We have three Abhiplavas of six days in the beginning, then follow Âyuḥ and Gau of one day each. Thus we have twelve days ; then follow ten days of a Dvâdas'âha sacrifice. Thus we have thirty days of a month ; we have to make up the deficiency of two days of the 7th month ; the thirty-first day is occupied in the performance of the Mahâvrata sacrifice and the thirty-second day in the performance of Atirâtra. Thus we have 180 days in the second half of the year called Dakṣiṇâyana. The Viṣuvân is a separate day ; if it is included, the total number of days comes to 181.

From the above analysis, we find that the Mahâvrat is the last but one day of the Gavâmayana ; it will, therefore, fall on or about the winter solstice. " It is not a bloodless sacrifice. There was either one beast sacrificed to Indra and Agni or a batch of eleven animals and in either case there is an additional sacrifice of a bull to Indra or to Prajâpati and in the former case of a goat to Prajâpati. Now at least in some cases the skin of the sacrificial animal was removed and used to form the drum (भूमिदुन्दुभि) on which with the tail of the victim the priest made solemn music."

महाव्रत described.

" To the left of the Agnidhra priest were placed two posts on which was hung up as a target a completely round skin or according to Lâtyâyana two skins, one for the chief archer and the other for any others who were good shots. At one point in the ceremony the king or a Rajput mounted the chariot and driving round the *Vedi* pierced with three arrows the skin leaving the arrows to stick in the skin." See Keith's Sankhâyana Âraṇyaka (Harvard oriental series, vol. xviii).

I would invite the attention of the curious reader to Tilak's Orion about the explanation of Ekâṣṭahâ which is the eight day of the dark half of Mâgha. He has discussed the different views on p.p. 43-54.

From the above analysis and the table given at p.p. 753-754, we see that the circle of the year is divided into 361 days, if we include the Viṣuvân. The 6th and the 7th months which are near the Viṣuvân are of 28 days and the 1st and the last months consist of thirty-two days. The rest of the months *viz.*, the eight months are of 30 days each. If we divide the circle into two parts we have two semi-circles of six months each ; in the first semi-circle we have 180 Somasutyâs each one consisting of three oblations. The order of the ceremony is reversed in the second semi-circle. This circle represents the year called Prajâpati, presided over by the twelve Âdityas of the twelve months into which a year is divided. Kuṇṭe considers it a ceremony in remembrance of the migration of the Âditya race of the Aryan tribe just as Angirasâmayana and Śâkyânâmayana are in remembrance of the migration of Angirasa and Śâkya races.

गवामयन according to the Vedic tradition. Gavâmayana is described in the Aitareya Brâhmaṇa in the 4th Pañchikâ, Chapter 18, Khaṇḍa 3. and verse 17.

गवामयनेनर्यंति गावोवाआदित्या आदित्यानामेवतदयनेनर्यंति । गावोवैसत्र
मासत शफाऊश्रृङ्गाणि सिषासत्यस्तासांदशमेमासि शफा: श्रृगांयजायन्तता
अब्रुवन्यस्मैकामाय दीक्षामह्यापामतमुत्तिष्ठामेति तायाउद्तिष्ठंस्ताएता-
श्रृङ्गियएय: । अथया: समापयिष्याम: संवत्सरमित्यासततासामश्रद्धया
श्रृङ्गाणिप्रावर्तंतता एतास्तूपराऊर्जंत्वसुन्वं तह्मादुता: सर्वानृतून्
प्राप्त्वोत्तरमुत्तिष्ठन्त्यूर्जं सुन्वन्सर्वस्य वैगाव: प्रेमाण: सर्वस्यचाऋ
तांगता: सर्वस्य प्रेमाणं सर्वं स्यचाऋतांगच्छति एवंवेद । आदित्याश्च
ह्वाअङ्गिरसश्च स्वर्गेलोकेऽस्पर्धंत वयंपूर्वएष्यामोवयमितिवेहादित्या पूर्वं
स्वर्गलोकंजग्मु: पश्चैवांगिरस: षष्ट्यां वावर्षेषु । यथा वा प्रायणीयो त्रिरात्रश्च-
तुर्विंशउक्थ्य सर्वेऽभिल्लुत्रा: षडह आक्षंयन्यान्यहानितदादित्यानामयनम् ।
प्रायणोयोतिरात्रश्चतुर्विंश उक्थ्य सर्वे पृष्ठ्या: षडहा आक्षंयन्यान्यहानि
तद्गिरिसामयनम् । सायथा स्तुति रंजसायन्येवमभिल्लुत्र: षडह स्वर्गस्यलोक-
स्याथ यथा महापथ: पर्यांणएवं पृष्ठ्य: षडह: स्वर्गस्यलोकस्य तद्घदुभाभ्यां
वैयन्नरिष्यत्युभयो: कामयोऽपाप्त्यैयश्चाभिल्लुत्रे षडहेयश्चपृष्ठ्ये ॥

" They resort to गवामयन because cows are suns; it is the session of the suns (आदित्य s); they therefore resort to this session. Formerly the cows desirous of hoofs and horns resorted to this session. Their horns and hoofs sprang forth in the tenth month. They said ' the purpose for which we were initiated is fulfilled; let us then rise '. They therefore rose these are the horns. And those that wanted to complete it within a year, resorted to it; by reason of their want of faith, the horn did not come out; they are, therefore, hornless but they, obtained vigour. They therefor e, having passed all the seasons, rose and obtained power. They became dear and charming to all. He who understands this becomes favourite and charming to all. The descendants of अदिति and अङ्गिरा competed for possession of heaven; ' let us go first, let us....' The descendants of अदिति (gods) first went to heaven; subsequently the descendants of अङ्गिरा went sixty years after. It is the session of the descendants of अदिति, where besides मायशीय and अतिरात्र चतुर्विंशउक्थ्य, all the अभिप्लवs are षडह. It is the session of the descendants of अङ्गिरस where besides मायशीय and अतिरात्रचतुर्विंशउक्थ्य all the days are occupied by पृष्ठषडह. Just as the highway leads through thornless path, so does अभिप्लवषडह lead one to heaven; just as the highway leads to alternative places, so does पृष्ठषडह lead one to heaven. One goes by two (feet) so that he may not fall; one therefore resorts to both the अभिप्लवषडह and पृष्ठ्यषडह so that both kinds of his desires may not fall short."

The same kind of description is found in Taittarîya Saṃhitâ Kâṇḍa VII, Prapâṭhaka 5 and Anuvâka 1 and the following.

From the above texts, we find that the Gavâmayana is of two kinds one lasting for ten months and the other for twelve months. It may be mentioned here that the Gavâmayana is the model sacrifice amongst all the annual sessions. If you perform a Gavâmayana lasting for ten months or 300 days, we have to omit five Ṣaḍahas from the first five months in the first semi-circle and 5 Ṣaḍahas from the 8th, 9th, 10th and 11th months in the 2nd semi-circle, because these are the only variable or elastic part of the Gavâmayana. The first and the last days of the Gavâmayana called the introductory and final Atirâttras, the 2nd day called the Chaturviṃs'a, the pentultimate day called the Mahâvrata, one Abhijit and the three Svarasâmas before the Viṣuvân and three Svarasâmas and one Vis'vajit after the Viṣuvân with ten days of Dvâdas'âha make up 22 days and constitute the fixed part of the Gavâmayana. See the list at p. p. 753-754.

The Gavâmayana is the model of all annual Sattras.

We also find in the above quotations that the Ṣaḍahas are of two kinds ; आदित्यानामयन and अङ्गिरसामयन. Abhiplava Ṣaḍaha and Priṣtya Ṣaḍaha. If the annual sacrifice of the Gavâmayana is performed with all the Abhiplava Ṣaḍahas it is called Âdityânâmayana but if it is performed with all the Priṣtya Ṣaḍas, it is called Angirasâmayana. If one wishes to adopt a lunar year consisting of 354 days, he shall have to omit six days from the above scheme. This उत्सर्गिनामयन. modified form of the Gavâmayana is called Utsarginâmayana. It is fully described in Tâṇḍya-mahâbrâhmaṇa in the 5th Chapter and Khaṇḍa 10. Sâyana in his commentary says that in every month, one day is omitted. According to the T. S.

"यदादिष्टमुत्सृजेयुर्यादृशेपुनः पर्यांप्लावेमध्ये षडहस्य संपद्येत षडहैर्मासा-न्त्संपाद्ययत्सप्तममहस्तस्मिन्नुत्सृजेयुः " ।

If one omits the ordained one which recurs repeatedly in the Ṣaḍaha, it shall be omitted on the 7th day on the same recurring after completing the months with the Ṣaḍahas.

Sâyana on commenting upon the passage says,

यदिशास्त्रोपदिष्टस्याप्युत्सर्गापेक्षयातदानी मपि यादृशे यादृश महज्योति रादिकं पुनः पुनः पर्यावर्तमानेषडहस्य मध्येसंपद्यते, तादृशमेवोत्सृजेत् । न तु प्रतिपदोक्तं विषुवदादिकमित्यध्याहरणीयम् । तस्मादभिप्लुव पृष्ठ्यैः षडहै मासम्पूरयित्वा पृष्ठ्य षडहादुर्ध्वभावि यत्सप्तममहस्तस्मिन्नहनि प्राप्तंज्योति-र्याग मुत्सृजेत् ॥

" In comparison with the omission of the one ordained by the scripture, that which of the Jyoti etc., recurs over and over again in the Ṣaḍahas shall be omitted ; but not the Viṣuvân etc., mentioned above should be filled up as an ellipsis. Completing a month by the Ṣaḍahas consisting of Abhiplavas and Priṣtyas, if the 7th day subsequent to the Priṣtya Ṣaḍaha happens to be the day of Jyoti, it shall be omitted." In this view there will be five such Jyoti days before Viṣuvân and there will be only one Jyoti day in the 12th month. So only six days will be omitted.

According to Keith the passage quoted from the T. S. is obscure ; but Tilak in his *Arctic home in the Vedas* is of opinion that in the Utsargi-nâmayana six days are omitted from the Gavâmayaṇa but he does not say which six days are to be omitted.

Tilak is of opinion that the year of the ancient Aryans consisted of ten months as that of the ancient Romans; this he says can be explained only by the fact that the Aryan lived in circumpolar region where it was possible for a year of ten months. This is one link in the chain to support his theory.

Tilak's theory.

I have described the Gavâmayana with all its modifications. If any one is desirous of knowing more about it, he can read the concluding Kânda of the T. S. or any Brâhmana or Śrauta Sútras.

PÂDA 6.

The author proceeds to deal with the right of persons to perform a Sattra. The opinion of Gânagâri according to As'valâyana Śrauta Sútra is that persons of the same Gottra can perform a Sattra but the opinion of Śaunaka is that people of different Gottras but of the same Kalpa can perform a Sattra. See at pp. 455 and the following of that work as published in the Ânaudâs'rama Sanscrit Series. What is a Kalpa? There are two sacrificial systems called the Naras'ansa and the Tanûnâpâta. They are the verses of the Rigveda repeated at the time of the Prayâja offerings. Those who repeat the Nâras'ansa verses belong to that Kalpa and those who repeat the Tanûnapâta verses belong to the Tanûnapâta Kalpa. According to our author the persons belonging to the same Kalpa though professing different Gottras are entitled to perform a Sattra.

The persons of the same कल्प are entitled to perform a सत्र.

कल्प explained.

Taking Kulâlayajña as a model sacrifice, it is said " एतेनराज पुरोहितौ सायुज्यकामौनौयजेयातास् " By this, the King and his priest desirous of salvation should perform a sacrifice? The term राजपुरोहितौ is explained; there are four views as set forth in जैमिनीयन्यायमाला (1) two priests of a King (षष्ठीतत्पुरुष) (2) a priest of one King and a priest of another King. (3) Two Kings who officiate as priests, (कर्मधारय) (4). A king and his priest (द्विगु). The author accepts the last view; in this view, the king and his priest are entitled to perform the Kulâlayajña.

राजपुरोहितौ explained.

Only a Brâhman is entitled to perform a Sattra; other two castes are not entitled to act as Ritviks. It is only of the family of Visvâmittra belonging to the same Kalpa that can participate in a Sattra.

A विश्वामित्र ब्राह्मण is entitled to perform a सत्र.

An आहिताग्नि is entitled to perform a सत्र.

Before a Sattra can be performed, it is necessary to perform the Agnyâdhâna; in other words, a person who is an Âhitâgni (who has established fire) is entitled to perform a Sattra.

New sacrificial vessels are to be constructed for a sacrifice.

The sacrificial vessels such as the Juhu etc., should be new; they should not be borrowed, because if the lender happens to die during the continuance of the sacrifice, the borrower shall have to return them to be burnt with the dead under the text आहिताग्निमग्निभिः दहन्तियच्च पात्रैश्च." "A person who has established fire, should be burnt with fire and the sacrificial vessels."

All twice born are entitled to repeat सामधेनी verses.

In a modified sacrifice, all the three castes are entitled to repeat the Sâmadhenî verses.

What are सामधेनी verses?

The Sâmadhenî verses are the fire-kindling verses and sticks are thrown on repetition of the verses in the fire. They are eleven in number and are given in T. B. III. 5·2. The use of these verses is fully explained in Sâyana's commentary on T. S. II. 2. 5.7-8. The poetical translation of the eleven Sâmadhenî verses is given by Eggeling in his translation of Ś. B. Part I, p. 102 (S. B. E.) By repeating the first and the last verses three times they are increased to 15 verses. They are all in the Gâyattri metre. Two Triṣṭubh verses are added to complete the number seventeen. See Ś. B. VI. 2·2·10.

PÂDA 7.

सर्व॑स्व is given in a विश्वजित्.

The author now proceeds to deal with those things that can be given in a gift. In connection with a Visvajit sacrifice it is said ' विश्वजितिसर्वस्वंददाति ' "He gives his entire wealth". What is the meaning of entire wealth? It includes everything over which a sacrificer has proprietary possession save the sacrificer's parents over whom he has no proprietary right,

What is सर्व॑स्व?

the landed property which is vested in the crown, the future property that does not exist and the past property that is spent. A horse cannot be given in fee because it is of no use for a priest and a pious and religiously disposed slave should not be given. Accordingly, ' Sarvasva ' means all kinds of moveable property over which a sacrificer has proprietary right and which is not forbidden. Such property in existence at the time of the performance of the sacrifice can be validly given as fee of the sacrifice to a priest.

The wealth is divided into three parts (1) that which is for one's own enjoyment ; (2) that which is for the sacrifice and (3) that which is for the priest's fee. If a sacrificer gives away all kinds of the above said wealth, what is to be paid for the ceremonies after the sacrificial bath ? The author, therefore, thinks that the ' Sarvasva ' consists of the wealth set apart as fee of the priests.

Entire wealth means only that portion which is set apart as the priest's fee.

What is the fee of the Vis'vajit which is performed in the beginning in an Ahargaṇa sacrifice ? It has eight days consisting of विश्वजित्, ज्योति, गौ, आयु, आयु, गौ, ज्योति and अभिजित्. It is the modified form of the Dvâdâsâha. We know in an independent Vis'vajit sacrifice the fee is 'Sarvasva', *viz.*, that portion of a sacrificer's wealth which is set apart as the priest's fee. The same is the fee in a Vis'vajit, and also in an Ahargaṇa according to ' Śabara, but according to Kumârila, it consists of 1,200 cows. We have followed Śabara's view in the interpretation of the Adhîkaraṇa treating of the present subject.

Fee in and अइर्गण.

In order to entitle one to perform a Vis-vajit ｜sacrifice, he should possess 1,200 or above 1,200 cows. A person, therefore, not possessing 1,200 cows or possessing less than twelve hundred cows is not entitled to perform a Visvajit sacrifice.

A person not possessing 1,200 is cows is not entitled to perform the विश्वजित् sacrifice.

In an Agnyâdhâna ceremony it is said *inter alia* that *unlimited* should be given (vide the text at p. 39f) What is the meaning of it ? According to our author it means ' a large gift '. As all the definite numbers up to 1,000 are mentioned, ' the large gift ' necessarily means any number above 1,000.

अपरिमित means a large gift over 1,000.

A Parakriti is the narration of the acts of one individual and a Purâkalpa is the narration of the acts of a community. They are denoted by the terms इति, ह and स्म. They are in the nature of an Arthavâda (supplementary sentences) in support of a Viddhi or Niṣedha. The acts of ancient people in the bygone ages are either good or bad. The acts of the former class are praised and held up as ideals to be followed and those of the latter class are censured and denounced, so that they may not be followed.

परकृति and पुराकल्प explained.

The author now proceeds to fix the period of the performance of a विश्वसृज्ञामयन

विश्वसजामयन,   मयनं. The extreme limit of it is said to be of 1,000 years. What is the meaning of 1,000 years in the text quoted at p. 399 ? There are eight views on this subject. The first view is that as one cannot attain the age of 1,000 years, the विश्वसृज्ञामयन is the sacrifice of the gods. The second view is that a man can attain the age of 1,000 years by use of *elixir vitæ* or prolong his age by other means, so the sacrifice can be performed by perfect men. The third view is that of काष्णाजिनि. A man can have the sacrifice performed in several generations by himself and his descendants for a period of 1,000 years. The fourth view is that by performing the विश्वसृज्ञामयनं a man attains the age of 1,000 years. The fifth view which is that of लाबुकायन is that a number of 250 persons can join in performing it and complete it within a period of 4 years thus making the total of 1,000 years, because a year in this view is used in a secondary sense. The sixth view is that a year is variable ; it is solar, lunar or seasonal : you can attach any sense to it. In this view, a year means ‘ a month.’; Accordingly, the विश्वसृज्ञामयन is of the duration of 83 years and 4 months. The seventh view is that a year means ‘ twelve nights ’ ; accordingly the duration of the sacrifice comes to 33 years and 4 months. The eighth and the last view is that a year means ‘ a day ’; accordingly the period of duration for the performance is 2 years, 9 months and 10 days ; this is the view of the author.

PÂDA 8.

The Chaturhotri is a homa which is performed with the object of propagation of one’s species. There are two portions of it ; one consists of the offerings

चतुहोतृ is performed in an unconsecrated fire.

and the other of the soma cup. The mantras that are pronounced are originally given in the T. A., but they are fully explained and commented upon by Sâyana at p.p. 388 and 389 of T. B. Vol. I of the Ânandâs'rama edition. As to the performance of the Chaturhotri homa, it should be done in an unconsecrated fire.

Similarly,' the Upanayna homa consisting of three oblations स्थपतीष्टि described at p. 313 and गर्दभेज्या which is performed as a penance by a religious student when his vow of chastity is unintentionally broken and in which an ass is sacrificed to निर्ऋति

उपनयनहोम, स्थपतीष्टि and **गर्दभेज्या** are performed in an unconsecrated fire.

are performed in an unconsecrated fire.

The time for the performance of देव and वैश्यकर्म.

The ceremonies are of two kinds (1) देव and (2) वैश्य. The देव ceremonies are also of two kinds (1) श्रौत and (2) स्मार्त. The स्मार्तदेव ceremonies are performed when the sun is in the north, in the bright half of a month and during the day. While on the other hand, the Paittrya ceremonies are performed when the sun is in the south, in the dark-half of a month and at night.

An initiated in a ज्योतिष्टोम has to beg alms and purchase soma.

An initiated one in a Jyotiṣṭoma has to beg alms for twelve nights for his maintenance and purchase soma; the wealth is immaterial. He shall have to do it under a Vedic precept whether he possesses wealth or not.

Certain permanent ceremonies.

Similarly, there are many other rites which are invariably performed and are therefore permanent as, for example, the Brâhmaṇa's milk diet, warrior's food consisting of gruel and a merchant's Âmikṣâ dish in a Jyotiṣṭoma; certain orders in the Dars'apûrṇamâsayâga, putting on grass dress performing संवत्सरहोम and recitation of the द्रव्यमंत्रs in a Vâjapeya. These ceremonies are performed whether the reason for their performance exists or not.

Relaxation of the rule as to breaking of the fast in the case of a digestive complaint.

The rule is that in a Jyotiṣṭoma sacrifice, a fast is broken in the midday or after the midnight; but if a sacrificer is suffering from any digestive complaint, he need not observe the rule strictly: and break the fast to suit his convenience.

In a Jyotiṣṭoma, it is said that an initiated shall sacrifice an animal to the dual gods Agni and Soma; but under a special text, a goat is specially ordained. The author has discussed many views upon the subject by reason of the difference of opinion as to the denotation and connotation of a term fully explained in the preceding pages of the introduction. The author's view is that the animal is genus and the goat is a species. As soon as one utters the word ' goat ' which is naturally connected with the sense, it brings before his mind's eye a certain figure of a quadruped which is classed amongst the species of the goat.

CHAPTER VII.
PÂDA 1.

The author in the first six chapters has dealt with Upadés'a. He now proceeds to deal with Atides'a in the remaining last six chapters. Before explaining Atides'a, it is necessary to define Prakṛiti and Vikṛiti.

प्रकृति and विकृति explained. The sacrifice is of two kinds namely (1) Sakalânga (2) Vikalânga. If a sacrifice is performed with all the details, it is of the former class and is technically called Prakṛiti because it is a model in itself and serves as a pattern to others. A crippled or Vikâlanga sacrifice is one in which some details are omitted; it is, therefore, called in the ritualistic literature Vikṛiti or modified sacrifice. They are also called archetype and ectype respectively. There are certain sacrifices which are models in themselves ; as for example दर्शपूर्णमासयागs are the models of all हविः, ज्योतिष्टोम is the model of all soma sacrifices and गवामयन is the model of all animal सत्रs and so on.

अतिदेश defined. There are some archetypal details which are transferred to the modified sacrifice. This transference of the details from the model sacrifice to the modified sacrifice is called Atides'a. The Apurva is laid down by a Vidhi text and applies to the model sacrifice ; the Chodaka text makes the details of the model sacrifice applicable to the modified sacrifice. The Atides'a is of several kinds as shown in the table given at p. 278.

Classification.

The common and differentiating features of श्येन and इषुयागs the ectypes of the ज्योतिष्टोम. There are two modifications of the Jyotiṣṭoma called Iṣuyâga and Śyenayâga. In connection with Iṣuyâga, it is said ' समानमितर च्छेयनेन ' the other is similar with श्येन. The Iṣuyâga and Śyenayâga have borrowed certain details from the Jyotiṣṭoma which form their *differentia* but over and above this differentiating feature the Iṣuyâga resembles Śyenayâga in other details. In this view, the text is an Atides'avidhi.

When the offering and their ब्राह्मणs are transferred from the वैश्वदेव to the वरुण प्रघास, the details are necessarily transferred. There is चातुर्मास्ययाग which is fully explained in the preceding pages ; in connection with the वैश्वदेव which is its subordinate part, eight offerings mentioned at p. 424 are laid down. In the Brâhmaṇa, these offerings are praised in the form of an Arthavâda. The details called Angavidhi are also described. The five offerings and their Brâhmaṇa are made applicable to the वरुणप्रघास

another subordinate part of the चातुर्मास्य. Now the question is whether the details are also transferred. The view of one side is that only the five offerings and their अर्थंवाद are transferable under the text " वत्ब्राह्मणा न्येव पंचहवींषिवद्ब्राह्मणनीतराणि ". The same Brâhmaṇa which applies to others applies to these five offerings ". The author's view is that the details with the offerings and their Arthavâda are made applicable to the Varuṇapraghâsa, because the transference of the offerings without the details is of no use. The Brahmaṇa includes both अर्थंवाद and Angavidhi.

Ekakapâlabrâhmaṇa is read in connection with Vais'vadeva and Aindragnabrâhmaṇa is read in connection with Varuṇapraghâsa. Both these Brâhmaṇas are transferred to the Sâkamedha another subordinate part of the Châturmasya. In view of the principle laid down above, the Brâhmaṇa includes both the Arthavâda and the details.

The same principle followed in transference of the ब्राह्मण to the साकमेघ.

The Ekakapâla Brâhmaṇa as we have seen is transferred to the Sâkamedha. We have Ekakapâla consecrated to heaven and earth in Vaisvadeva and another Ekakapâla consecrated to the lord of the universe in Varuṇapraghâsa. Which Ekakapâla is meant ? Whether it is the एक कपाल of the वैश्वदेव or that of the वरुणप्रघास that is transferred to the साकमेघ ? The author decides in favour of the tranference of the एककपाल of the वरुण प्रघास to the साकमेघ. The first reason is that

The एक कपाल of the वरुण प्रघास is transferred to the साकमेघ.

Reasons for the same.

the latter is very close to the वरुणप्रघास. See the description of the चातुर्मास्य in the preceding pages. (2). The ऐंद्राग्न ब्राह्मण which is read in connection with the वरुणप्रघास is also transferred to the साकमेघ and (3) the transference of the एककपाल from the वैश्वदेव is meaningless because the offering of the एक कपाल in the वैश्वदेव does not complete the sacrifice and further at the time of the sacrificial bath there is a double offering.

ब्राह्मण explained.

The word Brâhmaṇa used above is thus explained.

पूर्वेषांब्राह्मणंयत्तदुत्तरेष्वतिदिश्यते ।
चोद्यंतेयेन वाक्येनतत्तेषां ब्राह्मणंमतं ॥

" When a ब्राह्मण of the model sacrifices is transferred to the modified sacrifices, (by virtue of the) चोदक text under which it is done (it) becomes their ब्राह्मण." We have already noted the difference between the संहिता and ब्राह्मण. When the ब्राह्मण of the model sacrifice is transferred under a चोदक text to the modified sacrifice, it becomes the ब्राह्मण of the modified sacrifice. It includes both अर्थंवाद and अङ्गविधि.

PÂDA 2.

We have described the Vedic music at p. XCI of the introduction and explained many musical terms. In the present Pâda transference of certain musical air is explained. It is said that Kavatîs should be sung in Rathantara. The Kavatîs are certain verses of the Rigveda commencing with कयानश्चित्र etc. ; there is another verse अभित्वाशूरनोनुम which is technically called अभिवर्ती and is sung in रथंतर tune.

The question is whether रथंतर stands for this typical अभिवर्ती verse, the line marks (स्वरs) of the अभिवर्ती verse or the word रथंतर. The author says that such absurd questions cannot arise ; the text is simply a direction to transfer the air to the Kavatîs. The result is that the Kavatîs are to be sung in the low air called Rathantara tune. Singing in a sacrifice produces an invisible result, because it is under a Vedic command ; while singing with a view to learn it produces no invisible effect.

PÂDA 3.

In the preceding Pâdas, we have dealt with those transfers of the details which take place under the direct texts and which are technically called प्रत्वक्षश्रुतं (see the classification at p. 422.) Now we come to the change of names called नामातिदेश. We have seen what अग्निहोत्र is ; it is a name of a particular sacrifice. If an अग्निहोत्र is performed for a month continually, it is called Kundapâyina sacrifice ; it is, therefore, a sacrifice in which all the characteristics or qualities of Agnihottra are transferred. It is a case of change of names.

Change of name.

कुण्डपायिन is a modified form of अग्निहोत्र.

The first day of Dvâdas'âha is called Prâyanîya and the first day of the Gavâmayana is also called Prâyaniya. It is a compound word and is not a case of the change of name as enunciated above. The first day in a sacrifice is called Prâyanîya. There is therefore no transfer of the characteristic of the first day of the द्वादशाह to the first day of the गवामयन.

प्रायणीय is a compound word.

The author now proceeds to determine what Sarvapṛiṣṭha means in the text " विश्वजित् सर्वपृष्ठोभवति " A Vis'vajit, is Sarvapriṣṭha. We have explained the term Priṣṭha at p. XCII. The question is which Priṣṭha is meant to be sung in a Vis'ajit ? Is it a Priṣṭha of the Jyotiṣṭoma or that of Gavâmayan ? The author is of

In सर्वपृष्ट of a विश्वजित्, षड्ह songs of गवामयन are meant.

opinion that as in a Jyotiṣṭoma there are not many Priṣṭhas, though there are many Stomas, the Priṣṭhas of the Gavâmayana are, therefore, transferred; they are six in number *viz*, रथंतर, बृहत्, वैरूप, वैराज, शाक्वर and रैवत.

An अवभृथ in a वरुणप्रघास is borrowed from a सोमयाग.

In connection with the वरुणप्रघास, it is said "वारुणयानिष्कासेनतुषै इचाव धूमयंति." They go to the bath with the remnant of आमिक्षा and husk. The sense of the term 'bath' is to be determined. Which bath is meant, whether it is the bath of the full and new moon sacrifices which are the models of the वरुणप्रघास or that of a सोमयाग where it invariably takes place? In the new and full moon sacrifices water is sprinkled in all directions with the mantra given at p. 438. This sprinkling of water is figuratively called 'bath'. It cannot be a transferance of the so—called bath of the दर्शपूर्णमासयाग to the Varuṇapraghâsa.

But not its materials.

The result according to our author is that it is the bath of a Somayâga, that is borrowed. Now the question is whether the material of the Somayâga should be used in the sacrificial bath transferred or not. The author says that as the text quoted above expressly mentioned the materials, namely, the remnants of Amikṣa and husk there is, therefore, no necessity of borrowing the puroḍâs'a cake from the Somayâga.

What is the meaning of वैष्णव in the राजसूय sacrifice.

In a Somayâga, there is an Âtithyeṣṭi; in its connection, it is said 'Vaiṣṇavonavakapâla' which is a cake baked on nine potsherds in honour of विष्णु. In a राजसूय ceremony there is a cake baked on three potsherds in honour of Viṣṇu. Is it a case of transference of the cake of the Âtithyeṣṭi to the Râjasûya? The author says that it is not a case of borrowing; the word Vaiṣṇava (pertaining to विष्णु) is used in the derivative sense; so the principle of Agnihotranyâya does not apply.

It is used in a derivative sense.

The Râjasûya will have, therefore, cakes baked on three earthen pans in honour of Viṣṇu.

The same principle applies to निर्मंथ्य etc.

Similarly, *nirmanthya*, Varhi and Âjya are used in the derivative sense in the texts at p. 440 in connection with an animal sacrifice. By reason of these words occuring in the context of the Dars'apûrṇamâsayâga, it cannot be said that the peculiarities of an animal sacrifice are transferred to the Dars'apûrṇamasayâga. The Prayaṇiyanyâya therefore applies.

In connection with the Châturmâsyayâga, it is said " द्वयेाः प्रणयंति तस्भाद् द्राभ्यांयंति " " They carrying in two, therefore with two they go " There is an Agnipraṇayana ceremony in Dars'apûrṇamâsa and Somayâgahs. It consists in carrying three burning sacrificial sticks of Udamvara wood besmeared with ghee from the Âhavanîya fire of the Prâchînavams'a to the Uttaravedi in a soma sacrifice (See the plan in the frontispiece fig I.) During the ceremony the प्रैच्य mantras and other Mantras are recited at every stage of it. The Mantras are given in the Taittrîyasanhitâ 3152 at seq. of the Anandâs'rama edition. The description of Agnipraṇayana is also given in the Aittareya Brâhmaṇa 1st Pañchikâ, 5th Adhyâya, 2nd Khaṇda, verse 28. Now the question is, whether the Agnipraṇayana of Somayâga where it plays an important part or that of the Dars'apûrṇayâga which are the models of the Châturmâsya is meant. The author says that the Agnipraṇayana is used here in its derivative sense ; no principle of transfer (Atidesha) is involved. The next question is, what is the nature of the text quoted above ? Whether it is Parisankhyâ Guṇavâda or Arthavâda ? It is not a Parisankhyâ, for Parisankhyâ has three defects as said repeatedly. It is not a Guṇavâda as there is no description of a quality, It is a therefore an Arthavâda.

There are four parts of Châturmâsya as said in the preceding pages of the introduction in connection with the description of the Châturmâsya (1) Vais'vadeva (2) Varunapraghâsa (3) Śakamedha and (4) Śunâs'iriya. In connection with the text 'द्वयेाः प्रणयंति' there are three other texts to be interpreted ; the first is ' उपात्रवर्षंति ' " Here they make an offering " It is an Anâravyavidhi and means that in the northern altar, they make offerings. Then there is the prohibitory text " नवैश्वदेवेउत्तरवेदिषुपवयंतिनञुना‐ विरीये ". They do not construct a northern altar in a Vais'vadeva sacrifice nor in a Śunâs'irîya. If there is no Uttaravedi in a Vais'vadeva or Śunâs'irîya, there cannot be an Agnipraṇâyana. Then after this prohibition, we have the third text in the nature of Pratiprasava " उक्वारएतैायबस्व, यद्वरुणप्रघासः साकमेधश्च." " Verily they viz., वरुणप्रघास and साकमेध are the two thighs of a sacrifice ". The result is that the text Dwayopraṇayanti applies to the Varuṇapraghâsa, and Sâkamedha and the Agnipraṇayana ceremony takes place there.

The applicability of the principle of Dwayaḥpranayanti is very important in interpreting the smriti texts and the smriti commentators have very often resorted to it. It is a simple legal truth which is very often resorted to by the lawyers of the British

Courts of Justice *viz.*, the principle of estoppel " Ons should not bow hot and cold at the same time ". See Kishori Lal Sircar at p. 324.

The characteristics of स्वरसाम, एक कपाल and आभिक्षा are transferred.

There is a text in connection with Gavâmayana, " अभितोदिबाकीर्त्यँ नयस्वरसामान: " " On both sides of Divakîrtya there are three Swarasâmas ". The Divâkîrtya is the Viṣuvan day ; there are उस्वरसामः in both the semi-circles of Gavâmayan on both sides of the Dîvakîrtya which is like a diameter. See at p. 753. In these Swârasâmas by reason of the continuity of the Atigrâhya cups, there the Saptadas'astoma is sung. We have पृष्ठषडह in a Gavâmayana, in it we have Tribrit Pañchadasa, Saptadas'a, Ekavims'a, Triṇava and Trayâstriṃs'a songs. There is a transference of the peculiarities of the Swarasâmas to the Prıṣṭaṣaḍahas by virtue of the text " पृष्ठयः षडहः द्वौस्वरसामानौ." Prithṣṭa has six days and two Swarasamas. Similiarly we have the transference of the peculiarities of the Vais'vadeva cake to the आग्रयण sacrificial cake and the peculiarities of the Vais'wadeva Amikṣa to the मैत्रावरुणामिक्षा.

The meaning of the terms cloth and cart.

There is a text " वासोददाति अनोददाति." He gives cloth ; he gives a cart." Here the terms ' cloth ' and ' cart ' are used for cloth and cart when ready but not when they are being prepared by a weaver or a carpenter.

Fire means common fire.

In connection with गर्गत्रिरात्र, it is said " अग्निमुपनिधायस्तुवीत." " Having placed fire, he praises." Here in the text, ' fire ' means common unconsecrated fire. Unless there is a text to the contrary, ' fire ' means unconsecrated fire.

When the term ' यूप ' is applied to उपशय, it is in a secondary sense.

There are eleven sacrificial posts in an Ekâdas'inî sacrifice ; the last one from the south is called Upas'aya. Animals are tied to the ten sacrificial posts ; no animal is tied to Upas'aya ; consequently no ceremonies are performed. The Upasaya is a sacrificial post only in name ; the word ' sacrificial post ' applied to it, is in a secondary sense.

यूष is a common song in an अग्निचयन.

In connection with the Agnichayana ceremony, it is said " पृष्ठैरुपतिष्ठंते. " " They worship with songs ". The यूष is also sung in a Jyotiṣṭoma in Madhyandinasavana. It naturally arises in one's mind that the Prıṣṭa of the Jyotiṣṭoma is meant to be sung in the Agnichayana. The author says that the word ' यूष ' means a common song and any verse from the Rigveda would, therefore, do for the purpose of singing.

PÂDA 4.

The author now proceeds to deal with the inferential Atides'a the second division of Vachana (see the table at p. 422). We have explained साध्य, साधन and इतिकर्त्तव्यता in the preceding pages ; "अग्निष्टोमेन स्वर्गं कामोयजेत" "Let one who is desirous of heaven perform an Agniṣṭoma." In this text we have all the three elements of भावना mentioned above. Heaven is (साध्य) an end in itself ; sacrifice is the means (साधन) and the अग्निष्टोम is the इतिकर्त्तव्यता. But where in a text, the साध्य and साधन are mentioned but the इतिकर्त्तव्यता is not given, it shall be presumed to be of the model sacrifice. As for example सौर्यं चरुं निर्वपेद् ब्रह्मवर्चसकामः' ' A person desicous of Brahmaṇic splendour should offer boiled rice to sun.' Here we have all the elements excepting the Itikartavyatâ. Brahmaṇic splendour is the object and the Sauryayâga is the means, while the procedure is not known. The model sacrifice of the Sauryayâga is Dars'apûrṇamâsa sacrifice ; the procedure in the Sauryayâga is therefore governed by that in the Dars'apûrṇamâsayâgas. In such a case, the Itikartavyatâ will be presumed to be Vedic but not profane or secular.

Where in a text, the इतिकर्त्तव्यता, one of the elements of भावना is not mentioned it shall be presumed to be of the model sacrifice.

Further presumption is that it is Vedic.

The sentence or command on the strength of which a person acts or which prompts or induces a person to act or omit to act is a Vidhi. The Vidhyanta is the entire Brâhmaṇa with the Purodâs'a excepting the contrary the Vidhyadi consists of the the principal Vidhi, on Brâhmaṇa and Purodâs'a. The former is the procedure and the latter is the substantive law.

विध्यादि and विध्यंत explained.

the principal Vidhi, on Brâhmaṇa and Purodâs'a. the substantive law.

In a Hindu kitchen house when rice or any pulse or *khichri* is cooked, it is put with certain quantity of water into a cauldron or brass pot. The cauldron or the brass pot is placed on an oven and heated. The above said materials heated are not stirred by a spoon but after a certain time, the cook wants to know whether the material put on the fire is boiled or not ; he takes it out from the cauldron or the brazen pot by means of the spoon to ascertain the fact. From two or three grains of the materials that are taken out and felt by the fingers, inference is made from these sample grains about the whole class. This is a homely proverb amongst the Hindus even now and corresponds to the Latin maxim " *Ex uno disce omnes* " as said by Jacob in his

स्थालीपुलाकन्याय explained.

Loukikanyâyâñjali. In Logic, it is just the converse of the well known Aristotle's " *Dictum de omne et nullo* ". Sthalîpulâ kanyâya is, therefore, the inductive method of arriving at a universal proposition from the observation of two or more particular individuals of a class of which you predicate generally by reason of the similar situation in which they are placed.

The next question for determination is whether the Gavâmayana is governed by the procedure of Dvâdas'âha or Ekâha. In the गवामयन as we have seen, there are certain days called Jyoti, Gau and Ayuḥ ; as they last for more days than one, they come under a sacrifice, the model of which is a Dvâdas'âha. On the other hand, they have their names fixed conventionally, they are therefore Ekâhas. In this state of conflict between an inference and the conventional name, the author says that the name has preference over the inference. He, therefore, decides in favour of the procedure of the एकाह being applicable to the Gavâmayana.

The गवामयन is governed by the एकाह in its procedure.

CHAPTER VIII.

PÂDA 1.

The author having discussed the general features of the Atides'a in the preceding chapter now proceeds to illustrate it by means of the particular cases of it in Chapter VIII.

We have already seen in the preceding pages that the text which allows Sauryayâga to be performed contains the साध्य and साधन but not the Itikartavyatâ. How are we to determine it ? There is the word 'Nirvâpa' from which we can trace the origin or the model. We have a text in connection with the दर्शपूर्णमासयाग " आग्नेयमष्टकपालनिर्वपति " ' He offers a cake baked on eight potsherds to Agni '. We at once find the Vidyhanta in the Agneya. So the model of the Saûryayâga is Agneya and it is governed by the procedure of the latter.

The model of सौर्यंयाग is आग्नेय.

On the other hand Somayâga is a model in itself and is therefore not governed by the procedure of the Iṣṭis.

सोमयाग is a model in itself.

What is the Vidhyanta (procedure) in Aindrâgna? The procedure of the Dars'apûrṇamâsa governs the Iṣṭis ; in connection with the Aindragna, cakes baked on eleven potsherds are ordained ; the word used in this

ऐंद्राग्न is governed by the दर्शपूर्णमासयागs.

connection is ' निर्वाप.' It is an offering of ghee or other materials by means of an Agnihotrahavani in the दर्शपूर्णमास sacrifices. This indicative mark shows that the procedure of Aindrâgna is governed by the new and full moon sacrifices.

Similarly, the Agniṣomîya animal sacrifice is governed by the Vidhyanta of the Dars'apûrṇamâsayâgas, because the Vedic texts which permit Prayâja, Anuyâja and sprinkling of ghee on the animal, which are the peculiar characteristics of the Dars'apûrṇamâsayâgas show that the procedure of the Agniṣomîya is governed by that of the new and full moon sacrifices.

The procedure of दर्शपूर्ण-मास governs the अग्नी-षोमीय animal sacrifice.

The author says that the procedure of the Agnṣomîya animal sacrifice governs all other animal sacrifices viz., Savanîya, Nirûdha and Pas'uvandha. The indicative mark in the word ' आलभेत ' which is the common injunctive verb in all animal sacrifices shows that the procedure of the Agniṣomiya governs all the animal sacrifices. The second reason is that the procedure of Savanas is also common to all the animal sacrifices ; as " वपया प्रातः सवनेचरंति, पुरोडाशेनमाध्यंदिनें ऽगैस्तृतीय सवने " " They complete the morning libation with fat, the midday libation with पुरोडाश cake and the third libation with limbs ".

The procedure of अग्नी-षोमीय governs all the animal sacrifices.

The Savanîya is the model of the Ekâdas'inî sacrifice in which eleven animals are offered, because the two ropes by which animals are tied round a sacrificial post and the time for preparation of *soma* are common to both. While the Ekâdas'inî is the model of a Pas'ugaṇa sacrifice, because it is the former in which there are more sacrificial posts than one.

सवनीय is the model of the एकादशिनी, and the latter is the model of पशुगण sacrifice.

The model of the sacrifices of which the materials and the deity are not known is the Soma sacrifice ; the Dvâdas'âha is the model of the Ahargaṇa sacrifices from Dvirâtra to Śatarâtra. The Gavâmayana is the model of all the annual sacrifices such as Âdityânâmayana, Tapasvinâmayana etc.

The models of the indefinite sacrifices, अहर्गण and animal sessions.

There are sacrifices which last for days and are called by one name, Sadhyaskra and Sâhasra In them, the procedure of the preceding days is provided for, but not that of the succeeding days. In this state of uncertainty, the author says that the procedure of the preceding days governs that of the succeeding days.

The procedure of the preceding day governs the procedure of the succeeding days in सादस्क and साहस्र.

<table>
<tr><td valign="top" width="38%">

Untransferable ingredi-
ents of a sacrifice.

</td><td valign="top">

The author now proceeds to mention those ingredients of a sacrifice, which cannot be transferred. (1) The principal act (2) the fruit (3) the rule (4) the sacrificer (5) the aggregate or bundle of qualities which

</td></tr>
</table>

constitute the name of a sacrifice. When the modification of a sacrifice is a separate act, it resembles the model sacrifice in some of the minor details only. The fruit, the rule, the sacrificer, the name must necessarily be separate and cannot, therefore, be borrowed. These four above mentioned ingredients are the *differentiæ* of each sacrifice, either model or modified ; hence they are non-transferable entities.

<table>
<tr><td valign="top" width="38%">

The purificatory act is not transferable if its object is to benefit the sacrificer.

</td><td valign="top">

If an object pertaining to a minor act in a sacrifice is for the benefit of a modified sacrifice, it will be transferred from the model sacrifice with the object, to the modified sacrifice but if it is to benefit the performer of the sacrifice, it shall not be transferred. As for instance, it is said in connec

</td></tr>
</table>

tion with the Dars'apûrṇamâsayâgas ' गोदोहनेन प्रणयेत्पशुकामस्य उतास्मै गायतानर '. Let him carry water in a milk pail, if desirous of cattle ;

<table>
<tr><td valign="top" width="38%">

अपांप्रणयन explained.

</td><td valign="top">

O ! singer, sing for him ', I may tell you what Apam-praṇayana is ; it is described in the

</td></tr>
</table>

Satapatha Brâhmaṇa in Book I Chapter 1 Brâhmaṇa at p. 34 of the Â. S. edition. There is a note by the editor of it. An अध्वर्यु taking the चमस vessel made of वारण wood (Crataeva Roxburghii), in the left hand pouring water in it from the water vessel which he has in his right hand and placing it with the right hand on the northern side of the गार्हपत्य fire, asks ब्रह्मा " May I bring water " and orders the sacrificer to keep silence. The Brahmâ utters ' Bring to the sacrifice ' etc., in a low tone ; then he commands in a sufficiently loud tone so as to be audible to the Adhvaryu " well bring it ". Then the Adhvaryu taking the चमस vessel to the north of the Âhavanîya hearth places it on the spread out *darbha* grass on

<table>
<tr><td valign="top" width="38%">

प्रणीता water.

</td><td valign="top">

the external altar." See also Eggeling's Śatapatha Vol. I. p. 9. The water so carried is called Praṇîtâpaḥ and is used in the sacrifice.

</td></tr>
</table>

<table>
<tr><td valign="top" width="38%">

If the object is to benefit the sacrifice, the subordinate act is transferable.

</td><td valign="top">

There is a further text in the same connection , चमसेनाप: प्रणयेत् । गोदोहने नपशुकामस्य '. " carry water with a spoon ; if one desirous of cattle with a milk pail ". The Sauryayâga is the modified form of the new and full moon sacrifices. The carrying of water will be performed with the Chamasâ vessel ;

</td></tr>
</table>

because the carrying of it in a pail is with a particular object of a sacrificer; so it shall 'not be transferred. When the minor part is for the Kratvartha, it is transferable; as for instance ' खादिरं वीर्य्यकामायच्यू पं कुर्व्वीत '. "Let him construct a sacrificial post of Khadira wood, if desirous of strength." A sacrificial post must necessarily be constructed of some wood; it is not a modification but an essential element of a sacrifice; hence it is transferable.

In the Dars'apûrṇamâsayâga, there are two acts of Abhimars'an performed on the full moon day with Chatuhotra-mantras and new moon day with Pañchahotṛ-mantras. The Sauryayâga is the modified form of the Dars'apûrṇamâsayâgas. The question is, whether the Abhimar-s'ana is to be performed with the Chatuhotṛmantras, if it is performed on the full moon day and another with the Pañchahotamantras on the new moon day. The author says that in the Dars'apûrṇamâsayâga the time of performance is fixed but it is not so in the Sauryayâga; there will be, therefore, an option.

There is no time fixed for अभिमर्शन in सौर्ययाग,

The next question for determination is whether the Vidhyanta of any of the subordinate acts of the Dars'apûrṇa-mâsayâgas or of the Agneya as to boiled rice, is transferred to the Sauryayâga. The author decides in favour of the Agneya being the model of the Sauryayâga as to the procedure relating to the offering of the boiled rice, because the deity in both of them is one. The unity of the deity in both of them makes one the model of the other.

आग्नेय is the model of सौर्ययाग as regards the offering of the boiled rice.

Where there is a conflict between the indicative mark afforded by the deity and the offering in determining the procedure, the inference derived from the offer-ing prevails over that afforded by the deity; because the former is the internal part and the latter the external part of a sacrifice. As for example ' ऐंद्रमेकादशकपालं निर्वपेत् ' ' Let a cake baked on eleven potsherds be offered to इंद्र '. Here in the passage we have two words viz., Aindra and Ekâdas'akapâla which afford an indicative mark to determine the Vidhyanta. The former is governed by a Sannâya procedure and the latter is by that of the Puroḍâs'a. In this state of conflict between the deity and the offering, the procedure of the latter will prevail under the rule laid down above.

When there is a conflict between the procedure applicable to the deity and the offering, it is the latter that prevails.

In a Hiraṇya sacrifice there is a minor sacrifice called Satakrisnala. In it a hundred pieces of gold weighing one Krisnala each in the shape of wild rice are boiled in ghee and offered to Prajâpati. The question is what is the procedure? Whether it is governed by the practice that obtains in the oblations of ghee or that which prevails in the offering of the boiled rice. The author says that the gold pieces resemble the wild rice and are also boiled; so the procedure relating to the wild rice governs the one relating to the gold pieces.

The विध्यंत of boiled rice governs the offering of hundred gold pieces.

In connection with the Chitrâyâga, it is said ' दधिमधुघृतंधाना उदकं तंडुलाः तत्संसृष्टं प्रजापत्यंभवति '. ' curd, honey, ghee, fried rice, water and rice; all these mixed together are fit offerings to प्रजापति '. Here in the text we have a mixture called Madhûdaka (honey and water.) What is the procedure? Whether it is of Sannâya or of ghee oblations. The author says that ghee and मधूदक both resemble each other in colour and fluidity. The milking process which applies to Sânnâya is not applicable to Madhûdaka. The procedure of ghee oblations i.e., offering it in a low tone, therefore, applies to the मधूदक offering.

The procedure of ghee oblations applies to the मधूदक offering.

PÂDA 2.

The Iṣṭis are the models of the Vâjinejyâ and Sautrâmani, because Vâjina (whey), is the modified form of Sannâya and wine the ingredient of Sautrâmani is the fermented preparation from the vegetables. They do not, therefore, borrow the procedure of the Somayâga as is contended for by the objector.

The वाजिनेज्या and सौत्रामणि borrow the विध्यंत, from the इष्टि.

The procedure of Sannâya applies to the animal sacrifice for two reasons (1) the milk and flesh are both produced from an animal and (2) the Ukhâ which is used in Sannâya is also found in an animal sacrifice. For these reasons, says our author, the procedure relating to the Puroḍâs'a does not apply to the animal sacrifice.

The विध्यंत of सन्नाय applies to the animal sacrifice.

Now having established the procedure of Sannâya to be applicable to the animal sacrifice, the next question is whether the procedure relating to milk or relating to curd applies. Our author decides in favour of the procedure relating to milk applicable to the animal sacrifice for two reasons, (1) an animal is moveable and

The procedure of milk applies to the animal sacrifice.

milk is flowing; both are therefore moveable things, while curd is solid and thick. (2) Milk and flesh are directly obtained from an animal while curd is obtained from milk.

We have already explained Âmikṣâ and its preparation in the preceding

The procedure relating to milk applies to आमिक्षा.

pages. The question is, whether the procedure relating to curd, milk or both applies to it, because Âmikṣa is a modification of both. The author decides in favour of the procedure relating to milk applicable to Âmikṣâ, because in Âmikṣa the quantity of milk preponderates over the quantity of curd; and in the absence of curd, any other substance can be also put into the heated milk for thickening it and lastly milk is fresh and the deity to whom Âmikṣâ is offered is also fresh, while on the other hand curd is stale.

Division of सोमयाग.

The division of Soma sacrifices will explain the principle laid down here.

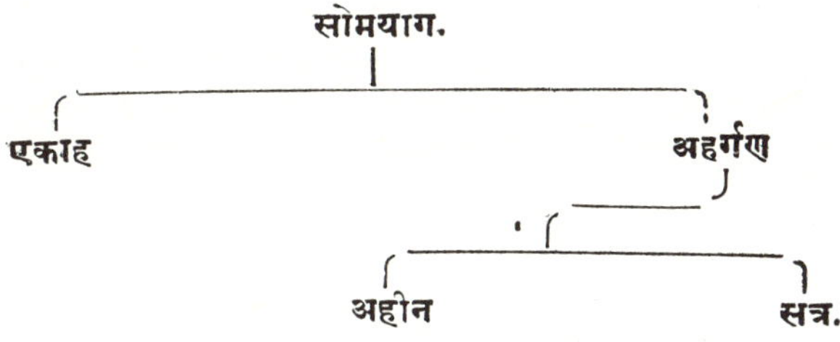

These Soma sacrifices have been explained in the preceding

An अहीन and a सत्र are governed by their respective procedure and are known by the injunctive verbs of each of them.

pages. One can also refer to As'valâyana's Śrautasûtara Chapter X. The sacrifice that lasts for a day is called एकाह; those sacrifices that take from 2 nights or upwards up to 12 nights are Ahînas and those that last from 13 nights and upwards upto 10,000 years are सत्रs. The Ahîna sacrifice is governed by the injunctive form of the Yajati verb; while the Sattra is governed by the injunctive forms of ' Upâsîran ' and ' Upeyuḥ '. The Dvâdas'âha which is one of Ahîna sacrifices is of several kinds; it partakes the nature of both Ahîna and Sattra. Now the question for decision is, what is the procedure in the Ahîna and Sattra? Whether it is the procedure of Dvâdas'âha ? The author's reply is that an Ahîna sacrifice is governed by the procedure of Ahîna and is indicated by the injunctive form of Yajati and a Sattra is governed by the procedure of a Sattra and is indicated by the injunctive forms of the verbs ' उपासीरन् ' and ' उपेयुः '. As a Dvâdas'âha partakes of the nature of both of them, these verbs, therefore, show the procedure to be adopted.

The next question for determination is the procedure that governs the Pañchadas'arâtra and Kuṇḍinamayaua. The former consists of fifteen nights made up of Trivrit, Agniṣṭut and Agniṣṭoma for three nights, Das'arâtra for ten nights, Udayanîya and Atirâtra each for one night. The latter con-

The procedure relating to a Sattra applies to the पंचदशरात्र and कुण्डिनायन.

sists of a monthly Agnihottra in the beginning and Das'arâtra Mahâvṛt, Udayanîya and Aratirâtra in the end. The dificulty arises by reason of the Atirâtra occuring at the end of each of them but not in the beginning. There is a text ' यदन्यतरतोतिरात्रस्लेनाहीन: ' ' because the latter part is अतिरात्र, therefore ' Ahîna '. It will, of course, follow as a corollary from the rule laid down above that both the sacrifices extending over a period above twelve days are Sattras and are, therefore, governed by the procedure pertaining to a Sattra. The author in addition to it relies on the injunctive forms of the verbs used in the Vidhi passages in connection with the पंचदशरात्र and Kuṇḍinamayana.

PÂDA 3.

The sacrifices belonging to a single deity and the dual deities are the models of the sacrifices in honour of a single deity and the dual deities.

There is a ceremony द्वादशाह is the model of जनकसप्तरात्र.

The procedure of the sacrifice in honour of a single deity is governed by that of the sacrifice pertaining to a single deity and that of the sacrifice held in honour of the dual deity is governed by that pertaining to the sacrifice in honour of the dual deity ; as for instance the Agneya is the model of S'uchidevata and the Agniṣomîya is that of the Agnâvaiṣṇava.

called Janakasaptarâtra which lasts for seven nights. It is described in As'valâyana S'ruta-sûtra at p. 406 of the Ânandâs'ram edition.

The question, is whether the procedure in the subsequent days is governed by the procedure of the first day as laid down in the preceding pages, or the procedure in Janakasaptarâtra is governed by what obtains in a Dvadas'âha. The author says that as in the text quoted at p. 483, the Agniṣṭoma heads the list of the Trivrit songs, so the procedure of the द्वादशाह applies ; the first four days will be occupied with the Trivrits headed by the Agniṣṭoma and then subsequently Pañchadas'a, Saptadas'a and Ekavims'astomas will come from the Dvâdas'âha.

What is the procedure in a Saṭṭrins'arâtra ?   Whether it is the procedure of a Dvâdas'âha or a Saḍâha. The Saṭṭrins'arâtra is a Soma sacrifice lasting for 36 nights.   The author says that the lower number of the Saḍaha *viz.*, six which divides the

A षडह is the model sacrifice of the षट्त्रिंशरात्र sacrifice.

number 36 is the criterion in order to determine the model sacrifice ; hence the Saḍaha is the model of the Saṭṭrins'arâtra sacrifice. The opinion of Bâdari is that it is

Opinion of बादरि.

governed by the procedure of the Dvâdas'âha.

We have explained the word 'संस्था' in connection with Jyotiṣṭoma sacrifice in the preceding pages. The objector says that as the संस्थाs happen to be in the Jyotiṣṭoma, the procedure therein is determined by that of the Jyotiṣṭoma. The उक्थ etc., are the Stomas. The rule is that the ceremony which ends in a particular Stotra song is called by the song of that संस्था. In the Dvâdas'âha days only, the names of the उक्थ etc., are possible ; so the procedure of a Dvâdas'âha is applicable to the Sansthâs.

The songs from the ज्योतिष्टोम are borrowed in a शतोक्थ्य and शतातिरात्र.

There are seven Sansthâs in a Jyotiṣṭoma and 12 Stomas as detailed below :—

Morning libation	1 बहिष्पवमानस्तोत्र
	4 आज्य स्तोत्रs
Midday libation	1 स्तोत्र
	4 पृष्ठ स्तोत्रs.
Third libation	1 आर्भव पवमान
	1 अग्निष्टोम performed by यज्ञायज्ञीय song.

There are no songs in a Dvâdas'âha. In a Śatokathya and Saṭâtiratra, the songs will be, therefore, borrowed from the songs of the Jyotiṣṭoma but not from the Dvâdas'âha where there is none.

There are Vedic metres such as Jagati, Anuṣṭup and Triṣṭubh. A Gâyatrî consists of 24 letters ; a Jagatî consists of 48 letters ; an Anuṣṭup consists of 32 letters ; and a Triṣṭubh consists of 44 letters. A Brihaspatisava is performed after a Vâjpeya and is a one day sacrifice. In it many verses

गायत्री means a ऋक् verse of 24 letters but not any combination of 24 letters.

of several metres are transferred from the Jyotiṣṭoma, the model sacrifice. The objector says that a Gâyatrî can be made by dropping letters of a Jagatî metre ; there are 48 letters in a Jagatî out of which you can drop 24 letters and thus convert it into a Gâyatrî metre. As there is an abundance of metres transferred to it from the model sacrifice, you can have Gâyatrî day in the सूक्तपतित्व by dropping letters from other metres and converting them into Gâyatrî metres. The author says, it cannot be so. The word 'Gâyatrî' is always used in a conventional sense ; it does not mean any combination of 24 letters, but it means an original verse from the Rigveda consisting of 24 letters.

PÂDA 4.

What is दर्वि ? In the present Pâda the author deals with Darvihoma. It is a word made up of Darvi and Homa. Darvi is a ladle and is thus described.

इध्मजातीय मिध्माद्धं प्रमाणं मेक्षणं भवेत् ।
वृत्तचांगुष्ठपृथ्वग्र मवदानक्रियाक्षमम् ॥
एषैवदर्वीयस्तत्र विशेषस्त महंब्र वे ।
दर्वींदुव्यंगुलपृथ्वग्रा तुरीयोनं तुमेक्षणम् ॥

See वाचस्पत्य.

" A Mekṣaṇa (a ladle) is half the size of Idhma (sacrificial fuel) belonging to the class of Idhma wood. It has a circle of the size of one thumb, an extensive front part and is fit for making an offering. It is also Darvî with the difference which I tell you and which is that it has the front part of two fingers and the Mekṣaṇa is less than 4 fingers ".

A दर्वि is a ladle and distinguished from a मेक्षण.

What is इध्म ? Idhma is described at p. 928 of वाचस्पत्य as follows :—

इध्म प्रमाणंचारत्निनरितिसन्धिः प्रकीर्तितम् ।

Then again.

समित्पवित्रंवेदं च कुर्यात्प्रादेशसंमितम् ।
इध्मस्तुद्विगुणःकार्यः परिधि स्त्रिगुणः स्मृतः ॥

" Idhma is said to be of one cubit by the educated persons. A Samit, Pavîtra and Veda should be made of the size of one span. An Idhma should be made double of this size and Paridhi should be three times of it in size."

समित्, पवित्र, वेद and परिधि explained.

Having explained the term Darvi, it is now very easy to explain Darvihoma. The question is whether the Darvihoma is a Guṇavidhi or Karmanâmadheya.

दर्विहोम is a कर्मनामधेय,

If one wishes to perform a *homa* with one, he shall do it with Darvihoma.
According to our author, it is the name of a *homa* wherein Juha etc., which are generally permitted are not used. The Darvihoma is both profane and religious. It is governed by the Juhoti Chodanâ or the injunctive form of the verb Juhoti, because Vidhiling form (जुहुयात्) is used.

It is both profane and religions.

Before I proceed further I may thus explain the dictum of Sinhâvalî-okana Nyâya. A lion on killing his prey looks backward and forward with a view to see whether there is any other animal of prey so that he may kill it as well, on his way to some solitary place. In grammar, when a word is connected backward and forward, the maxim is applied. Here the principal of Sinhâvalokitanyâya is applied to recapitulate the same thing which the author has already discussed previously.

सिंहावलोकितन्याय explained.

He says that Darvihoma can not be considered a Gunavîdhî (compound name) in which a ladle called Darvi is used, because there are many other things which are as well used.   It is a conventional term and is, therefore, a name of a ceremoney Karmanâmadheya.

दर्विहोम is not a गुणविधि

The next step is to find out its ectye or model? The first view is that it is governed by the procedure of a Somayâga.   It cannot be so, says the author, because (Vaṣaṭ) is used in a Somayâga while in the Darvi Homa, the word (Svâhâ) is used.

Different views as to the model of a दर्विहोम discussed.

The second view is that the Darvîhoma is formed by the procedure of a Nariṣṭahoma as both have the word ' Svâhâ ' along with the offering and have the injunctive form of the verb ' Juhoti.'.   The author says that the Nariṣṭahoma cannot be a model of Darvihoma because in a Triambakeṣṭi which is performed like the Darvihoma, grass, fuel, Anuyâja, Prayâja and Samadheni are prohibited. If Nareṣṭi had been a model of the Darvihoma, they would have found their place in the Triambakeṣṭi.

The third view is that the Patni Sanyâja is the model of Darvihoma. The author rejects this view as well, because if Patnisanyâja be considered its model, the procedure relating to ghee would apply ; but this is not the case.

The fourth view is that a Darvihoma is governed by Piṣṭikaraṇahoma and Phalîkaraṇahoma explained in the preceding pages. The author says that they are more in the nature of a pratipattikarma and cannot, therefore, be models.

The author after discussing the above four views and rejecting them says that a Darvi homa is a model in itself and has, therefore, no separate ectype or model.

It is a model in itself.

CHAPTER IX.

PÂDA 1.

The principle of ऊह explained.

Chapter IX treats of Ûha. When the details are transferred from the model sacrifice to the modified sacrifice and adapted to suit the circumstances, the modification or adaptation is called Ûha. As for i nstance the Âgneya is the model of the Saûryayâga ; in the former, the formula is 'I offer the pleased one to the fire': it is of no meaning. So the formula in the Sauryayâga will be thus modified 'I offer the pleased one to the sun'.

Different heads into which ऊह is divided.

The subject of Ûha has been treated under three heads as shown in the table at page 504. They are (1) Mantra (2) Sama and (3) Sanskâra.

प्रयोजक and निमित्त explained.

Before proceeding farther, it is necessary to explain Prayojaka and Nimitta. What keeps one engaged is Prayojaka. The Prayojaka is one that actuates any person to act in a certain way ; the existence of the thing which is a means for the engagement is Nimitta. An illustration will better explain them. You keep a gardener for the protection of your garden ; the protection of the garden is the end for which you engage the gardener and pay his wages. The garden is the means or nimitta. Take the reverse side of the same ; for a gardener, the monthly receipt of pay is the end or prayojaka which engages him in his work of gardening : the garden is the means by which he earns wages. One is a means and the other is an end. Similarly, the Apûrva which we have explained in the preceding pages is the prayojaka and the sacrifice is the nimitta. Now if a sacrifice be considered an end, there will be no necessity of the principle of Ûha ; any sacrifice would serve the purpose, but according to a Mîmânsaka an invisible result is produced by the performance of a sacrifice. According to the well-known verse,

अकामस्य क्रिया काचित् दृश्यते नहिकर्हिचित् ।
यद्यद्धि कुरुते कर्म तत्तत्कामस्यचेष्टितम् ॥

Manu II. 4.

No action is possible without an object in view.

" No where an action is possible for a person without any object in view. Whatever act is done, it is stimulated by a certain object. "

प्रयोजनमनुद्दिश्य न मंदो ऽपि प्रवर्तते ।

जगच्च सृजतस्तस्य किंनाम न कृतं भवेत् ॥

भट्ट quoted in सर्वदर्शनसंग्रह

An act is a means and the अपूर्व is the end.

" Even a stupid fellow will not act without a purpose in view ; could not there be His name by creating the universe ? "

To Mîmânsaka, therefore, every act presupposes an end ; the existence of the act is, a means called here Nimitta and the attainment of the extraordinary principle which surrounds a performer with an invisible halo and makes him fit for the attainment of heaven is the prayojaka. Having explained the rudimentary principle of the मीमांसा, it will be very easy to understand the nature of Ûha.

In connection with the Dars'apûrnamâsa, rice is pounded by a pestle and mortar and ground by a slab and muller. Before these sacrificial weapons (as they are called) are used, they are sprinkled over with water after repeating the Vedic mantras. This is called prokṣaṇa. The apparent object of pounding is to remove the husk from the rice ; if that were the simple object, there is no necessity of sprinkling of water on it : but over and above it, there is an invisible effect produced by the prokṣaṇa ceremony. In this view, if nails of a person are used in removing the husk from rice, instead of pestle and mortar, the principle of Ûha will come into play and the prokṣaṇa ceremony will be performed on the nails before they are used in peeling off the husk.

Again in connection with the Dars'apûrnamasayâgas, it is laid down

The principle of ऊह applies to a fruit and a deity.

' Let us obtain heaven ; let us be united with light '. It is as regards the fruit to be achieved. As to the deity, it is said ' let me obtain the highest victory after the victory of Agni ; let me obtain the highest victory after the victory of Soma'. In a Somayâga which is a modified form of Âgneya, a subordinate part of the Dars'apûrnamâsayâgas, it is said ' सौर्यं चरुं निर्वपेद् ब्रह्मवर्चसकामः ' ' let one who is desirous of Brahmanic glory offer boiled rice to Sun '. The deity and the fruit are different from those of the Dars'apûrnamâsayâgas. So the text quoted above will be modified to suit the circumstances of the Sauryayâga and will be read as ' Let me obtain the Brahmanic splendour ; let me obtain the highest victory after the victory of the sun '.

There is another objection to the applicability of the principle of ऊह. The different deities are worshipped in different sacrifices and their favour is secured. They are corporeal beings as described in the Vedic texts. In this view, no mantras should be uttered nor should they be altered to meet the exigencies of the different cases. The author's view is that the corporeal nature of the deity described in the Vedic texts is by way of allegory and the deities are subordinate parts of the sacrifice. The object is the Apûrva and the sacrifice is the direct means of attaining it. (Arâdupakâraka) and the deity is only a Sannipattyopakaraka in the language of the Mîmânsâ The uttering of मन्त्र and altering them to suit the nature of the modified sacrifice is, therefore, with a view to secure the अपूर्व. In this view, the principle of Ûha is indispensable.

The objection that the object being to obtain the favour of a deity the principle of ऊह does not apply, refuted.

The object is अपूर्व and the deity is subordinate.

Similarly, Prokṣaṇa प्रोक्षण on the wild rice ceremony on the wild rice is not for the wild rice but for the attainment of the Apûrva. Whatever is laid down in a Vidhi passage should be strictly observed to the letter in order to attain it. As for example low reading in a Jyotiṣṭoma before the Agniṣomîya, should be made in that part of the sacrifice where the minor oblations are performed but not in the entire sacrifice.

Low reading in a ज्योतिष्टोम.

In an Agnichayana ceremony, the bricks are pulled out and sprinkled with water. The question is whether the ceremonies of Vikarṣaṇa and prokṣaṇa are performed on each brick separately or on all of them simultaneously. The author says that these ceremonies are performed on all of them together, because the fire which is piled is one.

विकर्षण and प्रोक्षण ceremonies in an अग्निचयन.

In connection with a द्वादशाह, it is said 'पत्नीसंयाजान्तानि अहानि संतिष्ठते'. They maintain it up to the Patnîsanyâja days. *Prima facie* the text shows that all the days of a Dvâdas'âha are characterised by the Patnîsanyâja and the final day must end in it ; but the Linga shows otherwise. The whole text runs as follows " They maintain it to the end of Patnîsanyâja days ; no grass is subsequently brought and the sacrifice is, therefore, incomplete." It shows that the sacrifice does not end

All the days of the द्वादशाह excepting the last day are characterised by the पत्नीसंयाज.

with the Patnîsanyâja because the sacrifice is said to be incomplete. The result is that all the days of a Dvâdas'âha except the last day is charac-terised by Patnîsanyâja. Patnîsanyâja as explained in the preceding pages of the introduction consists of the offerings of ghee made at the end of a sacrifice to the wives of the gods.

We have already described the Samadhenî verses in the preceding pages of the introduction. We have also given the verses; they are originally eleven in number. They are increased to the number fifteen by repeating the first and the last, three times. In that connection the text is 'त्रिः प्रथमामन्वाह त्रिश्चरमामन्वाह'. He repeats the first verse thrice at the end and repeats the last verse thrice at the end." The question is whether the verses 'Pravovâja' etc,. should be repeated thrice. The author says that the verses 'Pravovâja' at any other place should not be repeated; it is only the first and the last of the eleven verses, that go under the name of Sâmadhenî verses and have been fully described in the preceding pages, are to be repeated thrice.

The first and the last of the सामधेनी verses should be repeated, but not any verse commencing with मनोबाज.

An Ârambhaṇîyeṣṭi which is a preliminary ceremony in connection with the Dars'apûrṇamâsayâgas and consists in a vow to be taken by a sacri-ficer to perform the Dars'apûrṇamâsayâgas for his whole life should be performed when they are commenced at first. It should not be repeated on the occasion of each performance of the Dars'apûrṇamasayâgas. It is only a vow to perform the sacrifices for one's life and the repetition of the vow with each repetition of the sacrifices is simply redundant and useless. In this view, the Ârambhaṇîyeṣṭi is a preliminary ceremony to the Dars'apûrṇamâsayâgas when commenced for the first time but not to the subsequent performance thereof.

If in the Nirvâpa mantras, the terms used do not convey the conven-tional sense or the names of the deities but they are meant to secure the favour by praising the deitiés, the principle of Ûha does not apply. As for instance, O ! Havi, I being inspired by सविता offer thee who art beloved of Agni with the arms of As'win and the hands of Pûṣa". The words ' Savita ' ' As'vina ' and ' Pûṣa ' are not the names of the deities ; they are not proper nouns but they are common nouns used in praise of the offering. (See the explanation at p. 522). In this view of the author, there will

If in the निर्वाप mantras, the terms used are common nouns but not the names of the deities, the prin-ciple of ऊह will not apply.

be no उह and the Nirvâpamantra quoted above will be read unaltered in the modified sacrifice.

When a word conveys a conventional sense, it is said to be Samaveta

समवेत and असमवेत explained.

and when it is not tied by convention and used as a common noun it is called असमवेत. Now the question is whether the term 'Agni' in the above quoted text is Samaveta or Asamaveta. It is used as a proper

अग्नि will be adapted in the above text.

noun and shall be adapted in the modified sacrifice in view of the principle enunciated above.

Principle deduced succinctly stated.

There are other illustrations given at p. p. 523 and 524 from which the principle deduced is thus succinctly stated.

When the sense of a term can be adjusted to the occasion, there will be no उह as the term can be used in any sense suited to the occasion but when the sense of a term is unchangeable, then there can be a substitution of any other word to suit the occasion in the modified sacrifice.

In the Dars'apûrṇamâsayâga there is a verse quoted at p. 524 and

When the term 'यज्ञपति' is subordinate, the principle of उह does not apply but if it is principal, the उह will come into force.

repeated to invoke इड़ा. The word 'Yajñapati' is used in a singular number. In a यज्ञ where there are many sacrificers, will it be in plural? The author says that the text in which the term 'Yajnapati' occurs, is asamavetavcthana and is in praise of इड़ा. It is with a view to stimulate a sacrificer by praising it and the sacrificer is, therefore, subordinate and not principal. The principle of Ûha will not apply and the text will be read unaltered in a यज्ञ. If the sacrificer is principal, the principle of उह will come into play; as for instance in the Dars'apûrṇayâgas, there is a hymn which is read at the time of Prastarapraharaña (throwing off the used up grass in the fire) and longevity of the sacrificer is prayed for. Here the sacrificer is principal and in a Mantra where there are more sacrificers than one, the plural number will be used.

क्रियाप्रकायक and फल-प्रकायक explained.

There are, therefore, two kinds of Mantras; one class consists of Kriyâprakâs'aka explaining the performance of an action and the other consists of Phalaprakâs'aka explaining the reward of an action. In the mantras of the former class, the principle of उह does not apply because the performer is there subordinate in relation to the action while in the mantras of the latter class the Ûha will come into play, because the performer is principal in relation to the fruit achieved.

In a Subrahmaṇyanigada in a ज्योतिष्टोम sacrifice there is a verse "O Indra! Who has horses, O ram of Medhâtithi O! lover of Vriṣaṇas'va's daughter, O! white attacker, O paramour of Ahalyâ, come ". This निगद is transferred to the Agnistuti under a chodaka text. There in the text the word Indra is Samaveta and it will therefore be adapted and the word Agni (fire) will be substituted but the other epithets used for Indra are Asamaveta and shall be read unmodified. Their significance is fully explained at P. 526. As to the explanation of the term 'Ahalyâyaijara' See Kumarilabhaṭṭa * quoted in the History of the Ancient Sanscrit Literature by Max Muller at P. 273 of the Pâṇini Office publication, Raja Shiva Prasad's Itihasatimiranasaka Part III., P. 11., S. Dayânanda Saraswati's Ṛigvedâdibhâṣyabhûmikâ P. 183 (Sanscrit edition) and Tilak's Arctic home at P. 347. The mythology of Ahilyâ and her paramour is too well known to be explained here.

The principle of जड explained in connection with सुब्रह्मण्यनिगद.

The mytrology of अहिल्या and her paramour.

In an Agniṣṭoma several animals are sacrificed to the different deities as for instance Agni, Aindragna and Sarasvatî To the last deity an ewe is offered. In connection with the Agni Ṣomiya, there is an Adhrigapraiṣa (a command to an अग्निषु priest) " उपनयतमेध्यादुरः आग्यासाना मेधवतिभ्यांमेध्यम् । प्रास्ना अग्निंभरत " See at P. 1005 of तैत्तिरीय ब्राह्मण of the Ânandâs'rama edition. "Place the consecrated animals at the gate for slaughter for the two masters of the sacrifice, (husband and wife or the sacrificer and the priest) for the sacrifice. For him, nourish fire ". The question is whether the अधिगुमेष should be recited in the सरस्वती sacrifice where ewe is offered. The author's reply is that it is a common command and as 'ewe' is feminine, the formula shall not be repeated at all. The question which is for solution, here, does not in the author's view, arise.

अग्निषुमेष shall not be repeated in the सरस्वती sacrifice.

Having dealt with the principle of जड as applicable to the मंत्रs, the author now proceeds to explain its applicability to the songs.

In the Jyotiṣṭoma sacrifice, song called Yajñayajñî is sung. In this connection it is said "The word 'girâ' should not be pronounced as girâ; if a singer pronounces 'गिरा' as निरा, he shall throw himself up and by making it 'aira' shall sing it. In the song the word 'गिरा' occurs. The question is whether Girâ should be pronounced with 'Ga' or without 'Ga'.

Modification of निरा to गिरा in a यसायज्ञीय song and to आइरा when set to music.

* See तंत्रवार्तिक Chap. I. pada 3 sutra 7 at p. 133 of the Chaukhambhâ edition.

The author's reply is that it should be recited without 'ग' as it is expressly laid down by the Vedic text. Further, it shall be set to music and sung as 'आहरा' as said in the text 'उदगवमाहुरावादवासा' 'should be sung as 'आहरा', 'वा' and 'Dakṣāsā'. The principle of Ûha, therefore, applies to 'गिरा' and it is be modified as 'हरा' and when set to music, it becomes 'आहव'.

PÂDA 2.

We have already explained what a Sâma is and how it differs from a Stotra. It is a song and conveys the idea of a tune. It is a generic term and रथंतर, बृहद् etc., are its species.

साम explained.

It is not principal but only subordinate. It is for the purpose of altering the words in a melodious way. It, therefore, exists for the purpose of another. When a Ṛik verse is sung it is pronounced melodiously. The verses sung while learning music are useless and do not serve the purpose of the sacrifice. A song is, therefore, a purificatory act (Sanskârakarma).

It is for purpose of a sacrifice and is a purificatory rite.

A Sâma consisting of three verses from the Rigveda is called a तृच; the first verse of a तृच is called Stotrîya, the second is called Anurûpa and the third is called पर्याय. According to the author each verse should be sung separately in order to constitute a group of three verses called तृच, because (Anavâna) singing *uno tenore* is possible when each verse is sung separately.

Each verse of a तृच is to to be sung separately.

As we have seen above in a तृच, there are three verses; the tune of the first verse governs the tune of the last two verses. The question is, what should be their measure? If the metre of the first verse is different from that of the two succeeding verses, there will arise two defects called Sans'ara and Viles'a. If the first verse is of larger measure *i.e.*, it has more letters than those in the succeeding two verses, the redundant portion from the first verse will have to be deleted in order to harmonise the song. This kind of defect is called संचर (superfluity). If on the other hand, the measure in the last two verses is longer *i.e.*, if it contains more letters than those in the first verse, the redundant portion of the two verses will be without a song. This kind of defect is called Viles'a (deficiency). In order to avoid these two defects, all the verses of a तृच should be of equal measure.

The verses in a तृच should be of equal measure.

संचर and विलेश explained.

योनि and उत्तरा explained. The first verse in a सूच is called Yoni and the last two verses are called Uttarâ. There are two treatises for the guidance of the singers; they are (1) Chhanda-grantha in which a variety of योनिs are given and (2) Uttara Grantha in which several varieties of Uttaras are mentioned. As said above, the tune of the Yoni is the tune of the Uttara; so the principle of Ûha applies to the Uttara.

Principle of प्रगाथ explained. On the other hand in a Pragâtha the rule that the verses of a Yoni and Uttara shall be of equal measure is not observed. I have fully explained Pragâtha at p. 542 with an illustration. I have shown how a verse of a Yoni and Uttara are adapted to the musical mode by changes and modifications. It is useless to repeat the same here. Different varieties of songs are produced by mixing two kinds of verses on the principle of Pragâtha.

Different modifications at the option of a singer. We have seen that the verses of the Rigveda are adapted to a certain tune. It is, therefore, optional to a singer to adopt any of the modifications of letters called Vis'leṣa, Vikarṣaṇa, Abhyâsa, Virama, Stobha etc.

A deity should be praised by a साम. In a Stotra the praise of a diety is prominent in the mind of a singer, while in a साम the idea of music is prominent. The Stotra and Sâma are both the same. It follows as a corollary that a deity should be praised by a Sâma.

Change of letters in the उत्तरा is effected at any place where 'इ' occurs. The change of letters called Vis'leṣa in the Uttara is not necessarily governed by the similar change in a Yoni. Any letter, where cerebral 'इ' occurs is changed into Âî under the rules of music.

स्तोभ explained. A Stobha is a musical stop. During the course of singing there are some expressions which are used by a musician to gain time. The first kind of expression is the repetition of the same word, as ' Adri ! 'अद्रि' ; it is called Adhika by our author. The second kind of pause is by means of a word without any meaning, as ओग्नाइ ; it is called Vivarṇa.

A स्तोभ is transferable. Though Stobha is a pause in order to gain time in singing, yet it is transferable ; if a song is transferred, it is transferred with all its incidents.

CLVI.

The author proceeds to deal with the third head of ऊह called the अह as applicable to the purifactory ceremony from the sûtra 40.

The principle of ऊह applies to purificatory rites.

The author says that the principle of ऊह applies to (1) the substance (2) quality (3) modifications, (4) transgression and (5) prohibition ; as for instance. (1) Prokṣaṇa ceremony is performed on Vrîhi (wild rice) before it is boiled and offered to a deity. If Nîvâra is offered instead of Vrîhi, the Prokṣaṇa will also be performed on it.

(2) The applicability of the principle of Ûha in the case of the quality ;

Other illustrations.

the text is " Let him eat honey or clarified butter when engaged in a sacrifice lasting for six days ". The author says that the same silence is observed in eating honey as is done when ghee is used in fasting.

(3) Applicability of Ûha to the modifications. The pestle and mortar are sprinkled over with water in a model sacrifice ; when nails are used in removing the husk from rice in a modified sacrifice, they are to be sprinkled over with water before they are used.

(4) The rule of Ûha in cases of transgression. The ceremonies in connection with a sacrificial post should be performed on a Paridhi when it is used in the place of the sacrificial post.

(5) The rule of Ûha in the cases of prohibition. When 'इरा' is uttered in music in place of 'गिरा' the former should be treated as 'गिरा' for all intents and purposes.

We have seen above in the illustration No. 4 that the ceremonies pertaining to a यूप are performed on a paridhi.

No change in the मैषमंत्र in case of a परिधि when treated as यूप

In the model sacrifice, there is a praiṣamantra (an order) to the effect "order for the anointed sacrificial post (Yûpa). The question is whether परिधि should be used in place of 'यूप' in the praiṣamantra. The author's reply is in the negative, because the paridhi becomes a Yûpa for all intents and purposes and no alteration will, therefore, be effected.

The ceremony performed on the praṇîtâ waters as explained in the preceding pages shall be performed on Sannâya,

The ceremonies of the प्रणीता on सन्नाय.

as an extraordinary principle is thereby produced.

The rule as to singing Rathantara is that a singer has to sing in a long tune by winking his eyes and looking up to heavens ; but when he sings Vrihat, he shall do so

Rule as to singing रथंतर and बृहत्.

in a high tune and meditate on the ocean. In a Rathantara, he praises heroes and in a Vrihat he praises pictures etc.

A Kaṇvarathantara is a modification of Vrihat and Rathantara and partakes of the qualities of both but where there are contradictory qualities of वृहद् and रथंतर, it partakes either of them at the option of a singer. Where the qualities are not contradictory it partakes of them collectively.

कणुवरथंतर explained

A little variation of Vṛihat and Rathantara constitues a Priṣṭha. The Priṣṭhas are Rathantara, Vṛihat, Vaîrûpa, Vaîraja, Śâkvar Raîvata. The Sâma of different tunes make up these Priṣṭhas. Târânâtha says, "In one Sûkta, when three Ṛik verses being repeated seventeen times under the rules of Brâhmaṇa, yield 17 *stomas*, then to such Stotras the term 'priṣṭha' applies, as seventeen पृष्टs." The rule of singing Rathantara and Vṛihat is different from each other in a Gosava where a double song (Dvisâmaka) is sung, both Rathantara and Vrihat being combined together.

A पृष्ठ explained

In a द्विसाम. both are combined together

Pârvaṇa homa is a collection of all the sacrifies pertaining to fire‘ cake and animal. The word is derived from पूषति to give, to make a donation ; it, therefore, means time when something is given ; it applies to all the sacrifices collectively whether they consist of ghee oblations, cake or flesh offerings. In this view, the Pârvaṇa Homa which is performed in the Agneya, the model sacrifice, is not transferred to Sauryayâga where no such collection of offerings is made.

A पार्वणहोम explained it; is not performed in a सौर्यंयाग.

The Dars'apurṇamâsayâgas are two different sacrifices ; they are Dars'ayâga and Pûrṇamâsayâga. A Dars'ayâga is performed on the new moon day and the pûrṇamâsayâga is performed on the full moon day. It is not a case of the performance of both the sacrifices on the new moon day and then again on the full moon day.

Rule as to the performance of the दर्श and पूर्णमासयागs

Samid, Tanûnapât, Eda, Varhi and Svâhâ are the names of the यागs but not of deities. The reason is that if they had been the names of the deities, they would have been in the dative case but not in the accusative case. As 'अग्नयेशायंजुहुयात्' He offers, an oblation to fire in the evening ; 'अग्निहोत्रंजुहोतीति'. ' He performs an अग्निहोत्र'. In the present case, we have साग्निधो यजति, तन्नुनपांत यजति, इडे यजति बर्हिर्यजति.

समिध् etc., are the names of the sacrifices but not of the deities.

स्वाहाकारंवषडि'. He performs Samid, he performs Tanûnapâta, he performs वषट्, he performs वषि he performs स्वाहाकार. These sacrifices or offerings have been fully explained in the preceding pages.

PÂDA 3.

The principal of ऊह to the मंत्र when the purpose is served by it.

Where the object of a मंत्र remains the same in the modified sacrifice as it is in the model sacrifice there is no change, but where the purpose is not served by keeping the word intact, there the principle of ऊह applies; as for instances 'अग्नयेजुष्टंनिर्वपामि' 'I offer the pleasing one to *Agni*'; 'व्रीहीणां मेधसुमनस्यमान:' 'O! essence of *barley* with satisfaction,' in the अग्नेय, the model sacrifice. Under the principle of Ûha, in the Sauryâyâga the modified sacrifice, the words *Sùryàya*, and सोबाराणां will be substituted, because reading the Mantra unaltered serves no purpose.

स्वरण मंत्र adopted to the circumstance of the modified sacrifice.

It is said "नौदग वषंनिर्वपेच्छ्रियै श्रीकामः" "Let one desirous of wealth offer boiled kidney beans (phaseolus mungo) to श्री". In that connection, it is said पौडरीकाणि वा दर्वीविभिमर्वंति' 'The lotuses serve as grass.' There the Staraṇamantra (a mantra uttered at the time of spreading grass) दर्भे: स्तृणीतहरितै:' 'Spread the green grass' is transferred under a Chodaka text. Will it be uttered unaltered when the *lotuses* which are red, are spread? To comply with the circumstances of the modified sacrifice, the स्वरणमंत्र will be adapted and will be read as पुंडरीकै: स्तृणीत रक्ते: " "Spread the red lotuses."

Expiatory ceremony in case a sacrificial post is touched ordinarily.

When a sacrificial post is touched under a Vedic ceremony no expiatory ceremony is performed but if it is touched ordinarily, a penance is performed and the mantra एषतेवायो' 'It is thine, O! Vâyu' is uttered; it shall be adapted to the circumstances of the case as directed in the text quoted in full at p. 564.

The पाय मंत्र is adapted and dual form is used when two animals are sacrificed.

In a Jyotiṣṭoma in connection with an Agnîṣomîya animal, there are two Pâs'amantras for tying an animal to a sacrificial post one has singular form and the other has plural form. "अदिति: पार्यमनुभो कृवेतम्" 'Let अदिति break this trap' and अविमो पाषान् मधुमेंसकृवेकान्" "Let अदिति break these traps ". The former is the reading of the Taittarîya branch of the Yajurveda while the latter is the reading of मैत्रारुणी branch. In a modified sacrifice where two animals are sacrificed and where two ropes or traps will be necessary, what mantra transferred under a Chodaka text should be recited? There are three views on the subject; the singular form being Asamavet should be recited; the second view is that the plural form should be recited, because the plural includes the dual. The third view which is the author's view is that the मंत्र should be adapted and dual form should be used.

In the अग्नीषोमीय there is an option.

In the Agniṣomîya sacrifice there will be an option as to the applicability of these two mantras; you can choose either of them; because it is the model sacrifice and both mantras are mentioned according to the different recensions of the black Yajurveda.

In connection with the Dars'apûrṇamâsayâgas, there is a text' ' Bring the vessel containing water; place the sacrificial fuel, cleanse the ladle and having adorned *the wife*, bring us clarified butter." *The wife* in the text means the wife of the sacrificer. The question is whether the term ' wife ' should be altered, if the sacrificer happens to have more than one wife. As the principle of Ûha does not apply to the model sacrifice as laid

The formula of पत्नीसन्नह्य will be read unaltered in the model and the modified sacrifices.

down above, the text will be read unaltered irrespective of the number of the wives of the sacrificer. As the text remains unaltered in the model sacrifice, it will be transferred to the modified sacrifice unaltered. The principle of ऊह, therefore, does not apply to the text whether read in the model or the modified sacrifice.

In Agniṣṭoma, Ukthya, Ṣoḍas'î, Atirâtra and the Sansthâs of a Jyotiṣṭoma, the number of Savanîya animals is increased from one to four. All of them are governed by the same Vidhi as that of the Agniṣomîya. In the Adhrigupaiṣa there is a passage " kindle fire for him ". We have already seen

In a ज्योतिष्टोम the principle of ऊह does not apply to the सवनीय animal sacrifice.

that the principle of Ûha does not apply to the Atirâtra in the case of Sarasvatîmeṣî ' an ewe consecrated to Sarasvati ' in the preceding pages.

In view of the principle laid down there and as laid down above, the principle of Ûha does not apply and the Praiṣamantra according to Śabara quoted at p. 569 will be read unaltered. But Mâdhava doubts the correctness of this dictum and says, ' There is an अत

The principle doubted by मधव.

under the principle laid down in connection with the ropes (Pasanyâya) in conformity with the linga and Vâkya, because Savanîya is a modification of Agnîṣomîya'.

The principle of ऊह does not apply to the मंत्र recited on the substitute.

When a substitute is used in the place of a material, the principle of Ûha does not apply and the mantra in that connection will be read unaltered ; as for instance Nîvara is sometimes used in place of Vrîhi ; a mantra which is given at p. 569 is recited on the occasion. In the mantra the term ब्रीहि occurs ; now the question is whether the term नीवार should be substituted in place of ब्रीहि. The reply in view of the principle laid down here is that there will be no substitution and the मंत्र will be recited unaltered.

The principle of ऊह does not apply to the organs in the double animal sacrifice.

In connection with the Adhrigupraiṣa quoted at p. 570 the different organs of the animal after its slaughter are described ' Let *eye* go to the sun and let *vital air* merge in the air." The question is whether the eye and other organ should be modified in a double animal sacrifice because there are two sets of eyes. The author says that there will be no Ûha as the light in the eye is one though there may be different eye balls.

The मंत्र in connection with the cutting off the skin of the animals will bɔ repeated as many times as there are animals.

There is another Adhrigupraiṣa "एकधाऽस्य त्वचमाच्छयतात्" " cut off his skin once." It is recited in connection with an Agnîṣomiya animal ; in the modified sacrifice where two animals are sacrificed, it shall be repeated as many times as there are animals because cutting off the skin will have to be repeated with each animal.

There is another Adhrigupraiṣa ; according to the Taittarîya branch it runs दैव्याः ग्रभितार उतमनुष्याश्रारारभध्वम् । उपनयतमेध्वा दुर ग्राग्रासाना मेधपतिभ्यां मघम्" "commence O ! divine and human Samita priests (whose duty is to kill the sacrificial animals), place the consecrated animals at the gate for slaughter for the *two masters of the sacrifice ;* and ye who are anxious for the sacrifice." In another recension the master of the sacrifice is in singular.

The मेधपालि formula shall be obtionally adapted according to the number of the beities in the modified sacrifice.

The question is whether the singular form should be read where one animal is sacrificed and the dual form where two animals are sacrificed. What is the meaning of the master of the sacrifice ? Does it mean the sacrificer or the god or both ? There are different views on the subject ; the first view is that in an Agnî Ṣomîya animal sacrifice there are two gods and one sacrificer and as the term master of the sacrifice includes both the deity and the sacrificer, both the formulas are unsuited in the model sacrifice. They are equally unsuited in the modified sacrifice and the principle of Ûha will, therefore, not apply. The second view is that when one sacrificer is meant, the singular form shall be used; if the sacrificer and god are meant, the dual form shall be used in the model sacrifice. When the formula is transferred to the modified sacrifice where more gods than two are worshipped, the principle of Ûha will come into play and the master of the sacrifice shall be used in the plural number. The third view is that when the sacrificer is single, the singular form is appropriate; but if the sacrificer and his wife are meant the dual form shall be used. According to this view also, the principle of Ûha applies and the change will be effected in the word 'मेधपति' according to the number of the sacrificers. The fourth and the last view is that the term मेधपति (master of the sacrifice) conveys the idea of a deity who is the master of the sacrifice; a sacrificer who parts with the proprietary possession of the property gifted, cannot be considered the owner or the master in law. Hence मेधपति is the god who fulfils all desires and hopes. In this view you can use the formula optionally in the modified sacrifice according to the number of the gods.

Where in the modified sacrifice where gods more than two are worshipped, the formula of the मेधपति will be optionally uttered in the singular or dual form provided the gods can be looked upon as a collective body. a sollective body as in an adapted and the मेधपति will be used in the plural form.

We have seen above that the Medhapati formula will be optionally used either in the singular or the dual form in the modified sacrifice where two deities are worshipped. Similarly, the same option will be exercised in the modified sacrifice where gods more than two are worshipped, provided they can be looked upon as one collective body; but where the deities are separate and cannot be so looked upon as Ekâdas'ini sacrifice; the formula will be

———

PĀDA 4.

There is an Adbrigupraiṣa for the removal of the ribs from the animal killed in a sacrifice. "*It has twenty six ribs* ; remove them from their places in their order." The Mantra is a direction to the priest to count the ribs and carefully remove them from the vertebræ to which they are attached. The question is, how is this Mantra to be repeated in a modified sacrifice where more animals than one are sacrified ? One view is that the मंत्र should be repeated according to the number of the animals killed. The second view which is the author's view is that the aggregate number of the ribs of the animals killed should be given as the ribs are principal in the *praisa* mantra. The result is that the principle of Ūha will apply and the formula will run as " द्विपञ्चाशदनयोावङ्क्रय:" " अष्टसप्ततिरेषां वंक्रय:".

The principle of ऊह applies to the मेषमंत्र as regards the removal of the ribs from the body of an animal killed in a sacrifice.

"They have fifty two ribs." "They have seventy eight ribs."

Number of the ribs in animals.

In a human body there are twenty four ribs ; twelve on each side ; in the body of an ordinary sacrificial animal, there are twenty six ribs.

"The ribs are elastic arches of bone, which form the chief part of the thoracic walls. They are twelve in number on either side ; but this number may be increased by the development of a cervical or lumbar rib or may be diminished to eleven. The first seven are connected behind with the vertebral column and in front through the intervention of the costal cartilages with the sternum ; they are called *vertebro sternal* or true ribs (costæ veræ). The remaining five are five false ribs (costæ spuriæ) ; of these, the first three have their cartilages attached to the cartilage of the rib above (*vertebro chondral*): the last two are full at their anterior extremities and are termed *floating* or *vertebral* ribs." Gray's anatomy, 17th edition p. p. 206 and 207.

A writer in the Encyclopædia Britannica (11th edition) vol. XXV. p. 171 says "The ribs in any given animal are always twice as numerous as the thoracic vertebræ in that animal." The thoracic vertebræ are also called dorsal vertebræ (See. P. 187 of Gray's anatomy.)

The dorsal vartebræ vary in number in the different species of the vertebrates.

CLXIII.

A hyppopotamus has 15	dorsal vertebræ ; and 80			ribs
A peccari	14 ...	...	28	...
A hog ...	13 ...	...	26	...
A dromedary	12 ...	...	24	...
A muskdeer	14 ...	...	28	...
A common ox	13 ...	...	26	...
A European vison	14 ...	...	28	...
A wild sheep of Tibet ...	13 ...	...	26	...
A Nubian giraffe	14 ...	...	28	...
A rein deer	14 ...	...	28	...
A common deer	13 ...	...	26	...

See Richard Owen's Anatomy of vertebrates (1866 edition) vol. II. P.P. 457-465.

In a horse sacrifice, there are many animals sacrificed as for instance "अश्वश्च्नूपरीगौतुगस्ते माज्ञापत्यबाः" "A horse, a hornless animal and *bos gaveus* are consecrated to Prajâpati. The horse of the Vajî species is said to have 34 ribs according the text of the Rigveda. The question is, how is the number of the ribs to be mentioned in the above Adhrigupraiṣa? The author says that as the number of the ribs of a Vajî horse is specially fixed by the verse of the Rigveda, the verse of the Rigveda quoted at p. 583 may be optionally repeated with the Adhrigupraiṣa.

अश्विगुमेध is to be modified as regards the total number of the ribs of the animals consecrated to प्रजापति.

There is a prohibitory text "Do not utter 34 but utter only 26"; it does not relate to the verse of the Rigveda ; it prohibits the mention of the number 'thirty-four' in the Adhrigupraiṣa but enjoins the repetition of twenty six there. As there are three animals consecrated to prajâpati having 34 + 26 + 26 = 86 ribs, the Adhrigupraiṣa will be modified and will be read as "चरुप्रीतिरेषांवंक्षृव:" etc.

The verse of the Rigveda fixing the number of the horse's ribs to be thirty-four may be optionally repeated with the मेषमंत्र.

A horse has 18 ribs on each side making the total of 36 ribs, some have even 38 ribs. A horse of the Vajî species is said to possess 34 ribs according to the Rigveda.

Number of the horse's ribs.

William Henry Flower and Richard Lydekker in the Encyclopædia Britannica 11th edition in Vol. XIII at P. 715 under 'Horse' say " The ribs are eighteen or nineteen in number on each side, flattened and united to the sternum by short stout tolerably well ossified sternal ribs."

There is another Adhrigupraiṣa ordering the priest not to pierce through the viscera considering it to be adipose tissue. See p. 585. In it, the word urûka occurs ; it means ' fat,' ' adipose tissue ' or ' omentum.' As in the modified sacrifice where there are many animals the principle of Ûha applies and 'urúka' will be used in singular, dual and plural forms according to the circumstances of the case.

The principle of ऊह supplies to ऊरूक.

Similarly in another adhrigupraiṣa "प्रशस्ताबाहू कृन्ततात्" " cut off the praise worthy arms. The discussion turns upon the term "prasasâ" which the author thinks to mean ' praise-worthy ' and qualifies the ' ar ns. In this view the principle of ऊह applies ; the pras'asâ will be adapted and used in dual and plural forms with the ' arms ' according to the number of the animals killed.

प्रशस्ता will be adapted according to the circumstances.

On the other hand when an Adhrigu is ordered to cut off the viscera in the particular shape of birds etc. Adhrigupraisa will be read in its entirety without any alteration. The reason is obvious ; the shapes in which the viscera is to be cut off are subordinate and will, therefore, be not effected by any change.

Where the organs are directed to be cut off in a particular shape, the principal of ऊह does not apply.

Every day an Agnihotra is performed by taking fire from the Ahavaniya to the Gârhapatya hearth. If it was out without the performance of the Agnihotra, then an expiatory ceremony in the form of a Jyotiṣmatî homa is performed. Now the question is, whether the Jyotiṣmatî homa should be performed, if the fire thus carried in the new and full moon sacrifices goes out. The author's reply is that as Jyotiṣmatî is an expiatory ceremony on a cause arising in the Agnihotra, it can not be transferred to the new and full moon sacrifices ; because the Jyotiṣmatî is performed when fire taken for an Agnihotra is extinguished, but not otherwise.

ज्योतिष्मती an expiatory होम is not performed in the दर्शपूर्णमासयागs.

For the same reasons, the Jyotiṣmati sacrifice shall not be performed when the preserved fire goes out. We have seen above that the Jyotiṣmatî is an expiatory ceremony and is performed when the fire is extinguished in an Aghihotra: it shall, therefore, be not performed when the fire preserved for

A fortiori it shall not performed when the preserved fire is extinguished.

some other object goes out.

When fire is carried for the performance of an Agnihotra, the Mantra given at P. 589 is recited. The question is, should it be recited when it is carried for the performance of the new and full moon sacrefices? The author's reply is that the Mantra is recited under a special injunction in the Agnihotra on the occasion of carrying the fire but there is no such direction in connection with the Dars′âpûrṇamâsayâga ; so there will be no recitation of the above said Mantra.

No मंत्र is to be recited when fire is carried in the दर्शपूर्णमासयाग.

In connection with the Jyotiṣṭoma sacrifice it is laid down " आदित्यः प्रावणीवः पर्विविषः" ' The first day (प्रावणीव) is with the boiled rice in milk to the sun-god." The question is, what procedure should apply? Does the procedure relating to rice or milk apply to it? If the former applies then the pounding and throwing it in the fire shall have to be done ; if the latter applies then sprinkling of water with the object of purifying it, is to be performed. The author says that as milk is the subordinate part for the object of boiling the rice, the procedure relating to gift shall apply to it i. e., utpavana etc. shall be performed. It is a ceremony of sprinkling of water for the purpose of purification ; it is described in कांड 1 chapter I. Brâhmaṇa 3 of the Śatapatha. There are two kus′a blades of the size of a span, called pavitras ; the water is taken by them and sprinkled with the Mantras given there. See for further information in the Vâchaspatya dictionary. " The St. Petersburg dictionary proposes the meaning ' an implement for cleaning ' for Utpavana in the passage 22 in Brahmaṇa 1 of Book I Chapter III of the Śatapatha-Brâhmaṇa." See the note 3 at P. 76 of Eggeling's Śâtapatha Vol. I.

The ceremony pertaining to the प्रावणीव shall be performed on the boiled rice in milk.

In an Abhyudayeṣṭi which has been fully explained in the preceding pages and which is an expiatory ceremony in a Dars′a Yâga, the procedure relating to the praṇita will not apply to the boiled rice in milk or curd ; the reason is obvious. There the sacrifice is already commenced under a mistaken idea of the Amâvasyâ (new moon) for which a penalty is paid in the form of an offering which is already there to a different deity. The procedure relating to gifts pradeyadharma, therefore, applies.

In an अभ्युदयेष्टि, the procedure relating to gift applies to the boiled rice in curd or milk.

On the other hand where the sacrifice is commenced afresh, the procedure relating to the boiled rice in milk or curd shall be governed by that of the pranîta like that of prâyaniya. The principle is that when a ceremony is a new one and performed for an object, the procedure in the boiled rice will be governed by the pranîtâdharma but not by the pradeyadharma ; but if a ceremony which is governed by the pradeyadharma is already commenced, the expiatory ceremony in which boiled rice is offered shall not be governed by the pranîtâdharma but by the pradeyadharma, the original procedure.

Where a ceremony is started afresh, the procedure relating to the प्रणीता governs the boiled rice.

Principle deduced.

In a Jyotiṣṭoma, milk is mixed with Soma and offered to Maitrâvaruṇa. What procedure will govern the milk here ? Whether it is pranîtâdharma or pradeyadharma. The author says that the procedure in it is governed by that of the pranîta as laid down under the prayaṇîya. The reason is that the milk is not for the purpose of gift to the deity but for mixing it with soma ; it is a subordinate part and shall, therefore, be governed by the procedure relating to the praṇîta.

Milk mixed with सोम in a ज्योतिष्टोम is govern- by the प्रणीताधर्मे.

Before I proceed further, it is better to explain paryagnikaraṇa. It is described in Kâtyayana Śrautasûtra Chapter VI. Sûtras 96-101. The Agnîdha with the brand of Ahavanîya fire goes three times round the space covered by the animal, ghee, slaughtering place, sacrificial post, the chatvala and the Ahavanîya hearth, or only that portion of the space occupied by ghee, animal and the slaughtering place. He then circumbulates after throwing the fire brand ; he then taking it goes to the north ; he takes the animal and the fire brand. Karka the commentator says that the Samita priest takes the animal by tying a rope round its neck. See at P. 890 of the Chaukhambâ edition of Kâtyâyana Śrautasûtra. See P. 187 Eggeling's Śatapatha Vol. II.

पर्य्यग्निकरण ceremony explained.

In connection with Asvamedha it is said 'ईशानाय परस्वत आलभते' ' He brings a deer for Is'âna.' 'परस्वत' is a species of a deer according to Mahîdhara and nvata. According to Mâdhava, it is a species of a wild animal. Monier Williams says that it means a wild ass. In the model sacrifice, it is said "पर्य्यग्निकृतानारेवानानुत्सृजति" " They relinquish the animals on whom paryagnikaraṇa is performed". Reading the

'आलभ' along with पर्य्यग्निकरण does not mean mere touching. It is an independent sacrifice.

two texts together, it appears *prima facie* that the 'आलभते' means touching the animal, because the other text suggests its relinquishment. The author says that the material and the deity are connected ; so the word, 'आलभते' means ' sacrificing.' In this view the texts mean the prohibition of the remaining acts after paryagnikaraṇa and lay down the offering of a deer to Îs'âna as an independent act.

There are texts in the model sacrifice वास्तटं वात्नीवतमालभेत "पर्यग्निकृत्वं वात्नीव तमुत्सृजति" "आज्येनयेषबुपस स्वापवति" "Let him sacrifice an animal belonging to Agni, to Twaṣṭri. He relinquishes a Patnîvat animal on whom Paryagni ceremony is performed. He finishes the remaining act with clarified butter." According to the principle laid down above, the Pâtnîvata sacrifice in honour of Twaṣṭri is a separate act from the ghee oblation.

END OF CHAPTER IX.

CHAPTER X.
PÂDA 1.

The author now proceeds to explain the principle of Vâdha in Chapter X.

The principle of वाध explained. We have seen how the author has explained the principles of Atides'a in general and particular and of adaptation. When certain details are transferred from the model sacrifice to the modified sacrifice under a Chodaka text they are sometimes modified and sometimes they are dispensed with. When the details are modified they are governed by the principle of Ûha, as fully explained in Chapter IX. When the details of the model sacrifice are dispensed with they are governed by the principle of Vâdha called suspension or omission.

Its classification. It arises in three ways ; first by implication, second by express text and third by prohibition.

The first principle laid down by our author is that those details of the model sacrifice of . which there is no necessity in the modified sacrifice are, therefore, suspended or omitted in the modified sacrifice. *Those details of which there is no necessity in the modified sacrifice shall be dispensed with.* As for instance, there is a modified form of a sacrifice called Śatakriṣṇâala homa, explained in the preceding pages. In the model sacrifice under a text, pounding is performed on the grains of Vrîhi in order to remove husk. As there is no husk to be removed from the golden pieces, the pounding shall not be performed. It is to be borne in mind that these golden pieces shall be boiled in ghee, because there is a direct text to that effect.

In a Râjâsûya ceremony there are offerings to the deities called Ratni. They are the modified forms of the Dars'apûrṇayâgas. It is said in connection with the Ratni offering that there is a self-constructed altar. In the model sacrifice when an altar is constructed, certain ceremonies are performed with recitation of the mantras. As in the Ratni, no altar is constructed and the ground in the natural state is used for altar without digging it, the ceremony in connection with the construction of the altar is dropt as being unnecessary.

The ceremony in connection with the construction of an altar is dropt in the रत्नि offerings.

In a Kâmyeṣṭi which is fully described at p. 601, boiled rice is offered to the Vis'vedevâs who are invoked, but if by any accident, boiled rice falls to the ground or sticks to the cudgel or wooden sword, Viṣṇuyâga is performed. As Vis'vedevâs are already invoked in the principal ceremony, there will, therefore, be no necessity of invocation of Viṣṇu separately and the recitation of the mantra invoking Viṣṇu will be dispensed with.

In a काम्येष्टि, the मन्त्र invoking विष्णु will be dispensed with.

In a Jyotiṣṭomâ, the Dîkṣanîya is transferred from the Dars'apûrṇamâsayâgas which are the model sacrifices. The Ârambhanîyeṣṭi which is a prefatory ceremony of the Dars'apûrṇamâsayâgas shall not be transferred, as the Jyotiṣṭoma has already its introductory ceremony in the form of Dîkṣaṇîya.

आरंभणीयेष्टि is dropt in the ज्योतिष्टोम, when दीक्षणीयेष्टि is transferred.

The cake baked on eight potsherds is offered to Anumatis in a coronation ceremony. These offerings are the modified forms of the Dars'apûrṇamâsayâgas though they are principal, yet each of them will have no prefatory ceremony. There will be, therefore, no Ârambhaṇîyeṣṭi.

No आरंभणीयेष्टि in the अनुमति.

There is no आरंभणीयेष्टि in an आरंभणीयेष्टि

A Fortiori there will be no Ârambhaṇîyeṣṭi in an Ârambhaṇîyeṣṭi.

In the Jyotiṣṭoma a sacrificial post is constructed for tying an animal and at that time a homa is performed. In a Sâdyaskrayyâga where a peg to which an animal is tied is used as a sacrificial post, the homa is dispensed with, because the text in the model sacrifice is that one desirous of cutting and making a sacrificial post shall

No homa is performed when a peg is used as a sacrificial post.

perform *homa* and as the peg is already existing, there is, therefore, no necessity of performing the said बाध.

When wood is removed from a tree for the purpose of a Yûpa, the remaining portion of the tree from the root upwards is called Sthanu; a certain ceremony in connection with it is performed and an offering is made with the recitation of the Mantra. He offers oblations in the lower part of the tree saying "arise, O! Lord of the forest with hundred offshoots". The question is, whether the Sthanvâhuti which is offered when a sacrificial post is constructed, should be made or not when a peg is used for the sacrificial post. It follows as a corollary from the preceding rule that when there is no sacrificial post constructed, there will be no ceremony of Sthanvâhuti. It does not benefit the sacrifice directly but only indirectly.

There is no स्थारावाहुति performed when there is no यूप

Similarly, Uttamaprayâja which is performed in connection with the Dars'apûrṇamâsa is only a purificatory ceremony of the deities. It does not benefit the sacrifice directly but only indirectly; hence the principle of Vadha applies. When a certain ceremony is Ârâdupakâraka, the principle of Vadha does not apply but when it is Sannipatayopakâraka the principle of Vadha comes into operation.

When a ceremony directly benefits a sacrifice the principle of बाध does not apply to it; but when it indirectly benefits it, the principle of बाध applies.

In the Agneya ceremony the two ghee offerings are made to Agniṣoma the dual deities. The first offering is to अग्नि and the second is to Soma; it is there said, 'O! Agni, bring Agni, bring Soma, bring Agni.' Agni is invoked to bring three deities namely अग्नि, सोम and अग्नि. The Agni to whom ghee is offered is different from the Agni to whom a puroḍâs'a cake is offered. The first offering of ghee made to Agni cannot be in the nature of a purificatory ceremony but it directly benefits the sacrifice. In this view, in the Sauryayâga which is the modified form of the Agneya the first affering to Agni is not dispensed with.

In the आग्नेय, the first offering to अग्नि directly benefits the sacrifice and the principle of बाध therefore does not apply to it.

A Pas'upuroḍas'a is described in Aittreya Brâhmaṇa Pañchika II Chap. VI, कंडs 8 and 9. Different victims are described in Khaṇḍa VIII and the sacrificial portion (मेध्य) changed forms and became transformed successively into various animals fit for sacrificial purposes. Passing from one animal to another,

पशुपुरोडाश described.

it ultimately became rice (Vrîhi). Rice is, therefore, fit for a sacrifice. In the 9th Khaṇḍa the rice is described as animal and its different parts are compared with the parts of an animal. In an animal sacrifice, a पशुपुरोडाश cake is, therefore, offered.

The principle of वध applies to the पशुपुरोडाश in an अग्नोषोमीय animal sacrifice.

In a Jyotiṣṭoma, there is an Agnîṣomîya animal sacrifice; after making an offering of *omentum*, a purodâs'a cake baked on eight potsherds is offered to Agniṣoma. According to our author, the pas'upurodâs'a being a subordinate act of the Agnîṣoma sacrifice, is a purificatory ceremony. It does not benefit the sacrifice directly but indirectly. In this view, the principle of Vadha applies.

वध means boiled rice and it is boiled in a pot.

What is the meaning of the word Charu ? The word is used in the sense of a 'pot' and 'rice'; according to our author, it means ' boiled rice'. Rice is boiled in a pot.

Different processes used in preparing a cake are dispensed with when rice is boiled.

As charu consists of a boiled rice offering, the different processes used in preparing a Purodâs'a cake are of course, dispensed with. They are Peṣaṇa, Sanyavana, संबपन, Santapana, Upadhâna, Prathukaraṇa, र्लंबी-करण, Abhûhya, Avajvalana and Vyuddhutya-sâdana; they are all fully described at p. 620 and the following pages. As they are not required in boiling rice, they are necessarily dispensed with and the principle of Vadha, therefore, applies.

<hr>

PÂDA 2.

Golden pieces shall be boiled like rice in a कृष्णलहोम.

We have explained what Kṛṣṇâlhoma is in the preceding pages of the introduction. The gold pieces weighing one ratti each are made in the form of 'rice'. As rice is boiled, these golden pieces shall also be boiled in ghee under a direct text "घृतेऽधपबति' " He boils it in ghee."

उपस्तरण and अभिघारण are suspen ded in a कृष्णालहोम,

Upastaraṇa and Abhighâraṇa are explained in the preceding pages; as these ceremonies of covering the purodâs'a with grass and sprinkling of ghee on it are not necessary in a Kṛṣṇâlahoma, they are, therefore, dispensed with.

In a कृष्णलहोम the golden pieces are sucked.

In the model sacrifice a cake is eaten; similarly in a kṛṣṇala homa the golden pieces boiled in ghee are sucked just as one sucks a sugar cane or a child sucks anything by making an onomatopœic sound 'चुषचुषा'.

The whole कृष्णल is to be taken by a ब्रह्मा priest at the allotted times without participation by any other priest.

In the model sacrifice, the Iḍâ food is divided into four parts and at the time of the repetition of 'यदु', all the parts are offered for eating. There in the Kṛṣṇalahoma, they are all taken together by the Brahmâ priest at their allotted different times without making any division thereof into the priests.

A fee paid to a Ritvik is in the nature of wages.

The fee that is paid to a Ritwik is in the nature of the wages in return of the labour done by him; it is not with a view to an accrual of the invisible fruit.

The eating of the remnants of the sacrificial food is by way of final disposal.

In the Jyotiṣṭoma and the Dars'apûrṇamâsayâgas there is the eating of the remnants called Iḍâbhakṣaṇa and Pras'itrabhakṣaṇa by the priests and the sacrificer. It is not in the nature of the wages of the priests, because the sacrificer has no longer any proprietary right left in the food by reason of its being offered to the deity of the sacrifices. It is in the nature of the Pratipattikarma i. e. by way of final disposal of the remnants of the sacrificial food.

In a सत्र, neither appointment of a priest is made nor is any fee paid.

We have explained what Satra is in the preceding pages. In it, the sacrificers themselve officiate as priests ; in this view there is no appointment. An appointment involves the idea of another person being engaged ; one cannot appoint himself. It, therefore, follows as a corollary that no fee for the labour is paid. If one does any work for himself, he does not charge for his labour. This does not necessarily prohibit any gift made out of any charitable or religious motive to a priest.

In an उदवसानीय, a fee is to secure the services of a priest.

In an Udavasânîya or otherwise known as Pṛṣṭas'amanîya which is performed after a Satra, a fee of one thousand is paid. This fee is for the purpose of securing the services of a priest, because Udavasânîya is an independent ceremony but not a part of a sacrificial session. A priest is appointed apart from the sacrificer and the sacrificers of a sacrificial session after its completion perform Udavasânîya one after the other.

Other gifts for production of invisible result.

In a Kameṣṭi sacrifice which is performed in a Sâraswata sacrificial session, a gift mentioned at p. 641 is made. As it is a part of a Satra the gift made therein is by way of charity for the production of invisible fruit but not for the purpose of securing the services of a priest. Similarly, a gift to an enemy in the new and full moon sacrifices is a charitable gift for the production of invisible effect, for no one engages an enemy to permform a sacrifice.

अस्थियाग explained; when any of the sacrificers dies during the continuance of a सत्र, a bone sacrifice is performed.

Certain acts belonging to a living person are not performed in an अस्थियाग.

When any of the sacrificers in a Satra dies during the continuance of the सत्र, his legal heir shall be initiated in his place and his burnt bones shall be placed in a pot seated on a deer's skin and shall be made to perform an Asthiyajña. This is symbolical only but the legal representative of the deceased in reality performs it. In it, the Mantras shall not be uttered, nor will there be any shaving, as these ceremonies are to be performed by a living person and the dead bones of the deceased sacrificer who is symbolically represented by them cannot possess the capacity to perform them. The Dìkṣaṇîyeṣṭi is also not performed for similar reasons. As no desires are left in a dead person, so no desire-accomplishing acts shall be performed.

सूक्तवाक is not recited in an अस्थियाग.

The Prayaṇîya is transferred from the Dars'apûrṇamâsayâga in the Asthiyâga; in the Prayaṇîya there is a Sûktavâka which is read by a Hotâ expressing the desires and hopes of the sacrifice. As the hopes and desires belong to a living man, the Sûktavâka is, therefore, dispensed with in the Asthiyajña.

No hopes and desires of a होता are expressed by a मंत्र in an अस्थियाग.

There are certain desires and hopes expressed by a Hotâ as for example in a Dvâdas'âha; as these desires are really the desires and hopes of the deceased sacrificer whom he represents, the representation comes to an end on the death of the sacrificer and the Hotâ cannot, therefore, express the said hopes and desires in an Asthiyajña.

The principle of कूटबार्चिंता applied.

These ceremonies are rightly dispensed with in an Asthiyajña and should not have formed the subjects of different Adhikaraṇas being based on absurd questions (Kṛtvâchintâ) which ought not to have been put forward for solution. They are so absurd that any person possessed of common sense can answer in the negative.

सर्वस्वार explained.

If a person wishes to go to heaven without any trouble, he shall perform a Sarvasvâra sacrifice ; he commences it and enters the fire in the third Savana with the accompaniment of the ârbhavapavamâna song after covering an Audumbarî branch with a new cloth and commands the Brâhmaṇas to complete the sacrifice commenced by him. It is, however, completed by the priest after the death of the sacrificer.

Cutting of the उदम्बर branch and touching of the शुक्र cup are done in a सर्वस्वार.

In the model sacrifice, a branch of an Udambara tree is cut off according to the measure of the sacrificer and the S'ukra cup is touched by him ; but as these ceremonies are for the sacrifice, they are performed by the priests after the death of the sacrificer in a Sarvasvâr. The same principle as laid down in an अस्तिस्वाग applies here.

A होता priest repeats the मंत्र expressing hopes and desires of the sacrificer.

A Hotâ priest pronounces the mantra 'आयास्तेयजमान:' "The sacrificer has hopes." This formula shall be repeated in a Sarvasvâra, because before the Ârbhavapavamâna song is sung, the sacrificer hopes to live in the interval

In a द्वादशाह, gift of gold to an आत्रेय and appointment of a priest are made.

In a Dvâdas'âha, there are certain ceremonies transferred from the model sacrifice, as for instance an appointment of a priest and gift to a priest of an Atri family. As Dvâdas'âha is a Satra, both should not be performed; but our author says that they should be performed in compliance with the Chodaka text and for production of an invisible effect.

On the omission of a subordinate part, the principal part is not thereby omitted.

When any subordinate part is omitted, the principal is not thereby omitted ; as for instance the Nirvâpa offerings which are made in an Agnihotra are made with an Agnihotrahavanî but when the Nirvâpa offerings which are made in the Pavamânesṭi a subordinate part of the establishment of fire, the sacrificial vessel Agnihotrahavanî is not used, because there is no occasion for its use in the Agnyâdhâna. The sacrificial vessel is subordinate and the Nirvâpa offering is principal. On the omission of a subordinate part, the principal part is not thereby omitted.

In a वाजपेय, in the text 'four handfuls,' handfuls are dispensed with.

In a Vâjapeya sacrifice, Charu is made of boiled wild rice in seventeen cups; but in the model sacrifice, it is said ' there are offerings of four handfuls.' In order to harmonise the applicability of these two texts, there are four possible ways. The first view is that both the handfuls and the number apply to the modified sarifice and the principle of suspension does not apply. The second view is that the four handfuls are not sufficient to fill up the seventeen cups, so both the handfuls and the number are dispensed with The third view is that one should be dispensed with; if the handful is suspended, you can measure the offering by any other means; if the number is suspended, you can have more handfuls to fill the cups. The fourth view, which is the author's view, is that the term 'handfuls' which happens to be at the end is suspended.

The words 'धेनु' 'वत्स' and ऋषभ explained.

There is a text "द्यावापृथिव्यांधेनुमालभेत' मारुतंवत्सं' ऐंद्रंऋषभम्." "Let him sacrifice a cow to heaven and earth; a calf to मरुत् and a bullock to इंद्र." The terms 'धेनु', 'वत्स' and 'ऋषभ' are conventionally fixed in their meaning and convey the idea of a 'cow', 'calf' and 'bullock.' They cannot mean a goat, kid and male goat. The former, therefore, dispense with the latter and the principle of बाध applies.

'श्वेत' means a white goat.

There is another text "वायव्यं श्वेतमालभेत भूतिकामः:" Let one who is desirious of prosperity offer a white (animal) to Vâyu." Here in the text, the term 'white' is used; it is an adjective: as in the model sacrifice a goat is sacrificed and there is nothing to the contrary to suspend the applicability thereof in the modified sacrifice the white, therefore, means 'a white goat.'

In a Sâdhaskra sacrifice, a peg is used in place of a sacrificial post.

When a peg is used in a साधस्क in place of a यूप, the ceremony connected with it is dispensed with and in a चित्रा sacrifice in the offering to प्रजापति the rice is not ground.

In the model sacrifice, the sacrificial post is made of Khadira wood and certain ceremonies are performed on it. As the peg in the Sâdhaskra is ready made, it is, therefore not constructed from Khadira wood nor are any ceremonies performed on it. In a Chitrâ sacrifice, an offering to Prajâpati consists of the mixture of curd, ghee, water, parched rice and common rice. In the model sacrifice, the rice is ground and converted into flour to make purodâs'a cakes for the deity but

In the Chitra sacrifice, the rice is mixed with articles of offering to prajâpati and grinding it into flour and making a cake from it are, therefore, dispensed with.

Cutting, hewing and setting up do not apply in the case of a peg used as a sacrificial post.

It follows as a corollary from the above view that cutting, hewing and setting up of a peg which are ordinarily done in the case of a sacrificial post are dispensed with, as the peg is ready-made.

Certain ceremonies being for the object of a sacrifice are perfor- used on the peg treated as a sacri- ficial post.

While, on the other hand, levelling of the ground with the Maitrâvaruna rod, sprinking of water, forcibly driving the peg in the ground and anionting it, being for the object of the sacrifice are, therefore, performed on the peg used in the place of a sacrificial post.

In connection with a Mahâpitryajña, there is a text "To Soma with the manes, cake baked on six potsherds; to the manes sitting on the kus'a grass parched rice (dhâna), to the departed souls whom the fire has

In the महापितृयज्ञ, the order is reversed.

consumed, a mixture called मंथ in the milk of a cow whose calf is dead." In the model sacrifice, the rice is ground first and then Puroḍâs'a cake made from it, is baked; but here in the Pitrimahâyajña this order is reversed; the rice is parched first in order to make it भात and then it is ground to prepare the mixture called Mantha. As to the preparation of Mantha see at p. 656.

— —

PÂDA 3.

When a principal act is transferred, the subordi- nate parts are also trans- ferred along with it.

When a principal act is transferred, the subordinate parts called Itikartavyatâ are also transferred along with it, as for instance Prayaja Aghara and Sâmadhenî.

In a sacrifice in honour of Vâyu, the verse recited as Aghâra Mantra is one from the 10th book of the Rigveda quoted at p. 663. In the model sacrifice, there are two offerings of ghee; the first offer- ing is made without any मंत्र and the second offering is made with the recitation of the

In a वायव्य sacrifice the हिरण्यगर्भमंत्र is recited in the subsequent offering of ghee.

Mantra of the Taittariyasanhitâ quoted at p. 664. As the first part of the offering is without recitation, the Hiraṇyagarbha mantra shall not be applicable there but in the subsequent part where the उत्तरवत् Mantra is recited in the model sacrifice, it is set aside by the Hiraṇyagarbha Mantra, because ' ka ' and ' Hiraṇyagarbha ' mean ' the lord of the universe '

(Prajâpati) and the 'ईश' of the Mantra of the model sacrifice is also 'lord of the universe.'

Placing of whey on an उत्कर and tying an animal to the परिधि are subordinate acts and are performed for visible results.

In connection with the soma ceremonies in a Chaturmâsayâga, it is said "They place whey on the tapering heap of mud dug out from the earth for the preparation of an altar (उत्कर) and tie an animal to the fence stick (परिधि)." It is contended that it is impossible to place whey on the Utkara which is pointed at the end and to tie an animal to the Paridhi which is very thin. The author says that the Utkara can be more broadened at the top and the Paridhi can be made stronger, because these acts are subordinate acts and are performed to achieve certain visible results.

The principle of समुच्चय explained with an illustration.

In an Agnichayana, there are Dîkṣâhuti. There are six offerings in the model sacrifice for which there are six Mantras quoted at p. 667 and similarly there are six mantras different from the Mantra of the model sacrifice in the modified sacrifice as quoted on p.p. 667 and 668. It is, therefore, contended that the offerings in the modified sacrifice will be accompanied with the Mantra of the modified sacrifice thereby setting aside the मंत्र of the model sacrifice. The author, however, says that both sets of Mantras will be combined together and twelve offerings will be made as there is a direct text to that effect quoted at p. 668. When the procedure of the model sacrifice is combined with that of the modified sacrifice it is called a combination or tacking (Samuchahya.) Where it is possible to combine the practices of the model and modified sacrifices, the principle of Samuchchaya shall be applied. In this view, the principle of Samuchchaya, therefore, applies here.

The principle of समुच्चय does not apply to the re-establishment of fire as far as fee is concerned.

There is Agnyâdhâna in which a fee is paid to the priests and in the punaradhâna which is the modified form of the Agnyâdhâna, another fee is provided for. As to the different fees payable in these ceremonies, see the texts quoted at p. 671. The principle of Samuchchaya as explained above does not apply in the Punarâdhâna (re-establishment of fire). The fees in both the model and modified sacrifices are specially laid down. The payment of the fee of the model sacrifice in the modified form of it shall, therefore, be suspended.

In the आग्रयण the principle of समुच्चय does not apply as far as fee is concerned.

In the Âgrayaṇa, the fee provided for consists of cloth and the first born calf; in the model sacrifice Anvâhârya is the fee. For similar reason, the principle of Samuchchaya does not apply; both have their separate fees.

अन्वाहार्य explained.

"The fees that are given at the funeral ceremony in the beginning and at the end and that are given on ths new moon day are called Anvâhârya." Vâchaspatya. अन्वाहार्य fee is described in the Taittarîyasanhitâ in Kâṇḍa I, Prapâthaka 7 and Anuvâka 3. It is cooked rice. See Kâtyâyana s'rautasûtra chap II. 148. Keith says at p. 100 of the Taittarîya Sanhitâ Vol. 1 "Anvâhârya is a mess food cooked with rice given to the priests as a Dakṣiṇâ." Eggeling says at p. 49 of part I of the Śatapatha Brâhmaṇa "Anvâhârya consists of boiled rice prepared from the rice grains that remain after the sacrificial cakes have been prepared. It is put on the (Dakṣinâgni) Dakṣiṇâ fire by the Adhvaryu for cooking after covering over the cakes and pouring out the water. Kâtyana II. 5. 27. Sâyana explains the term as that which takes away (anvâ-hri) from the sacrificer the guilt incurred by mistakes during the sacrifice, but the St. Petersburg Dictionary offers the more probable explanation of it as that which serves to supplement (anvâ-hri) the sacrifice."

The procedure of अन्वाहार्य applies to the fee paid in an आग्रयण.

In connection with the Anvahârya fee there is certain procedure laid down in the Kalpasûtra. A sacrificer orders the priests in the south to prepare the gift. To the priests in the north he says 'come from the south.' He gives them boiled rice (Anvahârya, saying'. 'This is boiled rice for you, O! priests, take it and go from the north.' This procedure which applies to the Anvâhârya fee in the model sacrifice applies to the fee consisting of cloth and calf in the Âgrayaṇa but cooking of rice which is done in the model sacrifice shall not be performed on the cloth and calf for obvious reasons.

Certain ceremonies dispensed with in an आग्रयण.

Similarly sprinkling of ghee which is performed in the model sacrifice shall not be done on the cloth and calf in the modified sacrifice.

A fee in a ज्योतिष्टोम consists of 1200 cows.

In connection with the Jyotiṣṭoma, a fee consisting of cows, horses, mules, asses, goats, sheep, rice, barley, sesamum and beans is laid down. According to our author the number refers to an animal, because the grains are not numbered but weighed. The word (तस्व) in the text quoted at p. 675 refers to the sacrifice. The number ' twelve hundred ' qualifies cows, because (1) she happens to be first amongt the animals mentioned in the text ; (2) horse cannot be an object of gift by reason of prohibition about its giving and taking and (3) she is the most useful domestic animal.

Distribution of the said fee amongst the priests unequally. The fee of twelve hundred cows should be divided amongst the 16 priests of 4 groups in the following order as shown in the table below :—

Group.	Name of the priests.				Share.	Number of cows.
I	अध्वर्युं	ब्रह्मा	उद्गाता	होता	1	576
II	प्रतिप्रस्थाता	ब्राह्मणाच्छंसी	प्रस्तोता	मैत्रावरुण	$\frac{1}{2}$	288
III	नेष्टा	अग्नीध्र	प्रतिहर्ता	अच्छावाक	$\frac{1}{3}$	192
IV.	पोता.	सुब्रह्मण्य	ग्रावस्तुत	उन्नेता	$\frac{1}{4}$	144

A cow is a fee in a भू sacrifice. In connection with a भू, an Ekâha sacrifice, the fee is thus laid down in the text quoted at p. 683 " its fee............ is a cow." As the text clearly prescribes a special fee in the Bhû sacrifice the entire fee as mentioned in the Jyotiṣṭoma is thereby suspended.

The gift of a three years old heifer in a साधस्क does away with the fee of the model sacrifice. In a Sadhyaskrayâga, purchase of soma is said to be made by means of a three years old heifer. In the model sacrifice it is laid down " he purchases it (soma) with a goat ; he purchases it with a bullock ; he purchases it with the hoof of a horse, he purchases it with a cloth," As the fee in a Sadhyaskrayâga is especially laid down, the fee of the model sacrifice shall, therefore, be dispensed with.

There is another text in connection with the Sadhyaskrayāga. "One whose soma is stolen shall give one cow as a fee ; on its being burnt, he shall give 5 cows." The gift of one cow or five cows replaces the number twelve hundred and leaves the gift of horse and grain etc, intact in the text quoted at p. 675 in connection with the fee of the Jyotiṣṭoma sacrifice.

The gift of one or five cows replaces the number 1,200 and leaves other objects of gift intact.

In an As'vamedha when an Adhvarya is given two gold stands for a lamp or two mirrors as a gift, his share of the fee is thereby suspended but not the entire fee of the sacrifice.

A present of two gold stands for a lamp does away with the share of an अध्वर्यु's fee in an अश्वमेध.

There is an Upahavya sacrifice which is not defined. In it the fee of the sacrifice consists of a dark horse of golden forehead. It is said that it should be given to the Brahmâ priest. This gift to the Brahmâ is in the nature of payment of the fee for the entire sacrifice and therefore suspends the payment of the entire fee mentioned at p. 675.

In an उपहव्य, the entire fee is suspended by a gift of a horse to ब्रह्मा priest.

Similarly, when it is said that a soma cup made of *Udambar* wood should be given to the Brahmâ in a भूतपेय sacrifice, the gift thereof dispenses with the entire fee of the sacrifice, because the gift of animals is therein prohibited.

The same principle applies in a भूतपेय sacrifice.

In a Vâjapeya sacrifice, a chariot yoked with a pair of oxen after reciting the Yajumantra is given as a gift to an Adhvaryu amongst other objects of gift. Does this gift do away with the other objects of gift ? The reply of the author is in the negative. In it, the gift consists of 17 chariots, 17 gold coins, 17 female slaves, 17 pairs of oxen, 17 cents of cows, 17 bundles of grass and 17 companions. All these are intended to be distributed amongst the priests. The chariots are, therefore, marked with certain symbols ; the one yoked with Yajumantra is given to an Adhvaryu, the one yoked with Rikmantra is presented to a Hotâ and the other yoked with Sâma Mantras is given to an Udgâtâ. In order to distinguish the chariots, they are thus marked out. The

The marking out of the chariot for an अध्वर्यु does not suspend other objects of gift.

marking out of the chariot does not do away with the other objects of gift to which the Adhvaryu is entitled. So here the principle of Vâdha does not apply.

PÂDA 4.

In an Agnichayana, the Nakṣatreṣṭi is performed. In the model sacrifice, there are Nariṣṭahomas. According to the author both the *homas* will be combined in the modified sacrifice. In a Śyenayâga, the priests with red turbans, red dress and sacred thread on the right shoulder move about. In the model sacrifice the sacred thread is said to be worn on the left shoulder. Here also both the practices will be combined ; it is not a case of supersession but that of combination. In a Pṛtyaṣaḍaha honey or ghee is eaten but in the model sacrifice, a Brâhmaṇa takes milk, a Kṣatriya gruel and a Vais'ya curd. According to the author both the practices shall be combined together. These are the cases of Samuchchaya but not of Vâdha.

Example of combinations.

The Śara supercedes Kus'a of the model sacrifice in the boiled rice offered to Soma and R udra ; similarly the sound of a moving chariot and that of a drum in a Vâjapeya sacrifice supersede the two blades of grass and the recitation of the Mantras of the model sacrifice. These are the examples of Vâdha but not of Samuchchaya.

Examples of superses- sion.

There are other examples of the applicability of the doctrine of Samuchchaya as for example the Bârhasppaty a cup in the Bârhaspatyasava is combined with the Indravâyû cups of the model sacri- fice. In a Vâjapeya, there are 17 animals delicated to prajâpati ; the animals of the model sacrifice are added to the already existing animals consecrated to Prajâpati in the Vâjapeya sacrifice. In a Sangrahaniṣṭi, the Âmanhoma is combined with the three anuyâja offerings of the model sacrifice. In the Mahâvrata which is a one day ceremony in a Gavâmayana the singing by the wives is in addition to the singing of the priests per- formed in the model sacrifice. In an Añjanâbhyañjana, the ceremony of an- ointment with incense lasting for 49 days is in addition to the anointment with butter, a ceremony of the model sacrifice. In the Mahâvrata, the upper garment is worn in addition to the lower garment of the model sacrifice ; and the *s'loka* songs are sung in addition to the songs of the model sacrifice ; but if the objects of the songs of the model sacrifice and that of the modi-

Other examples of co nbination.

fied sacrifice is not different and if the songs of the model sacrifice are subordinate, they shall be dispensed with, as Kautsa and Kâṇva etc., supersede the songs of the model sacrifice.

The songs of the modified sacrifice supersede the songs of the model sacrifice, in proportion to their number in the modified sacrifice ; as for example one song of the modified sacrifice shall set aside one song of the model sacrifice and so on. When the songs of the model sacrifice exceed the number in the modified sacrifice, the excess number left after supersession shall be combined with the number of the modified sacrifice but when the number of the songs of the model sacrifice falls short of that in the modified sacrifice, the songs of the model sacrifice shall be entirely superseded. The former is called Avâpa and the latter is called Udvâpa. In a Pavamâna song both Avâpa and Udvâpa apply.

The principles of आवाप and उद्वाप explained.

When the name of a deity has become associated with an injunctive word in a Vidhi passage, it cannot be substituted by any other synonymous word conveying the same sense or the same name of the deity, because that word has a special charm in it; as for example ,'वदाग्नेयोऽष्टाकपालो अमावास्यायां पौर्णमास्यां चाच्युतोभवति,'' " When one performs fire-oblations consisting of cakes baked on eight pans, he becomes infallible." Here in the text, the 'Âgneya' is very important and cannot be substituted by any of the synonyms of Agni. Similarly in the text "सौर्यंचरुं निर्वपेद्ब्रह्मवर्चसकामः" "(Let one desirous of Brâhmaṇic glory, offer boiled rice consecrated to the sun god.") the Saurya is connected with the injunctive part and is very important ; it can not be substituted by any other synonymous term denoting the sun.

In a विधि passage when the name is associated with a deity, no other synonym can be used in its place to denote the deity.

In the Âgnyâdhâna ceremony, there are Pavamâna offerings to the fire ; it is therein addressed as "purifying fire, holy fire" These two adjectives mean the same thing ; should they be repeated or in other words, should Agni be addressed with all his attributes ? The author says that Agni being a deity should be addressed with all the attributes ; but in the ghee oblations of the same ceremony where fire ceremony is described as Budhanvâna (inspiring), the god is not to be

In an अन्वाधान, अग्नि is to be addressed with his attributes but in the ghee offerings, the deity is to be addressed without the attribute as it qualifies the मंत्र but not the deity.

addressed with the epithet ' Budhanvân does not really qualify the god but the Puronuvâkya Mantra recited in honour of Agni.

In a ज्योतिष्टोम cow is addressed by 'उक्ष' but वनस्पति is not substituted by any other synonymous term.

In a Jyotiṣṭoma a cow is said to be an Anuvandhya animal; it should not be addressed by any other synonyms excepting Usra under a special text. Similarly Vanaspati, (herb) should not be substituted by any other synonym.

When an epithet is not Agni and Varuṇa are to be addressed with the epithet शिवष्टकृत in a sacrificial bath.

When an epithet is not Rûḍhi or used in a conventional sense but is a compound word Sanvijnanika or Yaugika, it may be applied to any deity; as for instance, he sacrifices to the "Sviṣṭakrit Agni and Varuṇa": though Agni is addressed as Sviṣṭakrit, yet as the word means 'completing the sacrifice excellently, it may apply to the dual deities like Agnîvaruṇa.

अग्नि is without the epithet in an अग्निषोमीय animal sacrifice.

On the other hand in an Agnîṣomîya animal sacrifice, Agni is to be addressed without Sviṣṭakrit in every proceeding in it as the deity in the sacrifice is described without the epithet.

In the Dars'apûrṇamâsayâgas, याज्या and पुरोऽनुवाक्या Mantras are subordinate parts in the new and full moon sacrifices.

In the Dars'apûrṇamâsayâgas, the Yâjyâ Mantras are recited while not in motion and Puronuvâkya mantras are recited while sitting. The difference in these two sorts of Mantras is that of posture. They are recited to help one's memory to remember the mantras; the result is visible. In this view, the Yâjyâ and the Puronuvâkya Mantras are subordinate but are not principal.

The principle of उह does not apply to the *manota mantra*.

There is an animal sacrifice in honour of Vâyu. In the model sacrifice where Agnîṣomîya animal is consecrated to the dual deities, the verse from the 6th Book of the Rigveda quoted at p. 714 and known as *manota mantra* is recited under a special text, because it is in honour of Agni singly. There the word 'अग्ने' has not been replaced by ' Agnîṣomaû.' As the principle of Ûha does not apply to the *manotu mantra* in the model sacrifice, it does not, therefore, apply to it in the modified sacrifice where it is transferred under a *chodaka* text.

कण्वरथंतर should be sung in its own Yoni.

Kaṇvarathantara is a particular tune like other tunes. The tune of the Yoni governs the entire song just as the Yoni of the Rathantara governs the Rathantara song and the Yoni of the Brihat governs the Brihat song. Similarly, the Yoni of Kaṇvarathantara governs the Kaṇvarathantara song. In a Vaisyastoma, there is a Priṣṭa song sung in the Kaṇvarathantara tune ; but in the model sacrifice the Priṣṭa song is sung in the various tunes as 'त्वामिद्धि हवामहे' in the Brihat, 'अभित्वाशूर' in the Rathantara and 'पुनानः सोम' in the Kaṇvarathantara tunes ; but here in the modified form of the song called Kaṇvarathantara which is the characterestic of the Priṭṣa in the Vais'yastoma, the song should be sung in its own Yoni.

उत्तरा verses follow suit.

We have explained in the preceding pages what a Tṛcha is ; it consists of three verses set apart for singing. The first verse is called Yoni and the last two verses constitute the Uttarâ. It is also said that the Uttarâ verses are invariably sung in the tune of their Yoni. It follows, therefore, that in a Kaṇvarathantara song, the Uttarâ shall be sung in the tune like its Yoni. Kaṇvarathantara is a mixture of Brihat and Rathantara.

The स्तोत्र and यज्ञ from the model sacrifice to an अग्निष्टुत् are transferred unmodified.

In an Agnîṣṭut which is a one day ceremony, the Stotra and Śastra praises in honour of different deities are transferred from the model sacrifice. As these praises are principal, so they will be transferred from the model sacrifice without any modification.

In a Châturmâsya ceremony the Anuyâja offerings are made with Pṛṣadâjyâ (a mixture of ghee with curd). The invocation mantra in the model sacrifice is "देवान् आज्यपान् आवह" "Bring the gods, the drinkers of ghee." This Mantra is transferred under the *chodaka* text to the modified sacrifice. The question is, whether the principle of ûha applies or not. There are 3 possible views of those who hold that the principle of Ûha applies. The first view is that the âjyapan dadhipân (drinkers of ghee and curd) should be substituted in place of Ajyapan (drinkers of ghee) in the invocation Mantra. The second view is that only Dadhipân (drinkers of curd) should be substituted. The third view is that Pṛṣadâjyapân (drinkers of the mixture of curd and ghee) should be substituted in the invocation Mantra. Our author rejects all these views and is of opinion that the principle of Ûha does not apply, because Pṛṣadâjya is not a different substance from the clarified butter ; it is coloured ghee purified by curd. In this view of the author, the invocation mantra is recited without any change in it.

PÂDA 5.

The first cakes of the model sacrifice are transferred.

There are texts permitting cakes baked on one potsherd to Heaven and earth, cakes baked on two potsherds to As'winas and cakes baked on three potsherds to Viṣṇu; but in the model sacrifice, cakes baked on eight potsherds are offered to Agni. As there are larger number of cakes in the model sacrifice, the question is, which cakes are to be transferred, the first ones or the last ones? The author's reply is that the first ones are to be transferred to the modified sacrifice and the last ones are to be omitted.

In a तृक्, the first तृच is transferred from the model sacrifice. A ऋक् is to be sung in a स्.

There is a Trik sacrifice in which there are three Pavamânas; in the माध्यंदिनपवमान one Tricha or a group of three verses is sung. In the model sacrifice there are three तृचs of different metres. According to the rule laid down in the case of the potsherd cakes, the first Tṛcha of the गायत्री metre will be transferred to the तृक् sacrifice. But in a Dhu song in the Trika sacrifice, only a Ṛik verse is to be repeated but not the तृच.

द्विरात्र is governed by the procedure of दशरात्र but not of द्वादशाह.

The first day in a Dvâdas'âha is called Prâyaṇîya and the last day is called Udanîya. The remaining ten days constitute Das'arâtra, the six days of which are called Pṛṣta days and the remaining four days are Chandoma. The Dvirâtra is governed by the procedure of Das'arâtra, because both of them have Râtri at the end and because the first day of the Dvirâtra is said to be the 2nd day of Dvâdas'âha and its second day is said to be the 3rd day of the Dvâdas'âha thereby eleminating the first and last days of the Dvâdas'âha and leaving the Das'arâtra as the model of the Dvirâtra.

आधूनन and वपन mantras are transferred to the अग्निचयन according to their appropriateness.

There are seven Adhûnana Mantras for establishing fire in an Ukhâ and fourteen Vapana mantras for putting fire in the Agni Kṣetra. These Mantras are transferred under a Chodaka text to the Agnichayana. Are these Mantras to be transferred according to the order? The reply of the author is that they are to be transferred to the Agnichayana, according to the appropriateness but not according to the order.

Transference of the songs from the modified sacrifice to the model sacrifice in the case of the विवृढ-स्तोमs.

We have seen in the preceding pages that some times it so happens that the songs preponderate in the modified sacrifice over those in the model sacrifice. Should the songs be transferred from the modified sacrifice to the model sacrifice ? Transference, as a rule takes place from the model sacrifice to the modified sacrifice but here in the case of Vivridhastoma sacrifices, the transference of songs takes place from the modified sacrifice to the model sacrifice in order to complete the number. Though importation from the modified sacrifice is improper, yet the repetition of the same songs of the model sacrifice which would otherwise happen in order to complete the number is equally improper. According to the author the importation of the songs from the modified sacrifice to the model sacrifice is justifiable under the circumstances.

In a बहिष्पवमान in the morning सवन only a ऋक् is imported from the modified sacrifice.

There is a Vahiṣpavamâna song in the morning Savana where the songs fall short of those of the modified sacrifice. As it is ordained in the model sacrifice that there shall be only one song, only one Ṛik verse will, therefore, be imported from the modified sacrifice.

Additional verses in the सामधेनी verses are to be imported from elsewhere.

There are eleven Sâmadhenî verses mentioned in the preceding pages and according to the text 'he utters the first and the last thrice', the number of the Sâmadhenî verses comes to fifteen ; but if you have to make the verses twenty one, you will have to import six verses from elsewhere, because there is no repetition of the verses sanctioned by the text save the first and the last as said above.

A षोडशी cup belongs to the model sacrifice and should be taken in the third सवन from the आग्रयण vessel with the accompaniment of praise.

In connection with a Jyotiṣṭoma, it is said "He who knows it, takes Ṣodas'î cup". The question is 'Where should Ṣodas'î cup be introduced'? According to our author, the Ṣodas'î cup is to be introduced in the model sacrifice i. e. in the Jyotiṣṭoma but not in the modified sacrifice. Further it should be taken from the Agrayana vessel but not from the ukthya vessel. He further says that it should be taken in the third savana. Fourthly, it is accompanied with praise songs both in poetry

CLXXXVI.

Practice in drinking
सोम

and prose. In a soma sacrifice there are several cups full of soma juice offered to the gods and drunk subsequently by the priests; they are called by different names. Amongst them is a Şodas'î cup which finds its place only in a Jyotişţoma. The juice therein is filled from the Âgrayaṇa vessel and drunk in the third Savana. Whenever any intoxicating juice is drunk, a song is sung just as it is the practice at the time of drinking *Bhanga* even at present in India.

In the Dvirâtra ceremony of the Angirasas, the Şodas'î song is sung on the second day. As there are several kinds of Dvirâtras laying down of Şodas'î in the Dvirâtra of the Angriasas is by way of a restrictive rule as regards it and a prohibitive rule as regards the Dvirâtras other than that of the Angrisas. Şodas'î is a soma cup and the song which is sung is also called Şodas'î song. They both exist together ; one cannot exist without the other.

बोडशी is sung on the second day in the Angiras's द्विरात्र

It is said in connection with the Şodas'î in the model sacrifice that it should be taken on the 4th day of a sacrifice lasting for more than one day. The words "4th day" are repeated twice. The question is whether the बोडशी should be taken on such successive fourth day in one Ahîna sacrifice or in various Ahîna sacrifices. The author's view is that the Şodas'î cup should be taken on the 4th day in various Ahîna sacrifices, because in one Ahîna sacrifice, there can be only one 4th day.

In an अहीन sacrifice the बोडशी cup should be taken on the 4th day of several sacrifices of the अहीन class.

In connection with a Jyotişţoma it is said "...................if it has a Jagat song, the cups preceded by Âgrayaṇa." The author's view is that as there is no Jagat- sâma in the Sâmaveda, it is a song from the Rigvâda produced from the जयती metre. It is sung in the Vişuvan and this Âgrayaṇa cup finds its place along with its accompanying Jagâtsama in the Vişuvan, the modified sacrifice.

The आग्रयण with its जयत्साम finds its place in the विषुवान्.

In connection with a Gosava it is said "Let him do both in a Gosava." In the model sacrifice, the verses of the Rig- veda commencing with Upa are sung in a Rathantara tune and those commencing with Agriya are sung in a Brîhat tune. These

There are no उपसत् and अग्निमती verses in the गोसव, etc.

verses will be, as a matter of course, transferred to the modified sacrifice but as there is neither Brihatpraṣta nor Rathantarapraṣta in the Gosava etc., the Upavatî and Agriyavati verses of the Rigveda do not find their place in the Gosava etc.

In a ज्योतिष्टोम sacrifice, some of the cups are arranged in the following order.

The ऐंद्रवायु cups should be taken first in their own class.

1st उपांशु
2nd अंतर्याम } आधारा class
3rd ऐंद्रवायव
4th मैत्रावरुण } चरा class

In connection with them, it is said "It is the tongue; they are the Aindravâyu cups, those who take Aindravâyava cups first, hold the tongue He takes them with the minute flow." The question is whether the above order should be broken and the Aindravâyava cups should be displaced and taken first or should they be taken in the order? The author says that there shall be no displacement of the cups and Aindravâyava cups shall be taken in the order given above. As they happen to be the first in the Adhârâ class of cups, so they are said to be first. Even in the desire-accomplishing ceremonies, they are to be taken in their own order and no displacement will, therefore, take place.

But आश्विन cups are taken first for the accomplishment of desires.

On the other hand in the Jyotiṣṭoma sacrifice the As'vin and Śukra cups shall be taken first, after displacement of the cups, because certain desires are said to be fulfilled on taking them first. As they also belong to the Adhârâ class of cups, they shall be taken before the Indravâyu cups.

Arrangement of the cups but the gift of the contents of cups is not displaced.

When the cups are displaced, the arrangement thereof is necessarily displaced; but the gift of the contents being principal is not, therefore, displaced.

A व्यूढ द्वादशाह is a modified form of a सँमूढ द्वादशाह.

उदयनीय explained.

There is a Dvâdas'âha sacrifice which lasts for twelve days. The first day called मांयणीय, the last day called उदयनीय and 10th day have Aindravâyu cups. Then on the remaining 9 days, soma is drunk in the cups called Aindravâyava, Sukra and Âgrayaṇa. As they are only three cups, they are thrice repeated in the same order. This repetetion of the cups is called Tryanîka.

In the Samûḍha dvâdâs'âha there are only 9 days in which cups of soma are drunk in the order given at p. 751. In the Vyûḍhadvâdas'âha which is the modified sacrifice, the cups are drunk in the order given in the second column at p. 751. The Vyûḍha is the modification of Samûḍha, because the former is a desire-accomplishing ceremony which is a modified form of a permanent one.

In a Gavâmayana which has been fully described in the preceding pages, the Tryanikas are repeated in 360 days. The Gavâmayana as we have seen, is divided into two parts; the first part is called Pûrvapakṣa. The Tryanîkâs of Samûdadvâdâs'âha which is the model of the Gavâmayana are repeated. The Pûrvapakṣa is divided into nine parts of 20 days making up the total of 180 days. The Tryanîkas as explained above, are repeated on the स्वस्वात्र Vivṛiddhi but not on the दंडकलित principle as explained in the preceding pages. It is done thus. The first six months of the Gavâmayana consisting of 180 days are divided into nine parts of 20 days. The first part consists of Âindravâyava cups; the second of Śukra and the third of Âgrayaṇa in their proper order (Anuloma), till all the parts are exhausted. In the second session of the six months, the cups are taken in the reverse order (pratiloma) till the 180 days are over, leaving the Viṣuvan day, which intervenes between the first half and second half, intact.

In the Vyûḍhadvâlas'âha the Bhakṣa, Pavamâna, Paridhi and Kapâal are transferred under a Chodaka text. There are Mantras in connection with them; the Bhakṣa mantra will be, as for instance in the three Savanas containing Gâyatrî, Triṣṭup and Jagati, transposed, i. e. the 'Gâyatrî' in place of Triṣṭup, Triṣṭup in place of 'जगती' and Jagati in place of 'Gâyatrî' under the text quoted at p. 757. The question is whether the metres and whole procedure will be interchanged i.e., Gâyatrî metre replacing the Tṛiṣṭupa metre etc. The author's reply is that the entire metre shall not be replaced by another metre but only a verbal change will be made under the principle of Ûha and 'Gâyatrî'.will be substituted in place of 'Triṣṭup'. Similarly in the case of Pavamâna, Paridhi and Kapâla.

PÂDA 6.

The tunes are to be sung in a दृच.	There are, as we have seen several kinds of tunes such as Rathantara, Brihat, Vairûpa Vairâjya, Sakvara, Raivata. These tunes are to be sung in a group of three verses (दृच.)

The verse 'अभिस्वर' should be sung in a रथंतर tune with the eyes closed till 'स्वर्दृश्य' in the text is reached

There is a verse of the Rigveda which is quoted at p. 759 and sung in a Rathantara tune. In the verse there occurs 'स्वर्दृश्य.' In connection with it, there is a direction to a singer 'let him shut his eyes, when a Rathantara tune is sung and let him wait for Svardris'a.' The author says that the text means the closing of the eyes till the singer reaches the word Svardris'a in the verse.

A पृष्ठ song in a गवामयन is to be song alternati-ly in वृहत् and रथंतर tunes.

In a Gavâmayana sacrifice there is a Prishtbya song lasting for six days. It is to be sung in Brihat and Rathantara tunes. The tunes will be sung alternately i.e. one day Brihat and the other day Rathantara for the period of six days.

In an एकादशिनी sacrifice, five animals are sacrificed on the first day and six on the last day.

In an Ekâdas'inî sacrifice, eleven animals are sacrificed. It is said in connection with them that they are to be sacrificed on the first and last days. How are we to divide the odd number into two parts? According to our author five animals are sacrificed on the first day and six animals are sacrificed on the (Udayanîya) (Prayaṇîya) first day and last day.

In a विश्वजित् all the tunes are sung in their order.

In a Vis'vajit all the six tunes are sung; it is, therefore, called Sarvaprṣtha. There is an intervening space between Mâdyamdinapavamâna and Maitrâvaruṇa song; should they be all sung in this space? The reply of the author is that though they are sung at one place, yet their order fixed by the text shall not be disturbed as the Râthantara tune in Pavaman, Brihat tune in Ârhhava and others in Madhyapavamâna. वैरूप tune is of a *hotâ*; Vairâja is that of a Brahmâ, Śakvara is that of a Maitravaruṇa and Raivata is that of an Achchâvâka.

In a पृष्ठ, उक्थ्य and षोडशी are to be sung in वैरूप and वैराज airs.

In a Jyotiṣṭoma sacrifice, there is series of songs called Ukthya and Ṣoḍas'î. Ukthya is sung in a Vairûpa and Ṣoḍas'î in a Vairaja tune. Do these tunes belong to the whole sacrifice? The reply of the author is that these tunes are to be sung in a Prṣtha as they are for its object, but they do not belong to the whole sacrifice.

Similarly when an Agniṣṭoma is said to consist of Trivṛit, it means the songs repeated thrice. The term Trivṛit has been explained in the preceding pages while dealing with the Vedic music. It does not refer to the materials thrice repeated but to the songs only.

त्रिवृत् refers to music.

In a double song, the Bṛihat and Rathantara tunes are combined together, because they are for the purpose of a Pṛaṣtha.

बृहद् रथंतर and tunes are combined together in a double song.

In a Gavâmayana as seen, in dealing with it in the preceding pages, there are two kinds of Ṣaḍaha. There are six songs, sung in षडह as Trivṛit, Panchadas'a, S aptadas'a, Ekavins'a, Trinava and Trayastrins'a.

Ghee or honey should be eaten at the end of a षडह

In the second kind of the Ṣaḍaha the above order is reversed. In that connection, it is said. "In a Ṣaḍaha when Pṛiṣtha is commenced, let him eat honey or clarified butter." The question is, whether ghee or honey should be eaten at the end or in the beginning of a Ṣaḍaha. The reply of the author is that it should be done at the end of the Ṣaḍaha, irrespective of the fact that the षडह ends in the Trayastrins'a or Trivṛit. If a षडह is repeated, the eating of ghee or honey shall not be repeated but it shall be done at the end of the last Ṣaḍaha, because the time for eating is fixed under a text. But

Exception to the rule.

in the first half of the Gavâmayana where Ṣaḍaha occurs in the first, second, third, fourth and fifth months, the eating of ghee or honey is repeated every month, because the last Ṣaḍaha of the first month is separated by the four Abhiplavas of the succeeding months. See at p. 753 of the book.

In a द्वादशाह all sacrificers are entitled to partake of honey.

In a sacrificial session of Dvâdas'âha where all the sacrificers are initiated as priests, they all partake of honey, because the prohibition of honey to a celibate does not relate to partaking of it in a sacrifice.

मानस day is the 10th day of a द्वादशाह.

There is a Mânasa day in a Dvâdas'âha in which earth is imagined as a cup and ocean as soma juice. The lord of the universe is the deity. Such a cup can be uplifted by imagination; cf the Barmecide feast in the Arabian nights. It is done on the 10th day of the Dvâdas'âha, hence the 10th day is called Mânasa day. There is, therefore, no separate day for it.

The model sacrifice of the sacrificial sessions (Satras) such as Dvâdasâha etc. is a Jyotiṣṭoma. As said in the preceding pages many persons are entitled to perform a Satra. The utmost limit is 24 and lowest number is 17. In it all the sacrificers act as priests; they are all initiated and do not get any fee for

In a सत्र there are many sacrificers and they all officiate as priests.

an obvious reason. Dvâdas'âha is both a Satra and Ahîna. In a Satra the chodanâ is governed by the verbal forms of Âsana and उपासि and there is a limited number of sacrificers not more than 24 and not less than 17.

In an Ahîna on the other hand the Chodanâ is governed by the verbal forms of Yajati and the number of the sacrificers is unlimited.

Difference between a सत्र and अहीन.

Further in a Satra all the sacrificers are initiated but in an Ahîna they are uninitiated.

There is a Paûṇḍarika sacrifice lasting for eleven days. About its fee, it is said "Let him give ten thousand, one thousand horses or eleven." The question that arises for solution is whether it is a daily fee or a fee of the whole sacrifice. The author's view is that it is the fee of the whole sacrifice.

The fee of the priest in a पौंडरीक consists of ten thousand cows etc.

The next question for solution is how is this fee to be paid? There are three views on the subject. (1) That one thousand cows should be brought everyday till the tenth day and one thousand horses on the 11th day and after the performance of the purificatory rite they should be given to the priest as their fee. The second view is that all the animals the objects of the gift

In a पौंडरीक sacrifice, the animals after division should be brought on each day and given as fees to the priests.

should be brought purified and given as fee at one time. The third view which is the view of the author, is that the animals should be divided first and then they should be given on each day after bringing them and performing the purificatory ceremoney on them.

In a modified sacrifice it is said "all the verses of Manu become Sâmadhenî verses." The question is whether the verses containing the word 'Manu' in the Rigveda should be imported and treated as Sâmadhenî verses. The reply of the author is that the number of the सामधेनी verses is limited to 15, 17, etc.; so only the limited number required should be imported but not

Only a limited number of the मनु verses required for kindling fire should be imported from the Rigveda.

all the verses containing ' Manu '. The Sâmadenî verses in general have been described in the preceding pages.

The soma creeper is purchased for a sacrifice. It is not weighed in a balance but it is measured in a piece of cloth. It is then carried in a Havirdhâna cart to the sacrificial ground. (See the figure no 1 in the frontispiece.) The piece of cloth which is used for measuring it, is then used for carrying it from the Havirdhâna cart to the place where it is kept for preparation of the juice.

In a ज्योतिष्टोम sacrifice the cloth for measureing soma is used in carrying from the cart to the sacrificial ground.

It is, therefore, the practice in a Jyotiṣṭoma, but in an Ahargaṇa where the sacrifice lasts for many days and the quantity of Soma is excessive, another piece of cloth is used for carrying it from the Havirdhâna cart to the place where *soma* juice is prepared. The piece of cloth for carrying it is procured at the time when it is so carried from the Havirdhâna cart to the sacrificial ground. Only the quantity sufficient for one day is taken out and fetched and the remainder is left there with the piece of cloth. As there are many days, so this process of carrying the soma from the Havirdhâna cart is repeated every day ; another piece of cloth for the purpose is, therefore, indispensable.

But in an अहर्गण one cloth is used for measuring it and another cloth for carrying it from the cart to the sacrificial ground. This cloth is procured at the time of carrying it.

PÂDA 7.

In a Jyotiṣṭoma, there is an Agnîṣomîya animal which is offered in the sacrifice ; the entire animal is not offered but it is killed and its parts are offered. The eleven parts which are specified and which are offered are the following :—

The eleven parts of an animal offered in a ज्योतिष्टोम sacrifice.

(1) the heart (2) the tongue, (3) the thoracic region. (4) the liver. (5 and 6) the two kidneys, (7) the left arm, (8 and 9) the lateral sides, (10) the right buttock and (11) a portion of the arms.

In a Sviṣṭakṛit however the following three parts are offered. (1)

Three parts are to be offered in a हविष्टकृत्.

अध्यूधनी is given to a hotâ in lieu of इडा food in the ज्योतिष्टोम.

The right shoulder, (2) the left buttock and (3) a portion of the arms. They therefore replace the eleven parts of an animal mentioned above. Similarly Adhyûdhnî is given to a hotâ priest in the ज्योतिष्टोम in lieu of Iḍâ food. What is Adhyûdhnî? It is a cow with large udders according to Vâchaspatya. According to Mâdhava, it is some organ other than the eleven parts of an animal enumerated above. Monier Williams says, " it is a tubular vessel above the udder or above the scrotum." According to Dhûrtasvâmî, it means flesh.

In an animal sacrifice.

In an animal sacrifice वनिष्टु is given to an अग्नीध as his food.

वनिष्टु explained.

Vaniṣṭu is given to an Agnîdha priest in lieu of his food. Vaniṣṭu is also, according to Mâdhava, an organ or viscera other than the eleven parts enumerated above. Somanâtha thinks it to be a muscle near the omentum. According to Dhûrtasvâmî, it is a particular part of the large intestine. Monier Williams says " A part of the entrails of an animal offerred in a sacrifice or the particular part of the intestines near the omentum."

A मैत्रावरण has one share in the remnants but a प्रतिप्रस्थाता has none.

A Maitravaruṇa priest gets only one share in the remnants of animal food in a Jyotiṣṭomâ sacrifice, because he assists both an Adhvaryu and a *hotâ* priest; but a Pratiprasthâtâ priest gets no remnants in the animal, because his duty is to boil *omentum*, the whole of which is offered to the deity without leaving any remnants behind.

A गृहमेधीय which is one of the parts of a चातुर्मास्य sacrifice is a model in itself.

and the chodaka texts.

There is a Châturmâsya sacrifice; in it there is Gṛihamedhiya in which the offerings are made to the *Maruts*. In connection with it, it is said " he offers ghee." What is the nature of the text transferred here under a *chodaka* text? There are eight views about it. The first view is that it is a repetition of what is there already in the model sacrifice. In this view, it is an Anuvâda and merely a tautology. The second view is that the text is neither a statement of facts nor does it lay down another sacrifice but it is to emphasise the offering of ghee by repeating the direct The third view is that the text is in the nature of praise and is, therefore, an Arthavâda. The fourth view is that the text inculcates a separate act and in that view it is not an Anuvâda, or an Arthavâda or a repetition to emphasise one action. The fifth view is that the text is by way of Parisankhyâ and shows that only the ghee oblations but not other details from the model sacrifice shall be transferred. The sixth view is that the text is not a Parisankhyâ by reason of its inherent three-fold defects ; why should you import the chodaka text from the model sacrifice when you have already a direct text in the modified sacrifice ? When there is no direct text, you can import it from the model sacrifice. The seventh view is that the principle of Atides'a applies and only the ghee oblations are transferred under the chodaka text. The eighth or the last view which is the view of the

In a गृहमेधीय, स्विष्टकृत् is borrowed under a text.

author is that the Grihamedhîya is a model itself and it has its own extraordinary principle. Only those details which are mentioned by the direct text are borrowed in the Grihamedhîya but no more. In this view, the Svistakrit offering which is directly mentioned is, therefore,

Remnants of स्विष्टकृत् are not eaten.

borrowed in the Grihamedhîya. Further the remnants of the Svistakrit offerings are not eaten in the Grihamedhîya as the text is silent about them and operates as Parisankhyâ.

In connection with a Jyotistoma sacrifice, it is said, " They sit up to the end of शंयु in a प्रावणीया but do not perform the Patnîsanyâja ; they perform an Âtithyâ up to the end of Idâ food but do not perform the Anuyâja. The question is whether the Prâyanîyâ is to be completed with the reading of Śanyu and the Âtithyâ is to be finished with the Idâ food. It will be better to explain the procedure in order to understand the text. In the model sacrifice, when ' तच्छंयो: ' is read loudly, the Adhvaryu priest throws the Paridhis in the sacrificial fire.

The प्रावणीय is finished with शंयुवाक and the अतिथ्या with the इडा food.

After this, from the remnants of the food, Patnîsanyâja is performed. The entire series of the procedure runs thus (1) the principal sacrifice (2) Naristahoma (3) eating of the Pras'itra etc., (4) eating of the Idâ food (5) Anuyâja (6) Sûktavâka (7) Śanyuvâka (8) Patnîsamyâja (9) Phalîkaranahoma (10) Prâyas'chittahoma (11) Isti by means of potsherds on which purificatory ceremony is performed. The objector's view is that in the modified sacrifice all the details enamurated above should be performed with the exception of the item no. (8) under the above quoted text which is in the nature of Parisankhyâ. The author's view is that the Prâyanîyâ should end with the item no.   7 and no further details should be performed. Similarly, the Åtithyâ should end with the eating of the Iḍâ food.

In the model sacrifice there are two sorts of Śanyuvâka and Iḍâbhakṣaṇa, one before Patnîsamyâja and the other after it. Which Śanyuvâka or Iḍâbhakṣaṇa is meant in the Prâyaṇîya or Åtithyâ respectively under the above quoted text? The author's view is that the first in both of them is meant, because the prohibition relating to the Patnîsanyâja in the text under consideration clearly shows it and further there is an authority which is quoted at p.p. 805-806.

The प्रायणीयो and अतिथ्या are to end in the first शंयुवाक and इडाभक्षण respectively before the पत्नीसंयाज

In a Jyotiṣṭoma sacrifice there are six Upasads, namely, Agni, Anîka, Soma, Śalya, Viṣṇu and Tejana. It is said about them that they are to be performed without Prayâjas and Anuyâjas.

The whole text in connection with them is " No other offering should be made first. If he offers other offerings first, he shall turn his face aside, because fire is the mouth of the oblations. He sprinkles ghee with a ladle ; he does not make any offering such as one to Agni, Anîka, Soma, Viṣṇu and Tejana. The meaning of the text is that an offering of ghee from the Sruva is made in the beginning of every sacrifice ; but if an ignorant man without making this preparatory ceremony makes any other offering in the Upasads, he gets into difficulties by this transposition. It is, therefore, incumbent that the preliminary offering of ghee from the Sruva should be made.

As to the interpretation of the text, there are three views (1) that Prayâjas and Anuyâjas alone should not be performed and the rest of the details should be performed in the Upasads. It is a prohibitory text as far as Pryâjas and Anuyâjas are concerned but is in the nature of Pratiprasava as to the performance of the rest of the details. The second view is that it is by way of Parisankhyâ and means that all the details should be performed with the exception of the Prayâjas and Anuyâjas. The third view which is the author's view is that the text is a pure statement of facts and the Upasads are models in themselves. Only the first ghee offering is made to Agni and the other offerings are made without ghee to other deities.

Pratiprasava means allowing a thing which has been prohibited once with certain conditions attached. As for instance, bathing is strictly prohibited to a patient but it is permissible to him with certain conditions attached.

प्रतिप्रसव explained.

A sacrificial bath in a ज्योतिष्टोम is a model in itself.

In a Jyotiṣṭoma sacrifice, there is a sacrificial bath resorted to with a cake baked on one potsherd to Varuṇa. In that connection, it is said, " he offers Prayâjas without varhi ; he offers two Anuyâjas without Varhi." There are three views as to the interpretation of the text ; the first view is that with the exception of the 4th offering in the Prayâja called Varhi and the 1st offering of the Anuyâja all the other offerings should be performed, because only the Varhiyâga is prohibited. The second view is that the text is in the nature of Parisankhyâ and the rest of the details excepting the ghee offerings are prohibited. The third view of the author is that the sacrificial bath is a model in itself, because if you look upon the text as a Parisankhyâ you split up one sentence into two by considering the laying down of the ghee offering and prohibiting the other details as two distinct commands. In this view, only that much which is expressly laid down should be performed.

Restrictive rule (नियम) as to materials in some sacrifices.

In a Vâjapeya sacrifice, a sacrificial post has been prescribed to be made of Khadira wood. A Yûpa is constructed from Khadira, Palâs'a or Rohataka wood. According to our author, the text in connection with the construction of the sacrificial post from the Khadira wood in a Vâjapeya is by way of a restrictive rule (नियम.) Similarly the text restricting a वृह to a वृहत tune and in a Traidhatavîya, the text restricting the making of the middle cake from barley are by way of Niyama.

The desire accomplishing sacrifices, have their own deities and materials but do not borrow them from the model sacrifice.

In the desire accomplishing sacrifices, the deity and the materials of the model sacrifice, are replaced by their own deity and materials specially enjoined for a special purpose. There is, therefore, no occasion for the application of the Chodaka texts which operate in the case of other details about which the texts are silent.

The text which allows खदिर-made sacrificial post to be used in a सौमापौष्ण is by way of नियम,

In a Saûmâpaûṣṇa sacrifice which is performed with the desire to possess cattle, a sacrificial post is specially prescribed to be made of Udambara wood ; but in the model sacrifice the sacrificial post is made of Khadira wood. In view of the principle laid down above, the sacrificial post made of Udambara wood replaces the sacrificial post made of Khadira wood and the text which lays down the Khadira wood for the construction of the sacrificial post is by way of Niyama.

It is said, " one who is desirous of Brahmaṇic glory shall offer Charu made of white wild rice and boiled in ghee to Soma and Rudra............ ", while on the other hand, in the model sacrifice barley is used. According to the principle laid down above, barley of the model sacrifice will be replaced by the wild rice of the special direct text which prescribes it in case one is desirous of the Brahmaṇic glory.

Wild rice is used as **व्रष** *for an offering, if one is desirous of Brahmaṇic glory.*

Before I proceed to explain the concluding *adhikaraṇa*, it is better for me to explain the terms Pañchâvattîya and Chaturvattîya. Pañchâvattîya is an oblation consisting of fivefold cuts of ladled ghee. Ghee is taken in a ladle : it is offered five times instead of offering it once to the fire. Sâyana has explained it in the Taittarîya Sanhitâ as " offering five times from the collected ghee." It appears that a certain family of priests makes Pañchvatta offerings and is therefore called Pañchvattîya and similarly the family of priests who make Chaturvatta offerings is called Chaturvattiya. The terms consequently came to denote the clans as explained at p. 818.

पंचावर्त्ती *and* **चतुर्वर्त्ती** *explained.*

There is a text in connection with the animal sacrifice in a Jyotiṣtoma " though a sacrificer is a Chaturvattî, yet the five offerings are to be made from the *omentum*." The objector's view is that the Pañchâvatta offering of a thing five times as explained above applies to the omentum only ; but our author says that the text quoted above applies to the other parts as well. In this view the fivefold cuts of an offering are applicable to the parts of an animal and the omentum as well.

पंचावत्त *applies to the parts of an animal and the omentum.*

<hr>

PÂDA 8.

There is a text in connection with the Mahâpitriyâga "he does not appoint a *hotâ*, nor does he repeat the names of the Ṛiṣis" ; but in the model sacrifice a priest is appointed and the gotra is repeated. As there is a Chodaka text which permits the appointment of a priest and repetition of the gotra and on the contrary there is a direct text which prohibits them,

The prohibition as to the appointment of a priest in a **महारपितृयाग** *is by way of* **पर्युदास.**

prima facie, it would appear that there is option in performing or not performing them. But according to our author the prohibitory direct text is by way of Paryudâsa or partial prohibition and means that the Mahâpitriyâga should be performed with all the details of the model sacrifice with the exception of the appointment of the priest and the repetition of the *gotra.* Similarly the text "............therefore in Anuyâja 'येयजामहे' is not uttered" is by way of पर्युदास and means that 'Ye Yajâmahe' should be repeated everywhere save and except Anuyâjas.

There are two Âjyabhâgas in the new and full moon sacrifices. Taking them as models, it is said, "he does not perform those two in an animal sacrifice nor in a soma sacrifice." The text cannot be considered a Paryudâsa in connection with the Somayâga and cannot therefore, mean that all the details of the new and full moon sacrifices should be performed in a Somayâga with the exception of the ghee offerings. It is not a Pratiṣedha as you cannot transfer the text to the Somayâga which is a model in itself. Consequently the text is an Arthavâda and therefore means that as the ghee offerings are not made in a soma sacrifice, so they are not made in an animal sacrifice.

Ghee oblations are not made in soma and animal sacrifices.

When there are two contradictory texts, they are optional. As for example, in connection with a Jyotiṣṭoma sacrifice it is laid down, "He takes Ṣodas'î cup in an Atirâtra; he does not take Ṣodas'î in an Atirâtra." The texts cannot be Paryudâsa, nor can they be in the nature of Arthavâda. In this view, taking of the Ṣodas'î is optional.

The optional nature of two contradictory texts.

In connection with an Agnihotra, it is laid down, "Let him offer gruel made of wild *sesamum,* let him offer gruel made of wild wheat................The wild *sesamum* and wild wheat are not fit for offerings. Let him offer them with milk." Here is an example of a pratiprasava ; first you prescribe the wild *sesamum* and wild wheat as offerings, then you forbid them but ultimately you permit their offering with milk. The above quoted verse is, therefore, by way of an Arthavâda according to our author and is in praise of milk.

Permitting of wild sesamum and wild wheat as an offering with milk is by way of अर्थवाद.

Similarly the text in connection with the Trambakahoma of Châturmâsya as to the determination of the performance or non-performance of the sprinkling of ghee and the text in connection with the establishment of fire as to the determination of the performance or

Other illustrations of the अर्थवाद nature of the texts.

non-performance of an Agnihottra are by way of Arthavâda and are in praise of the ceremonies which form the subject of the serious determination.

In connection with the establishment of fire there are texts which enjoin Varavantîya Yajñâyajñîya and Vamadeva songs; but it is also said there, "his fires are deserted by delay, if Brah mâ sings songs in an establishment of fire." As those two texts are contradictory, so the singing of Soma is optional.

Optional nature of the text as to singing of songs in the establishment of fire.

In connection with a Jyotiṣṭoma sacrifice, it is said, "An initiated does not make a gift, perform a sacrifice or cook food." There are 4 views as to the interpretation of the text. The first view is that all gifts, sacrifices and preparations of food are prohibited, because there is no word to limit it to anything special. The second view is that the text prohibits only those gifts etc., which are for the object of man (Puruṣârtha) because the object of the sacrifice (Kratvartha) is directly laid down and cannot therefore, be prohibited. The third view is that only those details which are transferred by a Chodaka text from the model sacrifice are prohibited. The fourth view which is that of our author, is that the text is by way of Paryudâsa and prohibits only the Puraṣârthâ, but not the Kratvârtha otherwise it will put a stop to the sacrifice itself.

पयु दास nature of the text which prohibits all initiated from making donation &c.

A special text predominates over a general text ; as for instance, there is a general text, " By whatever he offers in an Ahavanîya, his desired one is pleased ; (Anârabhyavidhi.)

A special text has a preference to a general text.

There are special texts (1) " he offers on a step ; he offers in the way, in a Jyotiṣṭoma (2) ; in a Râjasûya, it is said having taken the fat of a white ant, he makes an offering," (3) somewhere it is laid down " he makes Patnisannyâja offerings in a Gârhapatya fire." In this state of conflict between the Anârabhya and the special texts, the special texts according to our author prevail over the general text.

There is a general text to the effect " Let him pronounce seventeen Sâmadhenî verses at the end." Then again in Vaimridha and Adhvarakalpa etc., the same text is repeated. What is the effect of these two texts ? The author's view is that they are in the nature of compliment to each other. The Anârabhya text is an injunction and

Supplementary nature of the special text when it is a repetition of the general text.

he special text in the Vaimridha etc., is a supplementary text. Both of them form one complete text.

There is a general text, " Food is offered to the gods with Vaṣaṭ or Svâhâ ". In a Darvihoma which is a model, there is a special text "Svâhâ to the earth ; Svâhâ to intervening space ; Svâhâ to the wind." The special text is not a supplementary text, because there is no supplement in a Mantra. It is, therefore, for the purpose of emphasing the utterance of Svâhâ in order to attain the invisible fruit.

The special text in the दर्विहोम to utter स्वाहा। is not a supplementary text.

It is said, " He who knows this, piles up fire ;" again as regards cups, it is said, " It is the support of the sacrifice namely the Atigrâhya cup." The question is whether the Agnichayana and the Atigrâhya cup should be transferred to the modified sacrifice or not, because there is no *chodaka* text. The reply of our author is that just as other details are transferable, so also are the fire and cup, under the Atides'a or Upades'a, because these acts are of Samânavidhi for which there is a direct text prescribed in the model sacrifice and similar text in the m odified sacrifice.

Fire and the अतिग्राह्य cup are transferable, because they are of the class of समानविधि directing their transfer. समानविधि explained.

In connection with the Dars'apûrṇamâsayâgas it is said 'he offers four parts (Chaturvattam). The question is whether Chaturvatta applies to the Puroḍâs'a cake only or to the pouring and sprinkling of ghee. The reply of the author is that the Chaturvattâ applies to the pouring and sprinkling of ghee as well as the Puroḍâs'a cake. According to Monier Williams Upastaraṇa is pouring of ghee in a sacrifice and Abhighâraṇa is the sprinkling of the same. Chaturvatta is made up of pouring of ghee once, offering of cake once and sprinkling of ghee twice. These are the four parts.

चतुरवत्ता applies to उपस्तरण and अभिघारण as well along with the पुरोडाश cake.

There are silent offerings made in the new and full moon sacrifices called Upâms'u Yâga. The question is, whether Chaturvattâ applies to the Upâms'uyâga or not. The reply of our author is that it applies to the Upâms'uyâga also as it is the characteristic of a *homa*.

चतुरवत्ता applies to the उपांशुयाग.

Different views as to the interpretation of the text which permits cakes to अग्नि and ऐन्द्राग्न and milk in certain contengencies.

In connection with the Dars'apûrṇamâsayâgas there is a text, "Let him make one who has not performed a Somayâga, offer two Puroḍâs'a cakes consecrated to Agni and Aindrâgna; on the other hand, one who has performed *soma* shall be made to offer Sannâya." As to the interpretation of the text there are seven views; the first view is that it confers a right and is, therefore, a Śeṣa of another text, 'Let one who is desirous of heaven, perform a sacrifice.' In this view the text means that a person desirous of heaven should perform the sacrifice with these two Puroḍâs'a cakes. It is an Adhikâravidhi investing a sacrificer with a certain right to which he is entitled in case he is desirous of heaven and wishes to perform the sacrifice without *soma*. The second view is that the text is not a Śeṣa of an Adhikâravidhi but it lays down separate acts apart from the Dars'apûrṇamâsayâgas. In this view, the text means that an Asomayâjî desirous of heaven should offer sacrificial cakes to Agni and Aindrâgna. The third view is that the text is a direction for a priest. It therefore means that a person who is not a Somayâjî but is desirous of heaven should be made to offer these two sacrificial cakes. The fourth view is that the text lays down time; it therefore, means that when the sacrifices are performed by a person who has not previously performed a Somayâga he shall have to make an offering of the sacrificial cakes to Agni and Aindrâgna. The fifth view is that the text is by way of a statement of facts as far as the cake to Agni is concerned, because it is permitted in both the full and new moon sacrifices under a text quoted at the bottom of p. 838 and is a Vidhi in laying down the offering of the Aindrâgna in the full moon sacrifice only. The sixth view is that of Bâdarayaṇa; according to him the text lays down time. In this view the text is by way of a Pratiprasava as to the milk offering; the text, therefore, means that a Somayâjî and an Asomayâjî are both entitled to offer the Aindrâgna cakes optionally on the new moon day. The offering of the Aindrâgna cakes is before the performance of a Somayâga and there should be no offering of Sannâya subsequently. The seventh and the last is the author's view; he says that the text is in the nature of Annvâda as regards both the full and new moon sacrifices. In this view the text means that an Asomayâjî offers two Puroḍâs'a cakes, namely, Agneya and Aindrâgna and one who is a Somayâjî performs the offering with Sannâya.

Ghee offerings are made from the ध्रुवा vessel in an उपांशुयाग.

In the full and new moon sacrifices, an Upâns'uyâga is performed in the interval. In it, ghee offering is made from the Dhruvâ vessel. As to the figure of Dhruvâ see diagram No. 14 in vol. 1 of Dars'apûrṇmâsaprakâs'a of Ânandâs'rama series No. 93.

The deity of an उपांशुयाग is from the context where it happens to be.

The Upâns'uyâga is regulated by the context of slowly pronouncing the verses. The deity of the Vidhyanta is, therefore, the deity of the Upâns'uyâga. As the Upâns'uyága happens to be performed in the Dars'apûrṇamâsayâga the deity thereof is the deity of the Upâns'uyâga.

The other questions for determination are, who is the deity of the context that governs an Upâns'uyâga and when should it be performed whether on the new moon or the full moon day? There are several views on the subject discussed at length in the Adhikaraṇa. The first views is that Prajâpati is the deity of an Upâns'uyâga, because in a Prâjâpatya sacrifice everything is done silently. The second view is that the deity of the Upâns'uyâga is not Prajâpati but Agni. The third view is that, that an Upâns'uyâga is performed on a new moon day and the deity of the new moon sacrifice *viz.*, Viṣṇu is the diety of the Upâns'uyâga. The last view is the view of our author; he says that the Upâns'uyâga is performed on the full moon day and the deities are Viṣṇu, Prajâpati and Agnîṣoma under the text, " Viṣṇu should be worshipped with the silent offerings in order to avoid repetition ; the Lord of the universe should be worshipped with the silent offerings in order to avoid repetition ; Agnîṣoma should be worshipped with the silent offerings in order to avoid repetition." In support of his view that the Upâns'uyâga is performed on the full moon day, he relies on the Linga argument based upon the text which lays down fourteen offerings in the full moon sacrifice and the thirteen offerings in new moon sacrifice. The one offering in the new moon sacrifice is cut down by reason of the absence of the Upâns'uyâga in it.

There is a text in connection with the new and full moon sacrifices " He performs an Upâns'uyâga in the interval." We have seen that the Upâns'uyâga is performed in the full moon sacrifice. There are two kinds of full moon sacrifices ; one is performed before the performance of a Somayâga and the other is performed after it. In the first kind, only one cake is offered to Ágni and in the other, two cakes are offered to Agnîṣoma. The question is whether the Upâns'uyâga should be performed in the offering of one cake also. The opponent's view is that there cannot be an interval in the offering of one cake, so the Upâns'uyâga should be performed in the interval of the two cakes that are offered in the full moon sacrifice after the performance of the Somayâga. On the contrary, the author's view is that it should be also performed after the offering of one cake to Agni.

CHAPTER XI.

PÂDA 1.

The author treats of Tantra and Âvâpa in the eleventh chapter. An act which benefits many individuals or subordinate parts is called Tantra, while an act which confers benefit on one individual only is called Âvâpa ; as for example sifting of the husk from the rice by means of a pestle and mortar constitutes Tantra, as several grains can be thus cleansed at a time by this process but if you peel off the husk from an individual rice by your finger nails, this process is called Âvâpa because only one grain can be cleansed at a time, by means of it.

तंत्र and आवाप explained.

There is a text "Let one desirous of heaven perform new and full moon sacrifices." In the new and full moon sacrifices there are six sacrifices as for instance Agneya etc. Do all of them distributively or collectively conduce to the attainment of heaven ? According to the objector, each of them separately is the cause of obtaining heaven. When one orders another to besmear a Brâhman assembly with sandal paste, he thereby means to besmear each Brâhman constituting the assembly with sandal paste. The author's view is that it is absurd to hold that each constitutent part of the new and full moon sacrifice, is the cause of the attainment of heaven as there will be several heavens ; but it stands to reason that all of them constituting the new and full moon sacrifices contribute to the attainment of one main result. When it is said that a particular well was constructed by the whole village, it does not mean that each and every inhabitant of the village constructed it separately but what it means is that all of them collectively constructed it. The principle deduced from it is that if there are several principals and the object is one, the subsidiary act will be performed once for all, because they all

When the object of several primaries is one, the subsidiaries thereof should not be repeated but if the object of the primaries is different the subsidiaries shall be repeated.

collectively secure one object ; but if the object of each principal is separate, the subsidiary act will be repeated in the case of each.

Similarly the subordinate parts which constitute one whole sacrifice collectively, but not separately conduce to the attainment of the one main result of the sacrifice. As said repeatedly, the Bhâvanâ is made up of the Sâdhya, Sâdhanâ and the Itikartavyatâ. The subordinate parts come under the Itikartayatâ and therefore collectively achieve the main result of an act.

Subordinate parts of an act collectively contribute to the attainment of one main result.

There are several subordinate parts in a sacrifice ; there are amongst them which achieve certain desires of a sacrificer. Why should all the parts be performed when a particular desire is accomplished by performance of a particular part ? The reply of our author after discussing the different views is that a sacrifice should be completed with all its subordinate parts intact in order to achieve the main object of it under the chief injunctive text. The full and new moon sacrifices mean the principal sacrifice with their subordinate parts.

A sacrifice means a sacrifice with the principal and its constutuent parts.

The next question for determination is, whether the desire accomplishing acts should be performed once or repeatedly. The author says that as a man has desires at all times of his life, he should perform the desire accomplishing sacrifices repeatedly.

Repeated performance of the desire accomplishing acts.

When the object of an act is visible, it should be repeated till the object is accomplished, but where the object of an act is invisible, it need not be repeated and mere compliance with the text is sufficient. As for instance, where the object is to remove husk from the rice grains, the strokes of the pestle on the grains in the mortar should be repeated till the husk is removed from all the grains ; but in a religious act where the object is to achieve an invisible result, one stroke in order to comply with the injunctive text under which pounding is performed is sufficient to comply with the word of the text.

An act should be repeated in order to achieve the visible object but in a religious act where the object aimed at is invisible it need not be repeated.

The next question is whether the subordinate parts such as Prayâjas of a principal should be repeatedly performed to achieve an excessive fruit. The author says that they are the constituent parts of a principal. The principal and its subordinate parts all jointly achieve the main fruit of the sacrifice. In this view the subordinate parts should not be repeated.

Subordinate parts of a principal should not be repeated, as the object of all of them is to achieve the main result.

When a word is used in a plural number, it denotes the minimum number out of the numerals in the absence of any word denoting the contrary intention. As for instance there is a text "वसंताय कपिंजलमालभेत" "Let him bring the partridges for a sacrifice." The word 'partridges,' is used in plural; here there is no cardinal adjective to denote the exact number and means from three to million. The author's view is that when there is no cardinal adjective of quantity to denote the exact number, the plural substantive noun denotes the lowest number *viz.*, 3. The reason is obvious; the lowest number of partridges will cause the least sin arising from unnecessary slaughter of birds. There is also a Linga argument in

कपिंजन्याय explained.

therefore, the ' partridges ' means from three to million. The author's

The plural number denotes the lowest number three in the absence of any word conveying the contrary intention.

support of the author's view. "The black are consecrated to Yama, the arrogant to Rudra, and the sky coloured to the god of rains ; of them the tenth, therefore, belongs to Indra and Agni." The last tenth is possible only when each of the first three deities has three animals (mentioned in plural numbers) as their separate shares.

There is another text " Having controlled his tongue and milked three cows, he breaks silence and having commenced silence he milks *others*." Here ' others ' is used in a plural number. What does it man? Does it mean the ' three other cows,' as a plural number denotes the lowest number three under the Kapinjalanyâya?

In the text the other cows used in plural denote the entire number of cows possessed by a sacrificer.

The author says that here in the text a different intention is denoted. The cows are already milked and the remaining cows-whether their number be three or more-are to be milked, because there is a text which shows that no Agnihotra is performed with milk on that night, and no children get milk for drinking by reason of the milk of the entire stock of the cows being offered to the deity.

In the new and full moon sacrifices, Agneya etc., are the primaries and Âghâra etc., are the subsidiaries. The question is whether the subsidiaries in each primary should be separately performed or their performance once is quite sufficient. The objector's view is that the subsidiaries should be separately performed in each primary under which they fall; but our author's view is that they are all governed by one *vidhi* text and come under the general head of the new and

In the new and full moon sacrifices, the subsidiaries shall not be repeated with each primary but their performance once for all is quite sufficient.

full moon sacrifices; they all jointly contribute to the attainment of heaven, the main object of the sacrifices. Further there is no special direction for the performance of the subsidiaries; they are all on equal footing with respect to the performer, time and place. In this view, they are to be performed once for all and there is, therefore, no necessity for repeating them in the case of each primary.

There is a text " Let one competing for the foremost position bring a black-necked animal to Agni, a reddish brown animal to Soma and black-necked animal to Agni." Here we see that the first and the third animals are the same; why should not they be simultaneously offered on the principle of Tantra as explained above. The reply of our author is that they cannot be offered simul-

The principle of तंत्र does not apply when a different animal intervenes between two similar animals.

taneously, because first, time is an important factor and secondly, the reddish brown animal consecrated to Soma comes in the middle and if the first and the third animals consecrated to Agni are offered simultaneously, the order given in the text will be disturbed. For all these reasons, the principle of Tantra does not apply.

PÂDA 2.

In the foregoing Pâda the author has considered the principle of Tantra as applicable to the primary and now he proceeds to consider it as applicable to the subsidiaries.

The principle of Tantra does not apply to the Agneya etc., the primaries of the full and new moon sacrifices as regards space, time and agent; they are, therefore, governed in these matters by the principle of Âvâpa. This is the view of Śabara, but the view of other commentators is just the opposite of it.

The primaries in the दर्श and पूर्णमासयागः are governed by the principle of आवाप in matters of space, time and agent.

In the case of the subsidiaries that come under one primary the rule of Tantra but not that of Âvâpa governs time, space and agent, because the subordinate parts subserve the main object; they are not apart from the principal. The text with reference to space, time and agent governing the principal governs its parts also. If the materials and deities of the subsidiaries are combined with those of the primaries, the principle of Tantra will apply, because the subsidiaries therein come under their primary; but if on the otherhand, there is a separation, the principle of Âvâpa will apply, because in that case they are themselves primaries. The new and full moon sacrifices consist of two sacrifices called new moon sacrifice and full moon sacrifice each having six primaries. In a Râjasûya, there are Anumati etc., the fire oblations and Pavittra etc., soma offerings. Similarly in the Châturmâsya there are वैश्वदेव, वरुणप्रघास, साकमेध and. शुनासीरीय four independent sacrifices. The author says that the principle of Âvâpa governs the Iṣṭis, Râjasûya and Châturmâsya in their subsidiary actions; the reason is obvious. The Iṣṭi which consists of Dars'a and Pûrṇamâsayâgas has two independent acts. The subsidiaries of the full moon sacrifice shall, therefore, be performed on the full moon day and those of the new moon sacrifice shall be similarly performed on the new moon day. The principle of Tantra cannot, therefore, apply. The same principle holds good in the case of the Râjasûya and Châturmâsyas which are also made up of several independent acts.

The principle of तंत्र governs the subsidiaries under a primary in matters of space, time and agent.

The principle of आवाप governs the इष्टिs, राजसूय and चातुर्मास्यs.

There is a desire-accomplishing sacrifice called Adhvarakalpeṣti in connection with which it is said, " Let one whose enemy perform soma-Yâga offer cakes baked on eight potsherds to Agni and Viṣṇu in the morning and boiled rice to Saraswatî and Brihaspati and cakes baked on eleven potsherds to Agni and Viṣṇu in the noon and boiled rice to Saraswata and Brishaspati and cakes baked on twelve potsherds to Agni and Viṣṇu in the afternoon and rice to Saṛawata and Brihaspati." The question is whether the offerings of the three different times should be made on the principle of Âvâpa or Tantra. In the morning when people are aroused by the speech of the priests, says the objector, the performance should be made once for all in the morning. The author's reply is that the offer-

The आग्नेवैष्णव offerings should be made on the principle of आवाप in the अध्वरकल्पेष्टि.

ings should be made at the fixed time and their subordinate parts follow them. Each is to be performed with all its parts on the principle of Tantra ; but in relation to each other the performance is on the principle of Âvâpa, because they are independent acts *inter se.*

The principle varies in the case of वसाहोम.

Vasâhoma should be performed on the principle of Tantra where there is unity of deity and time of performance as in a Prâjâpatya where 17 animals are offered ; but where the deities are different at different times, it is impossible to apply the principle of Âvâpa will, therefore, apply as in and the offerings are made at different times, it is impossible to apply the principle of Tantra. The the case of an Ekâdas'inî.

A यूपाहुति is made once for all in an एकादशिनी sacrifice.

The Yûpâhuti should be performed once in the Ekâdas'inî, because an offering is made in the fire produced near the sacrificial post by friction but not in the Âhavanîya which is already there. It is done only once, lest in the several operations of friction the sacrificial posts might not catch fire.

In an अवभृथ ceremony the primary with all its subsidiaries is per-formed.

Avabhritha a sacrificial bath is performed at the end of the Jyotiṣ-ṭoma sacrifice. At that time a cake baked on a potsherd is offered to Varuṇa ; as there is no Ahavaniya, says the objector, the Âghâra etc., which are the subsidiaries shall not be per-formed. The author's view is that the primary with all its subsidiaries should be performed and nothing should be omitted. Water forms the part of the Avabhritha ceremony.

In the वरुणप्रघास the offerings in the northern and southern altars are performed separate-ly on the principle of आवाप.

In the Varuṇapraghâsa there are 8 offerings such as अग्नेय etc., made in the northern hearth and an offering of Âmikṣâ to Marut is made in the southern hearth. Here we have two altars separately. The text in connection with them is that " an Adhvaryu priest plaṇes the 8 offerings on the northern hearth and a Pratiprasthâta priest places the offering consecrated to Marut on the southern hearth." We see that we have two different altars where two different offerings are made by two different priests. The ceremonies cannot be performed on the principle of Tantra by reason of this difference ; the principle of Avâpa, therefore, applies and these two sets of offerings shall be performed separately.

In the Châturmâsya ceremonies of which Varunapraghâsa is a part, there are five priests namely Adhwaryû, Pratiprasthâta, Hotâ, Agnîdhra and Brahmâ. They all in combination perform the ceremonies. The Varunapraghâsa is no exception to it ; the offerings in the northern and southern altars as far as the priests are concerned are governed by the principle of Tantra ; and the same set of priests, therefore, performs the ceremonies in the northern and southern altars.

The same set of priests performs the ceremonies in the northern and southern altars in the वरुणप्रघास.

The Patnîsânyâjas which are performed in the Gârhapatya fire in the northern and southern Vîhâras in the Varunapraghâsa are governed by the principle of Âvâpa by reason of the difference of the priests. The Patnîsanyâjas in the northern hearth are performed by an Adhvaryu priest and those in the southern hearth are performed by a Pratiprasthâta priest. The principle of Tantra does not, therefore, apply to them.

But the पत्नीसंयाज are performed separately.

In the Vâjapeya sacrifice, seventeen animals are transferred from the model sacrifice. It is said in that connection "they relinquish those round whom fire has been taken ; they bring them to the sacrifice with the Brahmasâma. There are two views about it ; the first view which is that of the objector is that taking the fire brand round the victims and their relinquishment like that of the wild animals in the As'vamedha indicate the completion and bringing of the animals to the sacrifice indicates another act.

In a वाजपेय the subsidiary ceremonies after performing पर्यग्निकरण on the animals are postponed till after the bringing them to the sacrifice at the time of singing ब्रह्मसाम.

The author rejects the view as being opposed to the principle of unity of a sentence (Vâkyaîkatva). He says that the text is a prohibitory text as to the performance of the subsidiary acts and postponing them till after the bringing of the victims to the sacrifice at the time of singing Brahmasâmas.

On the other hand in the Pañchas'âradîya sacrifices which are Ahîna in their nature and performed annually for a period of five years, seventeen cows are sacrificed and seventeen oxen are relinquished as given in the text quoted at p. 901. Now the question is whether these seventeen oxen thus relinquished are to be kept in reserve for

The principle of the अश्वमेध wild animal governs the seventeen oxen of the पंचशारदीय sacrifices.

the fifth year or are to be relinquished every year. The author says that
the relinquishment of the seventeen oxen in the first year indicates the
completion of the sacrifice for that year and the same process is to be
repeated every year.   These annual sacrifices and relinquishments of
animals are to be repeated every year ; the principle of the As'vamedha
wild animals but not the Prâyâpatya animals, in the Vâjapeya governs
them.

In a coronation ceremony, there is Abhiṣechaniya, a one-day soma
sacrifice ; then there are offerings called
Samsripa and then follows Das'apeya another
Ekâha soma sacrifice. As there are two soma
sacrifices called Abhiṣechanîya and Das'papeya
sufficient quantity of soma is religiously pur_
chased. The question is, whether the subsidiary
ceremonies of these two soma sacrifices should
be performed once for all or separately, because

The subsidiary ceremonies of अभिषेचनीव and बथपेव are separately performed though सोम is purchased for them sufficiently in the beginning.

soma is purchased once for all for them. The reply is that they should
be separately performed. Though *soma* is purchased in the beginning
in sufficient quantity for the sacrifice, yet it is done nominally under a
command ("यः : सोमं क्रीणाति" "he purchases soma at once.") in the
Das'apeya.

In the Varuṇapraghâsa which is a division of the Châturmâsya
sacrifice, there is a sacrificial bath of which it is said. "They resort
to the bath with the remnants of husk and the curd dish consecrated to
Varuṇa."

In the Varuṇapraghâsa there are nine offerings ; the eighth offering
consists of the curd-dish to Varuṇa and the 9th
is an offering of a cake baked on one potsherd
to the Lord of the universe. A calf made of
barley flour is placed in the curd dish ;

The अवभृथ in the वरुणप्रघास is a separate act in itself.

having sacrifi ced it, and then setting about with the cake baked on one
potsherd, they go to bath with the remnants of the curd dish and the
husk of barley. About the resort to the bath with the remnants of the
curd dish and the husk of barley, there are three views ; the first is that
it is a separation of proceeding ; the second is that it is a mode of final
disposal (Pratipattikarma) and the third view which is the view of the
author is, that it is a separate act in itself.

In connection with

The उदयनीय च is an अर्थं कर्म.

the Jyotiṣṭoma it is said "with the remnants of the Prâyaṇîya they complete the Udayanîya." About the interpretation of this text, there are three views similarly. The first is that the Udayanîya is a separate act in itself like the sacrificial bath in the preceding *ahdikarna*. The second view is that it is a mode of final disposal (Pratipattikarma.) The third which is the author's view is that it is an Arthakarma and produces an Apûrva or invisible effect.

PÂDA 3.

In this pâda the author proceeds to determine the principle of Tantra as applicable to the subsidiaries which are performed on different occasions.

As regards, time, space and agent, the subsidiaries are governed by their primaries.

As a rule the time, space and agent of the subsidiaries are the same as they are in the principal but when a Vedic text directs otherwise it shall be so acted upon ; *e. g.* an altar is made in the forenoon on the new moon day (time) ; sacrificial bath is performed in water (space) ; and in a Saûtramaṇi there is difference of agents by reason of the difference of fees.

The ceremony of establishment of fire should be performed once for all on the principle of तंत्र at the appointed time before any sacrifice is performed.

There is special time fixed for various castes to establish fire under a text quoted at p. 908. The ceremony of establishment of fire (Agnyâdhâna) should be performed once for all. The fire can be taken for the use of any sacrifice that may be performed at a different time from that of the Agnyâdhâna, because it is indispensable in every sacrifice and should be performed before it.

The principle of तंत्र applies to the sacrificial post in a ज्योतिष्टोम, applies to the sacrificial post and there is no need of having many posts for the purpose.

In a Jyotiṣṭoma there are three animals *viz.*, Savanîya, Agniṣomîya and Anubandhya. They are sacrificed at different times ; one sacrificial post is quite sufficient for them. It is, therefore, constructed once for all. The principle of Tantra, therefore,

The principle of तंत्र applies to the purificatory ceremonies performed on a यूप.

Similarly the purificatory ceremonies such as washing, anointing, erecting and cutting of the sacrificial post are performed once for all on the principle of Tantra,

The principle of तंत्र applies to स्वरु used in anointing animals.

Svaru is an ornamental chip from the same wood from which a sacrificial post is prepared. It is used at the time of anointment of a sacrificial animal and then placed at the top of the post. The objector says that as soon as an animal is sacrificed, the Svaru is also thrown in the fire. The author on the other hand says that one Svaru is quite sufficient for anointing several animals and it is finally thrown in the fire when it is no longer required. It is impossible to have several Svarus when there is one Yûpa only, because it is prepared from the first chip. In the Ahargaṇa sacrifices where a horn of a black antelope is required for scratching the body, it is thrown away in a pit on the last day; the

A black antelope's horn is thrown away once for all on the last day in the अहर्गण:

reason is obvious, it is required every day during the continuance of the sacrifice which lasts for several days.

Silence should be broken once for all in the नानावीजेष्टि at the time of the final call of हविष्कृत्.

In the coronation ceremony, there is Nânâvîjeṣṭi in which various kinds of grains boiled or converted into Purodâs'a cakes are offered to various deities. In the model sacrifice, holy water is carried under a restraint of tongue and it is opened when a call is made on the Havṣkrit; it is transferred here. As there are several offerings of the variety of grains, there are several such calls. The question that naturally arises is, at what call should the vow of silence be broken? The author's reply is that it should be broken once for all after the final invocation.

The same principle applies to the अग्निषोमीय animal sacrifice.

Similarly in the Agnîṣomîya animal sacrifice where both animal and Purodâs'a offerings are made, the silence should be broken once for all at the end of both sets of offerings.

Joining of fire being for the primary, the release of fire takes place at the end of the primary in an अग्निचयन.

In the Agnîchayana, there are two ceremonies called Agnîyoga and Agnîvimoka. A fire oblation is made with "अग्निं युनज्मि" " I join fire ". It is called joining of fire. A fire oblation is made with इमं स्तनं ' this breast ' It is called release of fire. Should the latter ceremony be performed at the end of the entire ceremony consisting of the primary and subsidiaries? The author's view is that the ceremony of release of fire should be performed at the end of the primary, because the ceremony of joining of fire is performed for the primary.

In a Dvâdas'âha there is a time of Upasat called Pravargya where iṣṭis are performed. At that time, there is call of Subrahmaṇya. The question is, whether the call should be made once for all or should it be made on each day at the time of extraction of soma? The reply of the author is that the call should be made on each extraction of soma juice on the principle of Avâpa.

The call of सुब्रह्मण्य at the time of extraction of soma should be made on the principle of आवाप

As to the place and the priests that are engaged in the performance of a sacrifice, it is entirely at the option of the sacrificer to have a change or have the same place or set of priests for another sacrifice. There is no hard and fast rule governing the procedure regarding them. As regards the sacrificial vessels, the same set of vessels should be used in all sacrifices from the time of the establishment of fire till the death of the sacrificer who is cremated along with the sacrificial vessels. They are, therefore, scrupulously maintained till the death of th e sacrificer. The principle of Tantra applies to the use of the sacrificial vessels.

Rule as to place, priests and sacrificial vessels.

In the Vâjapeya, there is the animal sacrifice in honour of Prajâpati borrowed from the model sacrifice. In that connection it is said "subsequent to soma they commence with animals consecrated to Prajâpati". The order in the soma sacrifice in the third *savana* is as follows:—

The प्राजापत्य animal sacrifice should be performed at the end of all soma libations in the वाजपेय sacrifice.

The first is Ârbhâvapavamâna, (2) then the soma drink accompained with songs upto Vais'vadeva cups, (3) then the soma homa with songs, then Agnîṣṭoma songs and उक्थ्य etc., the modifications of soma. The question is, when should the Prâjâpatya animal sacrifice be performed? There are four possible views about it. The first view is that it should be performed after Ârbhâvapavamâna; the second view i s that it should be performed after drinking the soma cups; the third view is that it should be performed after the soma modifications and the fourth and the last view is that it should be performed at the end of all. This is the author's view.

In a Jyotiṣṭoma sacrifice, the Savaniya animal sacrifice is performed on the principle of Tantra and the cakes are offered incidentally. The text is "अग्निमारुता ऊर्ध्वं अनुयाजे ऽवरंति". "They commence अनुयाज after Agnimarut. Where Anuyâjâ are put off, the Sûktavâkas which follow them are also transferred forward. In the Sûktavâkas the deities of the Puroḍâs'a are praised. When the Sûktavâkas are transferred, are the deities of the Puroḍâs'a also transferred? The view of the objector, is that the Anuyâjâs following the animal sacrifice shall have the deities of the animal sacrifice but not of the soma libations. The author's reply is that the Sûktavâkas have the deities of the soma, as appears from the text quoted at p. 930 and it will be of no meaning if the deities of the Sûktavâka are disconnected. So on the transfer of the Sûktavâka, the deities thereof are necessarily transferred forward.

In the ज्योतिष्टोम savaniya animal sacrifice the deities of the सूक्तवाक are also transferred forward on the transfer forward of the सूक्तवाक.

PÂDA 4.

In a Râjasûya sacrifice there are many primaries. The question is, whether the subsidiaries therein should be performed on the principle of Tantra or Âvâpa The author's view is that they should be performed on the principle of Âvâpa, because there are several priests and their fees are separate.

In a राजसूय, the subsidiaries should be performed in each primary.

From the above view of the author, it follows that there is no rule as to the appointment of the priests ; they may be appointed at the change of procedure. The author says that if the priests are changed on the change of each procedure, it will be considered fickleness ; the priests are, therefore, appointed once for all for the entire ceremony of the Râjasûya.

In a राजसूय sacrifice, priests are appointed once for all for the entire sacrifice.

In the coronation ceremony (Râjasûya) there is an Aveṣṭi consisting of five offerings. As there are different fees prescribed, the subordinate parts should be separately performed on the principle of Avâpâ. In an Agnyâdhâna there is a Pavamâneṣṭi in which fire is worshipped under different names as Pavamâna, Pâvaka and S'uchi. According to the author when any desire is connected, in the first offering to Pavamâna, the subsidiary parts should be per-

In an अवेष्टि the subordinate parts should be performed separately.

In an Agnyâdhâna there is a Pavamâneṣṭi

Principles of आवाप and तंत्र applicable to पवमानेष्टि.

formed separately and in the offering to the latter two, the subsidiaries should be performed once for all ; but when the desire is to obtain Brahmaṇic splendour there is the joint application of all the above offerings.

In a Dvâdas'âha ceremony, there are Dîkṣâ, Upasada and Sûtyâ. How should they be performed ? There are 4 views as regards their performance ; the first view is that the Dîkṣâ and Upasada should be separately performed on separate days each having twelve days and Sutyâ should be performed on the last day thus having the total number of 25 days. The second view is that they should all be performed on each day at noon thus not going beyond the twelve days of the Dvâdas'âha. The third view is that they should be performed at a time on the 4th day on the principle of Tantra. The fourth and the last view which is that of the author, is that they should all be performed separately for twelve days. In this view, Dîkṣâ will last for twelve days, the Upasad will also last for twelve days and the Sutyâ will have twelve days allotted to it. The total of days will, therefore, come to 36 days and is supported by the Linga in the text " this Dvâdas'âha consists of 36 d ays.

In a द्वादशाह, the दीक्षा, उपसद and सुत्या are separately performed on separate days thus making up the total 36 days.

The subsidiaries, such as Savanîya animals in the Dvâdas'âha, should be performed separately, because the subsidiaries, time of which is not different from that of their primaries should be performed on the principle of Âvâpa.

The principle of आवाप applies to the subsidiaries that are performed along with their primaries.

In a Jyotiṣṭoma there is a Mantra " come, O ! Maghava, on such and such day ". The mantra is transferred to the Dvâdas'âha ; but in it the time being different from that of the principal, how is it to be repeated ? The reply is that it should be repeated once without inserting any numeral in the place of " on such and such day " unlike the practice of the model sacrifice where it is modified according to the circumstances.

The invocation मंत्र in the द्वादशाह is repeated once without modification.

There are three things essential in cooking animal food. (1) Kumbhi is a small pot in which parts of an animal are cooked. (2) S'ûlas are pieces of wood on wh ch heart and visceras of an animal are baked ; (3) Vapâsrayani is a cauldron in which omentum is boiled. As a general rule, one set of vessels is sufficient for cooking animal parts but if the flesh of various animals takes different time in cooking, there will, then, be different sets of vessels required for the purpose.

One set of vessels is sufficient for cooking parts of animals ; but if the parts of different animals take different time, several sets of vessels are required.

In an- As'vapratigrabeṣṭi where cakes baked on four potsherds ar offered to Varuṇa in proportion to the number of horses receivei as gift. In it, various potsherds are required ; one is not sufficient.

Different potsherds in an अश्वप्रतिग्रहेष्टि.

In the new and full moon sacrifices, rice is threshed in a mortar by means of pestle to remove husk from it. The mantra ' protecting heaven from the killing enemy ' is recited. It is recited once for all and need not be repeated with each stroke as there is one act and one substance.

In the new and full moon sacrifices the mantra should be repeated once.

On the other hand in the coronation ceremony where a variety of a cereal grains are threshed in Nânâvîjeṣṭi, its constituent part, the threshing mantra quoted above should be repeated on the occasions of threshing each cere al grain.

In a नानाबीजेष्टि, the threshing formula is repeated separately.

There are four kinds of ceremonies mentioned in the adhikaraṇa XIII viz., (1) Nirvâpa, (2) Lavana, (3) Upastaraṇa (4) Âjyagrahaṇa. (1) In the new and full moon ceremonies a Nirvâpa is made of four han lfuls of offerings. The Mantra recited is ' I being inspired by god Savitâ make a pleasing offering to thee, Agni, with the hands of Pûṣâ and the arms of As'winis, (2) In Lavana, four handfuls of grass for sacrificial purposes, are cut with the well-known mantra, " I cut thee O ! grass the seat of the gods ."

In निर्वाप, लवन, उपस्तरण and आज्यग्रहण, the मंत्र are recited on each occasion on the principle of आवाप.

3. In Upastaraṇa, grass is spread on an altar three times or five times with the Mantra "I spread thee, soft as wool."

4. In Ajyagrahaṇa, ghee is taken four times in a Juhû vessel with the mantra, "I take thee, the resplendent ghee in the resplendent vessel for the gods at every place in every ceremony." The question is, whether

the mantras mentioned above should be repeated once for all in each of the above said ceremonies or should be repeated on each occasion in the ceremonies. The reply of the author is that the mantras should be repeated on each occasion in the above said ceremonies.

There is a ceremony called (Vediprokṣaṇa) sprinkling of water on an altar three times with the Mantra "O ! grass, thou art altar." As the purification of the altar is one act and enures for the benefit of the whole sacrifice, the mantra is repeated once for all.

The मंत्र in the वेदिप्रोक्षण is repeated once.

In the Jyotiṣṭoma sacrifice, the body is scratched by the sacrificer by means of the horn of a black antelope. If an irritating sensation simultaneously arises in different parts of the body, they may be scratched by the horn but the mantra accompanying it is recited once only.

The मंत्र on scratching the parts of the body in a ज्योतिष्टोम is recited once

Similarly in the Jyotiṣṭoma, if an initiated sees bad dreams, crosses streams, gets wet in rains or happens to see impure things, he shall recite the mantra suitable on each occasion, once only. If he starts on a journey, the mantra shall be recited once for all but not on each march in course of it.

The principle of तंत्र applies to the recitation of mantras on the occasion of seeing bad dream etc., in a ज्योतिष्टोम.

In the Jyotiṣṭoma there is (Uparava) a pit for the extraction of soma juice. Over it soma is ground ; it is so called by the increasing sound of the grindstones. These pits or ground-holes are dug under the shafts of the southern of the two carts which are four in number. See p. 400 of the तैत्तिरीयसंहिता of the Ânandâs'rama. The first mantra from the first book and third chapter of the तैत्तिरीयसंहिता as quoted at p. 954 of the Mîmânsâ is recited. The question is, whether this uparava mantra should be recited once or should be repeated on the occasion of digging each pit. The author's reply is that the mantra should be repeated on digging each pit, because it is associated with each act of digging.

The principle of आवाप applies to the उपरव mantra.

Similarly, the Haviṣkrit mantra in the Jyotiṣṭoma, the Adhrigu Praiṣa in the Vâjapeya, Puronuvâkya and the Manota mantra are recited repeatedly. The principle of Avâpa applies, otherwise there will be a great confusion. As to the different mantras, see at p. 955.

The principle of आवाप applies to the हविष्कृत मंत्र and others.

CHAPTER XII.

PÂDA 1.

The author has explained Tantra and Âvâpa in the preceding Chapter; he now proceeds to explain Prasanga in Chapter XII. As we have seen that in a Tantra, a single performance of the subsidiaries in one primary is sufficient and no repetition thereof is necessary in other primaries; but in an Âvâpa the performance of the subsidiaries is repeated in each primary. In a प्रसंग, though the subsidiaries are performed in one primary yet they ensure for the benefit of the other primaries as well. As for example a lamp lit on a royal palace is primarily for illuminating the royal palace, but it also sheds light on the highway adjoining it. The Prasanga is Tantra looked from another point of view. It may be considered an extended application of Tantra. In it the performance of the subsidiaries is with the main purpose of one primary, yet it benefits other primaries indirectly. It differs from the Tantra in which the performance of subsidiaries is with the object of benefitting many primaries once for all; while in the former the performance of the subsidiaries is mainly for the benefit of one primary only but it enures for the benefit of other primaries as well.

प्रसंग explained and distinguished from तंत्र.

There is an Agnisomîya animal sacrifice in which an Agnisomîya animal is sacrified and Purodâs'a cakes made of animal flesh are also offered. Now the question is, whether the subsidiary acts performed in the animal sacrifice should be repeated in the offering of the पुरोडाश cakes; the author says that the principle of Prasanga comes into play and the repetition of the subsidiary acts is not needed in the Pus'upurodâs'a; of the subsidiary acts is in the animal sacrifice, the offering of the cakes made of animal flesh as the text about it is read in connection with the animal sacrifice. This does not prohibit any subsidiary acts as Âjyâbhâgas which are borrowed from elsewhere in the Pas'upurodâs'a and which are not performed in the animal sacrifice.

The principle of प्रसंग applies, to the offering of the animal cakes when the subsidiary acts are performed in the अग्निषोमीय animal sacrifice.

though the performance yet it benefits indirectly

But the subsidiary acts borrowed from elsewhere shall be performed.

Principle of प्रसँग further applied.

For the same reason, there is no necessity of having a separate altar in a Somayâga ; the big altar which is constructed there, is quite sufficient for all purposes. Similarly, the vessels such as cups and spoons are quite sufficient in a soma sacrifice but in those rites which are transferred from the Dars'apurṇamâsayâgas, the Juhû and Upabhrit must be used and the vessels used in the Somayâga will not suffice.

Animal cakes are cooked in the शालामुखीय but not in the शामित्र fire ; but in the कौण्डपायि नामयन, cooking is done in the मार्जहित fire.

In the sacrifices, the Ahavanîya fire is first burnt in the Uttaravedi ; then the Gârhapatya fire is burnt in the प्राचीन वंश stall (see figure 1 in the frontispiece). The fire that is burnt on the eastern side of the stall is called शालामुखीय and that burnt in the western part of it is called मार्जहित and is principal Gârhapatya fire and the Śâlâmukhîya fire is Gârhapatya fire in the secondary sense. Sâmitra fire in which flesh is cooked is subsequently burnt. The question is, whether the animal puroḍâs'a cakes should be prepared in the Samitra fire or in the Śâlamukhîya fire which is already there. The principle of Prasanga applies and the animal cakes should be prepared in it. But in the कौण्डपायिनायनम् which is a modified form of the अग्निहोत्र, the cooking should be performed in the मार्जहित which is the principal Gârhapatya fire but not in the Śâlâmukhîya fire which is a गार्हपत्य fire by courtesy.

Another cart should be brought in a Somayaga in a निर्वाप offering.

Certain ceremonies are performed to the west of the domestic fire after mounting on the right wheel of a cart. There are two Havirdhana carts containing the sacrificial materials in the हविर्धानमंडप at a distance from the place where the ceremony is performed. The question is, whether one of these carts can serve the purpose or not. The reply of the author is that if you bring one of the Havirdhana carts to the place of the ceremony, there is a fear of the soma ceremony being spoiled ; another cart should, therefore, be brought in. It is supported by the the fact that the word ' carts ' in the text is used in plural and therefore denotes 'three ' under the कपिंजलन्याय as exaplained in the preceding pages.

In प्रायणीया, initiation and vigil should be separately kept.

In a soma sacrifice, the vigil is kept on the day of initiation ; in the context of the Dars'apûrṇamâsayâga, it is said to be kept on the औपवसथ्य day. It is transferred to the Prayaṇîya under a Chodaka text. There the time thereof falls in the middle.

The question is whether the vigil should be separately kept or the vigil that was kept on the initiation day enures for the benefit of the entire sacrifice. The reply of the author is that it should be separately kept as it is transferred there from elsewhere under the Chodaka text. The principle of Prasanga does not, therefore, apply.

In the वरुणप्रघास, the मंत्रs should be repeated for each separate act.

In the Varuṇapraghâsa, there are several hearths; there are mantras for taking ghee, sprinkling water and touching. As there are different acts, mantras should, therefore, be separately repeated.

In a soma sacrifice, there are Iṣṭis like दीक्षणीया etc. Now the question is, whether fire should be separately kept for them or the Agnyâdhâna of the soma sacrifice will enure for the benefit of the entire sacrifice. The author says that the fire that is established for the soma sacrifice enures for the benefit of the entire sacrifice; there is, therefore, no necessity for re-establishing fire separately for the Iṣṭis. Similarly, the vows taken in the soma sacrifice enure for the benefit of the entire sacrifice and there is, therefore, no further need to take another vow in the Iṣṭis, the subordinate parts of the soma sacrifice.

There is no necessity of the re-establishment of fire in the इष्टिs, the subordinate parts of the soma sacrifice.

No need of separate vows in the इष्टिs in a soma sacrifice.

The principle of प्रसंग applies to the reception of the gods in a सोम sacrifice.

The same principle of Prasanga which applies to the soma sacrifice and its Iṣṭis in the case of the establishment of fire, applies to reception of the deities. The gods are invited and received on the previous day and worshipped on the subsequent day. In this view, the same deities who are invited and received as guests serve the purpose of the whole sacrifice.

Equipment of one's wife in a soma sacrifice lasts for the whole sacrifice.

At the time of initiation, the sacrificer ties a girdle round his waist and puts a grass rope round the waist of his wife; in the view, which the author takes of the soma sacrifice, this tying round of grass rope which is called equipment here, lasts for the whole sacrifice; so there is no necessity of separate equipment for the Iṣṭis, the subordinate parts of the soma sacrifice.

Food prescribed in the soma sacrifice enures for the benefit of the entire sacrifice.

Similarly, the food prescribed in the soma sacrifice is quite sufficient for the whole sacrifice and there is, therefore, no necessity to resort to the forest food transferred under a Chodaka text to the Prâyaṇîya.

The principle of प्रसँग does not apply to the eating of the remnants of food.

The same principle does not apply to the remnants of food ; their object is not maintenance but purification. In this view, eating of the remnants of food is transferred to the Iṣṭis, the subordinate parts of the soma sacrifice from the new and full moon sacrifices.

In the Dars'apûrṇamâsayâgas, services are hired with the food prepared with rice. In the Somayâga, there is a fixed fee of 1200 ; the gift prescribed in the new and full moon sacrifices is transferred under a Chodaka text to the Iṣṭis, the subordinate parts of the Somayâga. The question is, whether this gift of the food prepared with rice should be separately paid in the Iṣṭis. The reply of the author is that the priests are engaged for the whole sacrifice on the fee of 1200 and there is, therefore, no need of making this gift over and above the fee. It is distinguishable from the eating of the remnants of food which is for the object of purification.

The principle of प्रसँग applies to the fee paid for the engagement of the priests in a सोमयाग.

In the new and full moon sacrifices, a *hotâ* is appointed ; the appointment of the hotâ is transferred to the Iṣṭis in the Somayâga. In the latter also, there is an appointment of a *hotâ*. The question is, whether a *hotâ* should be separately appointed in the Iṣṭis. The author's view is that as a *hotâ* is appointed after the commencement of the sacrifice for the production of the invisible effect, he should be separately appointed for the Iṣṭis and the principle of Prasanga does not apply.

The principle of प्रसँग does not apply to the appointment of a *hotâ* in the इष्टिs in the सोमय ाग s.

Sprinkling should be performed on the वर्हि grass separately in the उपसदs etc., if it is performed for the benefit of the आति-थ्या only

Water is sprinkled on the front part of the वर्हि grass and its lower part is washed in an आतिथ्या. The same grass is required in the Upasadas and the Agniṣomîya. The question is, whether the sprinkling of water should be separately performed in the उपसदs and the Agniṣomîya. The author's reply is that if the sprinkling is performed for the benefit of the Âtithyâ only, it should be repeated separately in the उपसदs and the अग्नीषोमीय.

In the Âtithyâ, grass is spread with a Vedic mantra quoted at p 974.

स्तरण मँत्र should be repeated in the अग्नीषोमीय.

Does it enure for the benefit of the अग्नीषोमीय? The reply of the author is that it should be repeated, because the प्रग्वंश where it is spread is different from the northern altar and the object of spreading the grass is purification.

As seen above the वर्हि grass is purified in the आतिथ्या place and carried ceremoniously after arranging and fastening it to the Agniṣomîya place with the accompaniment of the mantras. There are two mantra quoted at p. 974; the one is recited at the time of arranging and fastening the grass and the other when carrying it to the Agniṣomîya

सम्प्रैन हरण मँत्रs shall not be recited when grass is arranged and carried from the प्रग्वंश to the northern altar.

place. As laid down above these mantras should be repeated but our author says that the object of the Starna mantra is different and the mantras which are technically called सम्प्रैन हरण मँत्रs are recited in the model sacrifice at the place where the grass is cut but not when it is carried from the Gârhapatya hearth to the Ahavanîya hearth ; *a fortiori* they will not be recited when the grass is taken from the प्रग्वंश to the northern hearth.

PÂDA 2.

Sacrificial fire is used for sacrificial purposes only.

Does the principle of Prasanga apply to the sacrificial fire ? Can you cook any food in it ? The author says that the sacrificial fire is intended for the Vedic rites only and cannot be used for the culinary purposes.

CCXXIII

The animal of the अग्नीषोमीय sacrifice is transferred to the सवनीय sa- crifice.

In the Agnîṣomîya animal sacrifice, Puroḍâs'a which is prescribed, is for covering the fissure made in the body of the animal killed to take out omentum. This animal cake is transferred to the Savanîya animal sacrifice under a Chodaka text. As the fissure made in the body of the animal can be covered by the cake prescribed in the सवनीय, there is no necessity of having an animal cake of the अग्नीषोमीय. The author says that the object of the animal cake being purificatory, it should be made and covering of the fissure made in the body of the animal is by way of Arthavâda.

The principle of प्रसंग applies to the call of the हविष्कृत्.

As to the call of the हविष्कृत् when it is made once, there is no necessity of repeating it again; one invocation is sufficient for the entire sacrifice.

Nocturnal sacrifice is governed by its own *tantra.*

There is a Nis'iyajña which is a Kâmeṣti and is performed to ward off the demons, on the night of the new moon. By what Tantra is it governed? Is it govened by the तंत्र of the new moon sacrifice? The author's reply is that the nocturnal sacrifice being performed with a certain object in view, is governed by its own *tantra* and is a separate act independently. Sâyanâchârya, however, holds that the nocturnal sacrifice is governed by the Tantra of the new moon sacrifice.

As to observing of a fast and constructing an altar the nocturnal sacrifice is gover- ned by the तंत्र of the new moon sacrifice.

In the new moon sacrifice, a fast is observed and an altar is cons- tructed; should the fast and the altar be separately observed and constructed in the nocturnal sacrifice described above. The author's reply is that the altar is already cons- tructed for the new moon sacrifice and the fast is observed in that connection; so no useful purpose will be served by demolishing the altar and constructing another and breaking one fast and keeping another. The principle of Prasanga applies.

The fuel and grass procured for the new moon sacrifice being not sufficient for the Nis'iyajña, so grass and fuel will be separately procured for it and in this view the principle of Prasanga does not apply. Similarly the re-establishment of fire if made for the reception of the deities should be separately performed. The reason is obvious ; the gods are received in the evening and the sacrifice in their honour follows the next day.

The principle of प्रसंग does not apply to procuring of grass and fuel and re-establishing fire with the object of receiving deities.

We have seen at p. p. 520 and 521 that Ârambhanîyâ the initial ceremony is once performed in the new and full moon sacrifices when they are first commenced and is not repeated in the subsequent performance thereof. Now the question for solution, is whether this preliminary ceremony called Ârambhaṇîyâ should be performed in the modified sacrifice or not. The reply of the author is that the Ârambhaṇîyâ performed in the beginning of the new and full sacrifices on the first occasion enures for the benefit of the new and full moon sacrifices, but its performance therein cannot confer benefit on other sacrifices that may be performed in one's life. The principle of Prasanga, therefore, does not apply to the present case.

The आरंभणीया performed in connection with the new and full moon sarifices does not enure for the benefit of the modified sacrifice.

There is a Pañchadas'arâtra ceremony lasting for 15 days; the first day is called Agnistut day and borrows the सुब्रह्मण्य call from its model Agnistut. It is, therefore, called आग्नेयी सुब्रह्मण्या. Then follow Jyoti, Gaû and Âyu ; the question is, whether the call in the remaining eleven days should be the आग्नेयी सुब्रह्मण्या or the ऐंद्री सुब्रह्मण्या of their own model sacrifice. The reply of the author is that in this state of conflict, the details of the majority prevail over those of the minority. In this view the ऐंद्रीब्रह्मण्या will govern the remaining days.

The characteristics of the majority prevail over those of the minority in case of conflict.

In the Kâmyeṣṭi Kâṇḍa, there is a text quoted at p. 985. There are seven minor ceremonies ; the two Âjyâbhâgas are performed by Tantra ; Dadhiyâga and the Indrayâga have वृधन्वती verses recited as Puronuvâkya and in the last three offerings of honey, clarified butter and water, the Vârtaghni verses are recited. According to the author's dictum laid down above, the Vartaghnî verses being in abundance will have preference over the Vṛidhanvatî verses.

वार्त्तघ्नी verses being abundant prevail over the वृधन्वती verses.

When the character-
istics borrowed are
equally balanced, the
characteristics of the
one that happens to
be first governs the
whole procedure.

On the other hand when the conflicting characteristics borrowed are equally balanced on both sides, the first in order shall prevail. As for example in the text quoted at p. 985 the cakes consecrated to Agni and Visnu are borrowed from the Aindrâgni cere-mony and the Sârasvata sacrifice is a modi-fied form of an Upaus'uyaga. As both are equal in number, the procedure of अग्नावैष्णव governs the whole ceremony.

The characteristics of
the principal prevail
over those of the
subordinate parts.

When there is a conflict between the details of the principal and its subordidate parts, the former shall prevail ; as for instance in a Jyotiṣṭoma there is a Dîksa-nîyâ ; it is said " Let him who performs a sacrifice by means of the Iṣṭis, animal and soma, do so on a new or full moon day." The order is first Dîkṣâ, then three Upasads and the flfth extraction of soma juice. What is the order in the soma ceremony when performed on the Parvi days ? Though Dîkṣâ is first, still the exraction of soma being principal shall have preference.

The rites pertaining to
the परिधि should be
performed on the परिधि
when it is used as a
sacrificial post.

A Paridhi is a stick used as a boundary mark ; there are such three sticks in number. A yûpa is a sacrificial post to which an animal to be slaughtered is tied. Sometimes the Paridhi is used in emergency for tying the animal. The Yûpa is anointed, erected and tied round with a rope ; while the Paridhi is rough and laid prostrate on the ground. What ceremony should be performed on the Paridhi when it is used as a sacrificial post ? One view is that both sets of rites pertaining to the secrificial post and Paridhi should be performed, provided they are not inconsistent. The second view is that the rites pertaining to the sacrificial post should alone be per-formed. The third view which is the author's view is that only the rites pertaining to the Paridhi should be performed so that it may not lose its character as Paridhi. It is used as a sacrificial post under a special text but does not lose its character as Paridhi.

तँत्री and प्रसँगी explained

When any primary falls in the middle of another primary the latter is called Tantrî and the former is called Prasaugî. Accordingly the whole will be governed by the Tantri. The तंत्री but not the प्रसंगी governs the procedure.

As for example in the Savanîya animal sacrifice, the morning *savana* is performed with omentum, the midday *savana* with the animal cakes and the evening *savana* with the parts of the victim ; here the animal cake falling in the middle of the Tantra of the Savanîya animal sacrifice is a Prasangî and the animal sacrifice is the Tantri. The whole procedure is, therefore, governed by the Tantra of the Savanîya animal sacrifice.

There are permanent ceremonies which are performed on the new and

When the model and the modified sacrifices are of the same तंत्र, the तंत्र of the latter prevails.

full moon days as for example the दर्शपूर्णमासयाग but the desire accomplishing acts which are their modified forms are also performed on the same days as for example Saûryayâga. The latter ceremonies falling in the middle of those ceremonies which are obligatory during one's life are *prima facie* Prasangi according to the principle enunciated above ; but as the modified ceremonies are performed with certain objects in view, the *tantra* thereof shall prevail. They are, therefore, Tantrî but not Prasangî.

In an Āgrayaṇeṣṭi there are three offerings (1) Aindrâgna (2) Vais'vadeva and (3) Dyâvâprithivî.

In the आग्रयणेष्टि, though flowering grass of the द्यावापृथिवी is used, it is not a तंत्री of the other two offerings named ऐंद्राग्न and वैश्वदेव but is a प्रसंगी by its position.

In the model sacrifice of the first two, there is no rule as to grass; it may be either flowering or non flowering : but in the Dyavâprthivi, the flowering grass is used. As there is no rule about the use of grass in the ऐंद्राग्न and Vais'vadeva offerings and as its use is optional, the flowering grass of the Dyâvâprithivi offerings though last in order may be used under the well-known maxim of कांस्यभोजिन्याय as explained at p. 990. It does not necessarily follow that the Tantra of the Dyâvâprithivi governs all other offerings ; the द्यावापृथिवी offering is a Prasangî but not a Tantrî. According to Pârthasârathi and Râme'vara Sûri, the Aindrâgna offering being first in order governs all of them and is a Tantrî but according to Mâdhava all the three offerings enumerated above are Tantrîs in themselves.

PÂDA 3.

There is an Ahîna sacrifice called Aṣṭarâttra which lasts for eight nights.

In an अष्टरात्र the upper and lower garments should be worn through-out.

On the first day there is Vis'vajit ; then follow Ṣaḍahas called Jyoti and then on the 8th and the last day there is Abhijit. To the Vis'vajit calf's skin which is enjoined as the upper garment in the model sacrifice is transferred, under the Nâma ; similarly new lower garment from the Jyotiṣṭoma, the model of the Jyoti is taken. The question is, which dress should be adopted in the Atirâtra sacrifice ? There are four possible views ; one is that the principles of Nâmadheya and Atides'a being equally balanced, there is an optin of dress. The second view is that the Vis'vajit being first in order, the calf's skin should be worn throughout. The third view is that as the dress of the model sacrifice of the majority of days is new and unwashed lower garment, such a dress should be put on throughout the whole sacrifice. The fourth and the last view which is the view of the author is that both kinds of dress should be worn ; the upper garment for the upper part of the body and the lower garment for the lower part.

In the अग्निचयन. the offering of the animal cake being first in order is the तँत्री of the entire action.

In connection with the Agnîchayana, it is said that after the offering of the animal cakes eight offerings to the अग्निगृहपति, सोमवनस्पति, सवितृसत्यप्रसव, रुद्रपशुपति, बृहस्पति, वाचस्पति, इन्द्रज्येष्ठ विश्वसहस्रव and वरुणधर्मपति should be made. What Tantra will govern the procedure ? The author's view is that though the offerings to the eight deities are more in number, yet as they fall in the middle of the offering of the animal Puroḍâs'a cake, they are Prasangi and are governed by the Tantra of the offering of the animal cakes.

The principle of समुच्चय applies to all modes of sprinkling of ghee in the new and full moon sacrifices. When any one of the substances is sufficient for the object, the principle of option applies.

In connection with the new and full moon sacrifices, it is said. " In sprinkling (ghee) he sprinkles straight, he sprinkles continuously, he sprinkles in front." Here the act of sprinkling is one, all modes of sprinkling will be used and the principle of (Samuchchaya) combination but not option, applies. When there are two or more substances for one purpose, and any one of them is sufficient any of them may be optionally used. The principle of Samuchaya does not apply.

CCXXVIII.

Expiatory rites for involuntary and voluntary acts or omissions.

There are two kinds of expiatory rites; one for voluntary acts of commission or omission and the other for those acts of commission or omission over which a sacrificer has no control. In the former case, all rites prescribed under the text should be performed but in the latter case, you have an option; you can perform any of the expiatory rites prescribed for an involuntary act or omission.

The prohibition as to the Vedic study on the पर्व days does not relate to the recitation of the mantras in the sacrifices held on those days.

On the Parva days, the Vedic study is prohibited and no classes are held just as Sunday is considered *dies non* for all purposes in Christian countries; it is not *dies juridicus*. The question is, whether the recitation of the Vedic mantras in the new and full moon sacrifices which are held on the Parva days should be made or not. The reply of the author is that the prohibition of the Vedic study relates to the acquisition of knowledge but does not relate to the repetition of the mantras on the occasion of a sacrifice held on those days.

The Vedic mantras should be sung according to the direction contained in the मंत्र पाठ but a mantra which is not read in the मंत्र पाठ but takes it origin in the ब्राह्मण should be read according to the direction contained in the ब्राह्मण.

The Vedic mantras are read with a particular Svara indicated in the mantra pâṭha with certain line marks as explained in the preceding pages of the introduction. It is called प्रातवचन or प्रातवचनस्वर; while in the Brâhmaṇa sometime they are read with different स्वर called भाषिक स्वर or भाषास्वर. The question is, " how are they to be read in this state of conflict ? " The reply of the author is that the Vedic mantras should be read according to the direction given in the Mantrapâṭha; but the Mantra which is not read in the Mantrapâṭha but takes its origin in the Brâhmaṇa should be sung as directed in the Brâhmaṇa.

The whole of mantra should be recited.

The question is, whether the whole of a mantra should be recited or only a portion of it. The author's view is that the whole of a mantra should be recited in the performance of a ceremony.

In an Agnichayana ceremony, there, is one offering of ghee made up of 12 cuts of it by means of a ladle made of Udam bara wood of the size of a fathom by uttering the mantra from the Taitariya Sanhitâ quoted at p 1001. This ceremony is called Vaşordhara in the liturgical terminology. Then follow eleven offerings with the remaining verse. The question is whether the portions of the Mantra should be read with each set of the offerings considered as one. The view of the objector is that only a portion of it should be read in order to obviate the delay which would be otherwise caused by reason of the oblation keeping pace with the recitation of the entire mantra. The author's view is that the entire mantra should be recited ; there is no need of the oblation keeping pace with the recitation of the mantra.

The whole mantra should be recited in वसोधार, offering.

In Âghâra also ghee should be kept in a ladle dripping in the Ahavanîya fire till the entire mantra is recited ; at the end of it, the whole should be offered.

In an आघार the whole mantra should be recited.

Where there are several mantras for one object as for example two mantras for division of the puroḍâs'a cake quoted at p. 1002, you have an option and can recite any mantra you like ; but where there number is given you have no choice left, and the principle of Samuchchaya applies as in the case of the text quoted at p. 1002 where the number is mentioned in clear language.

Option when there are several mantra for one object, but the principle of समुच्चय applies where the number is fixed.

When in a Brâhmaṇa there are several Mantras given for an act as for example two mantras quoted at p. 1003 for extending a Puroḍâs'a cake, the principle of option applies. You can make a selection of any mantra you like.

Option in case of the mantras given in a Brahmaṇa.

There are mantras for erecting a sacrificial post and fixing it by tying a rope round it. All these mantras should be recited as the principle of Samuchchaya applies. Similarly, the mantras, which are to be recited by a *hotâ* should also be read together, because they are recited by him to remind the Adhvaryu to perform the acts pertaining to his position as such.

The examples where the principle of समुच्चय applies.

PÂDA 4.

There are mantras which are told in a low tone on a rosary ; they are

The principle of समुच्चय applies to the जप मंत्र.

called Japa mantras. They are of three kinds; they are eulogistic, benedictory or descriptive. The object of the mantras being the production of the invisible effect they should all be told and the principle of combination applies.

The principle of option applies to the recitation of the याज्या and पुरोनुवाक्या verses.

There are mantras which are called Yâjyâ and Anuvâkyâ. A pair of each of them is given at p. 1007, their object being to remind the performer of the deities; the principle of option applies and you can exercise your choice in uttering either of them.

The purchase of soma is made with all the commodities mentioned in the text.

Soma creeper is bartered with certain commodities mentioned in the Vedic texts; it should be purchased with all those commodites; the reason is obvious, if you pay a higher price, you can strike off the bargain easily.

The principle of समुच्चय applies to the गुदोप यजन ceremony, being a प्रतिपत्तिकर्म.

There is a Gudopayajana ceremony in the Agnişomîya animal sacrifice in which the rectum and other useless parts of an animal are sacrified. What is the procedure when several animals are sacrificed as in a Pas'vaikâdas'inî, where eleven animals are sacrificed? The reply of the author is that the offering of all these useless parts should be made as an act of final disposal (Pratipattikarma). The principle of Samuchchaya, therefore, applies.

The principle of option applies to the payment of fee in an अग्निचयन ceremony.

In an Agnichayana ceremony it is said as to the payment of fee "One should be given, six should be given, twelve should be given." Here if the principle of combination were to apply, it will clash with the express number given in the text. As for instance, if you add one to six, the result will be seven which is nowhere sanctioned. Accordingly, the principle of option will come into operation. You can in this view either pay one or six.

In a पत्नी संयाज the principle of option applies to the offering of an animal's tail.

In the Dars'apûrnamâsayâgas the wives of the gods are worshipped; this ceremony is called पत्नीसंयाज. In it, the tail of an animal is offered. It is transferred to the Agnîşomîya animal sacrifice. The question is whether all the tails of the animals sacrificed or any of them may be offered ; or in other words, whether the principle of Samuchchaya or option applies. According to the author, the offering of the animal's tail is an essential act but not an act of final disposal, because it is commanded to be performed by a Vedic text. In this view, the principle of option applies and any tail may be offered in the Patnîsamyâja performed in an Agnîşomîya animal sacrifice.

We have explained Ukhâ fire in the preceding pages. It is kept in

The उखा fire being permament should not be combined with the desire accomplishing fires of the desire accomplishing acts.

an iron vessel which is tied round the neck of a sacrificer with two slings. He carries it for a year before he performs an Agnichayana. It is a permanent act (Nityakarma). When a sacrificer has any desire to be accomplished, he obtains fire in the way given in the text at p. 1013 Now the question is, whether these various fires which are mentioned in connection with the desire-accomplishing acts should be combined with the Ukhâ fire. The reply of the author is that there is a difference of fires which cannot, therefore, he combined. The principle of Somuchchaya does not apply. It is, therefore, optional to use any fire. In other words the permanent fire should be used in permanent acts and derire accomplishing fires in the desire accomplishing ceremonies.

The उखा fire is consecrated fire and the fire for desire accomplishing acts is un- consecrated.

The Ukhâ fire is a consecrated fire and the fire obtained for the desire accom- plishing acts is unconsecrated fire in which no Agnyâdhâna ceremony is performed.

We have seen that the Ukhâ fire is tied round the sacrificer's neck for

उखा fire should not be tied round the sacri- ficer's neck always.

a year ; the question arises whether it should be tied round his neck always as the Ahavanya fire is always to be maintained under a Vedic text ; the author's view is that it should not be tied round always, because it replaces the Âhavanîya fire.

In a सत्र and अहीन there are certain ceremonies such as touching of the Śukra cup by the sacrificer and measuring of an उदुम्बर stick with the size of the sacrificer. As there is a large number of sacrificers in a sattra and Ahîna who should perform them? The reply of the author is that any one may do them but the master of the sacrifice is the proper person to perform them. As these acts do not benefit any one in particular, any one of the sacrificers can perform them. On the other hand, the purificatory acts such as anointing the body or applying collyrium in the eyes being for

In a सत्र or an अहीन, acts which confer no particular benefit should be performed by the गृहपति but the purificatory rites should be performed by all the sacrificers.

the personal benefit should be performed by all.

The next question for determination is, who is entitled to officiate as a Ṛtvik ? The author's reply is that a Brâhmaṇa alone is entitled to act as a Ritirik for the following reasons. (1) He alone is entitled to drink soma while others are not entitled to it, but to phalachamasa drink ; only a Ṛtvik has to drink soma, so a non-Brâhmaṇa cannot officiate as such. (2) Sannâya cannot be drunk by a non-Brâhmaṇa, it is only

A Brahman alone is entitled to officiate as a ऋत्विक्.

Reason for it.

a soma drinker who is entitled to it. (3) It is only a Brâhmaṇa who is entitled to the remnants of the food in the full and new moon sacrifices ; the non-Brâhmaṇa are expressly prohibited to partake of them (4) The Anvâharya fee which consists of boiled rice is given to a Brâhmaṇ alone. For the above reasons the author arrives at the conclusion that a Brâhmaṇ alone is entitled to officiate as a Ṛtvik.

A note on the application of the Mimansa principles to Hindu Law.

We have seen that the Mîmânsâ was mainly written in helping one in understanding the Vedic rites and thus in interpreting the Vedic texts in connection thereof. Sâyana is the first available commentator who referred to the Mimansâ in his introduction to the commentary of the Rigveda. (See P P. 6 et seq. of Max Muller's Rigveda, 1st edition 1849.) In his commentary on the Taittereya Samhitâ, he has referred to Jaimini at the end of each chapter of the seven books, into which it is divided.

The commentators on the Smriti texts have very freely resorted to the application of the Mîmân-â rules in the interpretation of the texts. It will be useless to multiply instances from the commentaries on the Smritis; the principles explained in the preceding pages will help a reader in understanding the smriti texts if he is disposed to study them ; it will be a pedantry and tautalogy to cite examples from the smriti commentators. Take the well known maxim of द्वयो: प्रणयंति explained by me at. P. CXXXV of the introduction; it is referred to by Vijñânes'wara in chapter II. 135 and 136 at P. 201 of Moghe's 3rd edition. Jîmûta Vâhana the founder of the Bengal school of Hindu Law refers to it in XI. 5. 16 at P. 194 of Jîvânand's edition of Dâyabhâga.

Kishori Lal Sircar, the Tagore Law lecturer (1905) has written a special thesis on the 'subject which one cannot ignore in the study of the Hindu Law as developed in the courts in British India. Every Indian writer on Hindu Law has dealt with the Mîmânsâ rules in explaining it. It will be a mere repetition, if I were to explain the principles which have been dealt with in the introduction or in the body of the book. It is only with a view to show the importance of the study of the Mîmânsâ, that I have mentioned the fact by the way.

Sanskrit grammarians have also referred to the Mîmânsâ maxims as for instance निषादस्थपति न्याय, कपिंजलन्याय & c.

The High Courts in British India have referred to the Mîmânsâ rules in their judgments ; I shall now proceed with those cases in which the rules have been explained by the learned judges.

In Gopal Narhar Safray v Hanmanta Ganesh Safray I. L. R. 3 Bom. 173 at P. 280, Westropp C. J. says.

" Nilkanth quotes the text of Caunaka, already given. enjoining in adoption equality of class and allowing affiliation by Śûdras of " a daughter's son and a sister's son." Mr. Shanta Ram argued that Nilkanth, while strongly urging nay insisting on the affiliation of a daughter's son or a sister's son by a Súdra does not prohibit such an affiliation by a member of any of the three regenerate tribes. But this argument is inconsistent with Nilkanth's mention of the adoption of such persons by a Súdra as an exception and therefore inconsistent also with the rule *exceptio unius exclusio alterius* as well as with his observations in placitum 10 to the effect that the adoption of a daughter's son or sister's son is for Súdras alone. And although he in the next placitum treats such an adoption as " the most proper for Súdras " and in pl. 36 says " Of sudras (adopting) the daughter's son or sister's son is to be taken and no other," We see no reason for supposing that he intended to relax the interdiction of such adoptions by Brahmans, Kṣtriyas and Vais yas partly expressed and partly implied by Saunaka and expressly imposed by Sakala, Devananda Bhatta and Nanda Pandita"

The above quotation should be read with the original at pp. 43 *et seq* of Gharpure's edition of the Vyawahâra Mayûkha.

The dictum to which the learned Chief Justice refers, has been fully explained by Chandavarkar J. at p. 282 of Gangu *v.* Chandrabhagabai. I. L. R. 32 Bom. P. 275. "According to a well-known rule of interpretation in Hindu Law (1) when there is a collocation of two texts, dealing with the same subject, and in the first of them two words and expressions occur, of which only one is repeated in the second text, the other word or expression must be excluded as not applying to cases falling within that second text. So here in the first text which specifies the persons excluded from inheritance, it is said that those persons *shall be maintained (Bhartavyâh)* but that they are *incompetent to inherit (Niramshakâh).* In the text relating to their wives, only the word *Bhartavya* ("shall be maintained") is repeated. Hence, according to the rule, disinherison was not intended to apply to them. Further, had it been a rule of Hindu Law that the disqualification of a husband *per se* attaches to his wife that also would have been specified in the first text among the grounds mentioned in it as excluding a person from inheritance." Further the learned Judge at 283 says " And it is a canon of interpretation in Hindú Law that a

---

(1) For an illustration of this rule see Bhattoji Dikṣita's *Siddhânta Kaumudi* p. 55 (The Sri Venkiṭas'wara Press edition). For another application of the rule, which answers to the legal maxim *expressus unius est exclusio alterius*, see Westropp, C. J's. judgment in I. L. R. 3, Bom., 280 (Chandavarkar J.)

* As to the explanation of the maxim, see Broom's Legal Maxims, p. 504 (8th edition).

special text forming an exception to a general text should be construed strictly and applied only to the cases falling clearly within it " (1).

Knight J. who is the colleague of Chandavarkar J. concurred with him.

In Anandi v. Hari Suba. I. L. R. 33 Bom. 404 Chandavarkar J sitting with Heaton J. says at p. 409.

" And it is a rule of construction (Mimansa) according to Hindu Law, that where an exception exists to a general rule, the exception should be confined within the strictest limits so as not to unduly encroach upon the general rule. See this rule of construction explained in *Gangu* v. *Chandrabhagabai* I. L. R. 32 Bom. 275 at p. 283."

In Gangadhar Bogla v. Hira Lal Bogla I. L. R. 43 Cal. 944, which is a three judge decision of the Calcutta High Court consisting of Sanderson C. J., Woodroffe and Mukerjee J J., Mukerjee J. at p. 966 says.

" Further, it is plain that the argument of the appellant involves an *Atides'a* upon an *Atides'a*, that is a fiction upon a fiction, or a remote analogy on a remote analogy ; the adopted son by a fiction be a real son of the adopter, and, then, by another fiction, a real son, not only of the adoptive mother but of all the other wives of the adoptive father ; a train of reasoning most repugnant to a Hindu jurist."

At p. 967 he says.

" Why should we impute to Vijnaneswara, manifest violation of an elementary rule of interpretation namely, that he uses the same word in two different senses in the course of the same discussion [Dattaka Mimansa II, 35; Vyavahâra Mayûkha chap I. sec. I, 11-15 Dayabhaga chap. III. sec. II, p. 30 which furnish illustrations of the Arthaikatva Axiom, to a word or sentence occuring at one and the same place, a double meaning should not be attached (सकृद्वरितन्यरुः सकृदेवार्थगमयति)]; for let it not be over looked that although in the translation by Coolebrooke, the text of the Mitâkṣarâ is divided into distinct paragraphs, in the original the passage appears as one continuous and unbroken discussion."

He says at p. 969.

" There is thus plain indication that even in archaic times, the rule was deemed harsh and an endeavour was made to restrict its operation. Consequently we should not extend its application to cases, not only not comprised strictly within its letter but undoubtedly beyond its true spirit; in this connection we may bear in mind that Hindu jurists quite as much as English jurists [Ebbs v. Bonlnois 1875 L. R. 10 ch.

---

(1) " For this canon, see the chapter on " impurity," in the section on *Prayas'chitta*, Mitâkṣarâ (Moghe's third edition) p. 292* It is:—वावत्ववाधिते ऽनुपत्ति प्रथमोनभवति ताब्द्राधनीयम् (" The general rule ceases to apply only so far as is necessary for the purposes of the exception"). The canon is also given by West and Buhler in their digest, third edition p. 880 footnote (c). [Chandavarkar J.]

* The passage occurs at p. 296.

App. 479,484] recognise the well known canon of interpretation that a special text or statue forming an exception to a general text or statue should be construed strictly and applied only to the cases falling clearly within it ; the Mitâkṣarâ itself recognises the principal that where an exception exists to a general rule, the exception should be confined within the strictest limits so as not to encroach unduly upon the general rule Gangu v. Chandrabhagabai.   I. L. R. 32 Bom. 275 Anandi v. Hari Suba I. L. R. 33 Bom. 404, 409, Duttaka Chandrika sec. v. 27, Mitâkṣarâ on Prâyas'chitta ed. Moghe p. 292 (6) यावत्यबाधितेऽनुवृत्ति मध्यमोन भवति तावद्राघनीयम्

There was a dispute as to the succession between mother's sister's son and maternal uncle's son before a Bench in the Madras High Court consisting of White C. J. and Krishna Swami Ayyar J. in Appandai Vuthiyar v. Rajubali Mudaliyar, I. L. R. 33 Mad. 439. The learned judges at p. 442 say "There is a rule of the Mimansa that effect should be given to the order in which persons and things are named unless the sense requires a different order ; see *jaiminiya Nyâyamala chap v. Adhikarana.* In the absence of any decisive principle dictating a different order the duty of the interpreter of the law is to accept the order in which they are named as based upon some rule which they may be unable to discover or upon the mere *ipse dixit* of the law-giver."

The rule of law laid down by the learned judges of the Madras High Court was expressly dissented from by the Allahabad High Court consisting of Banerji and Piggott J J. in Ram Charan Lal v. Rahim Bux I. L. R. 38 All. 416. In this case, the Mimansa rule of order seems to h ave been half-heartedly argued by the learned counsel for the appellant as he referred to Sircar's Tagore lectures in his argument at p. 419. The learned judges without referring to the Mimamsa rule of interpretation decided the case on the texts and the case law.

Edge. C. J. in Beni Prasad v. Hardai Bibi* says at page 71 of the report,

"Let us see what was Mr. Colebrooke's opinion of the Mimansa of Jaimini. It is to be found in the transactions of the Royal Asiatic Society, vol. I, page 457. As I have not a copy of the transactions before me, I shall quote the passage from them which is set out at p. 74 of Golapchandra Sircar's Hindu law of adoption. As to the Mimansa philosophy of Jaimini Mr. Colebrooke said 'The disquisitions of the Mimansa bear, therefore, a certain resemblance to juridical questions, and, in fact the Hindu law being blended with the religion of the people, the same modes of reasoning are applicable, and are applied to the one as to the other. The logic of the Mìmansâ is the logic of the law ; the rule of interpretation of civil and religious ordinances. Each case is examined and determined upon general principles ; and from the cases decided the principles may be collected. A well ordered arrangement of them would constitute the philosophy of law : and this is, in truth, what has been attempted in the Mimansâ …..Instances of the application of reasoning, as taught in the *Mimansa,* to the discussion and determination of juridical

---

*I. L. R. XIV All. 67.

questions, may be seen in two treatises on the law of inheritance translated by myself, and as many on adoption, by a member of this society
Mr. Sutherland. (See Mitâkṣarâ on inheritance, 1, 1, 10 and 1, 9, 11 and
2, 1, 34 ; *Jimuta vahina* 11, 5, 16-19. *Datt. Mim.* on adoption 1,35,41
and 4, 65,66 and 6, 27,31. Dutt. Chand. 1, 24 and 2,4.) Golap Chandra
Sarkar in his Hindu Law of adoption page 74, gives much useful information as to the Mîmânsâ of Jaiminî and also as to the Vedânta. He
there says, 'Mîmânsâ, however is the name of a school of Hindu philosophy
founded by Jaiminî, the object of which is to establish the cogency of
precepts contained in the scripture, and to furnish maxims of interpretation, by means of the rules of reasoning.' And further on at p. 74, he
says, 'The Vedanta school of philosophy, the founder of which is Vyâsa,
is also denominated Mîmânsâ, and in order to distinguish it from Jaimini's
philosophy, the Vedanta is called the Uttara or posterior Mîmansâ ;
and the other, the Pûrva or prior Mîmânsâ. The division is similar to
that between the Vedas and Upanishads and based upon the same
principle ; the Mimansa of Jaimini deals with the practical or ceremonial
precepts ; whereas that of Vyasa relates to the theoretical or theological
precepts contained in the Upaniṣads. But as the school founded by Vyasa
has a distinct name of its own, the word Mimansa when used without
qualification means Jaimini's philosophy. The latter Mimansa is supplementary to the prior and they are parts of one whole. The two together
comprise the complete system of interpretation of the precepts and
doctrines of the scriptures both practical and theological. The rules
furnished by them are followed by the commentators as authoritative while
discussing doubtful questions of law'. I have thus at length by giving
the above quotations, to the Mîmânsâ of Jaimini or the Pûrva Mîmânsâ
as it is desirable to keep in mind that the rules of the Pûrva
Mîmânsâ, although there may sometimes have been overlooked or not
attended to by Hindu as well as English commentators and text writers
and by English translators, are no new rules of construction but are
authoritative rules for the construction of texts of the sacred law of the
Hindus.''

The same learned judge continues at the bottom of page 72 of the
report. "After giving his translation of the text of Vasiṣṭha which I
have already quoted* Mr. Mandlik says—'This text on the most approved
principles of criticism must also be treated as a recommendatory one,
in as much as it contains a precept that is intended for a certain
specified purpose. It is a rule of the Purwa Mimansa that all texts
supported by the assigning of a reason are to be deemed not as *vidhi*
but simply as *arthavâda* (recommendatory.) When a text is treated
as an *arthavâda*, it follows that it has no obligatory force whatever.
Śabara swâmîn constructs an *adhikarana* (a topic) on this head which
he calls *hetuman Nigada'dhikaraṇa* (a topic in regard to texts which
contain a clause containing a reason of the precept) out of five *sutras* of
Jaimini etc.''

The learned judge continuing says on page 73 of the report, " Ap
plying the rule of construction of the Mimansa of Jaimini to the text
of Vasiṣṭha, I am of opinion that that text, so far as it applies to the

---

*Seet at pp. 69-70 of the report.

adoption of an only son, is to be construed as a religious recommendation and not as a positive and imperative prohibition as we find the reason given in the text for the precept.

If the continuation of the text of Vasiṣṭha which I have been considering is correctly translated by Mr. Colebrooke as 'nor let a woman give or accept a son unless with the assent of her lord' or if the more correct translation is ' a woman shall not give or accept a son except with the assent of her husband' it is to be noticed that according to the rule of construction to which I have referred, the text as to a woman not giving or taking a son in adoption gives no reason for that precept and hence that precept might be construed as a positive and imperative prohibition against a widow adopting a son to her deceased husband without authority from him."

Sir John Edge has referred more than once to Jaimini's rules of Mimansa in his learned judgment extending over 32 pages of the report.

The case went up to the Privy Council in appeal. Their Lordships of the Privy Council say at P. 425 of Radha Mohan *versus* Hardai Bibi I. L. R. 22 Mad. 398 " In examining this question, their Lordships are again at great disadvantage in not knowing Sanscrit. In the absence of agreement among Sanscrit students they cannot adopt the representations made though by learned men to the effect that as a matter of grammar Vasista's injunction imports admonition rather than command. So with respect to what has been called Jaimini's rule which is so much relied on by Chief Justice Edge. *The author who wrote in the 13th century* appears to have been received as a high authority in the interpretation of Smriti texts. He lays down the rule that all precepts supported by the assignment of a reason are to be taken as recommendatious only. That, if sound would be conclusive as to Vasishta's text. But it is rather startling and a very intimate acquaintance with the Smritis would be needed before admitting its truth. It has not been brought forward in any case prior to this case from Allahabad. It may, however fairly be argued that one who having the power to give an absolute command gives an injunction not expressed in unambiguous terms of absolute command but resting on a reason, is addressing himself rather to the moral sense of his hearers than to their duty of implicit obedience. So far Vasishta's reason, founded as it is on temporal and not on religous considerations, gives some, though not very strong support to the respondent's theory."

The passage in Italics in the above quotation is mine. It may be remarked here that their Lordships of the Privy Council have accepted the date of composition of Jaimini's Mîmânsâ to be in the thirteenth century of the Christian Era from the judgment of Sir John Edge. (See at P. III of the Introduction.)

The case is also reported in I. L. R. 21 All 460. At P. 466 their Lordships are reported to have said.

" Again a rule had been applied or canon of construction termed Jaimini's rule: to the effect that in construing the ancient 'Sanscrit texts a precept was to be held only a recommendation not to be obligatory as a law where a reason for the precept was given. This rule had not yet been applied by any court."

They did not accept Sir John Edge's interpretation of Vasiṣtha's text with the aid of Mîmânsâ rules of interpretation.

In a subsequent case (Bhagwan Singh v. Bhagwan Singh. I. L R. 17 All. 294) when there was a question as to the validity of the adoption of the sister's son directly and that of daughter's son and mother's sister's son indirectly by a twice-born before the Full Bench, the learned Chief justice again refers to Jaimini's rules of interpretation applicable to the Smriti texts at p. 378 of the report.

"It appears to me that what Nanda Pandita was trying to demonstrate was that the sentence in Saunaka's text which Mr. Sutherland has translated as "For the three superior tribes, a sister's son is nowhere mentioned as a son" was a reason given for the immediately preceding sentence of the text ; "But a daughter's son and a sister's son are affiliated by sudras," and reading the two sentences together Saunaka had in the opinion of Nanda Pandita, expressly prohibited the adoption amongst the three regenerate classes of a daughter's son and a sister's son. Assuming for the moment that Nanda Pandita was correct in construing the sentence; " For the three superior tribes, a sister's son, is nowhere (mentioned as) a son " as the reason for the statement contained in the immediately preceding sentence of Sanuaka's text, and applying the rule of construction of the Mimansa of Jaimini which is to be applied to the ancient Sanscrit text of the sacred Hindu Law, the two sentences together must be deemed to contain an admonition only and not a positive prohibition against the adoption amongst the three regenerate classes of a sister's son and a daughter's son. The rule of the Mimansa of Jaimini is thus stated by Mandlik at page 499 of the Vyavahara Mayúkha :—" It is a rule of the Pûrva Mîmânsâ that all texts supported by assigning of a reason are to be deemed not as *vidhi* but simply as *Artha-váda* (recommendatory). When a text is treated as an *Artha-váda*, it follows that it has no obligatory force whatever. I have shown in my judgment in *Beni Prasad v. Hardai Bibi* I. L. R. 14 All at p.p. 70 *et seq.* that the rules of Mimansa of Jaimini, although they may sometimes have been overlooked or not attended to by Hindu as well as English commentators and text writers, and by the English translators, are no new rules of construction, but are authoritative rules for the construction of texts of the sacred law of the Hindus. The Mimansa of Jaiminî is older by many centuries than Dattaka Mimansa of Nanda Pandita. Its authority is undoubted. It has been applied by, amongst others, Jagannâtha Tercapanchanan who complied Colebrooke's digest and is referred to in the notes in that digest. This is what was stated by Mr. Colebrooke as to the Mimansa of Jaimini. The written law, whether it be *Sruti* or *Smriti*, direct revelation or tradition is subject to the same rules of interpretation. Those rules are collected in the Mimansa which is a disquisition on proof and authority of precepts. It is considered as a branch of philosophy, and is properly the logic of the law. In the eastern part of India, viz. Bengal and Behar, where the Vedas are less read, the Mimansa less studied than in the south, the dialectic philosophy, or *nyaya* is more consulted and is there relied on for rules of reasoning and interpretation upon questions of law, as well as upon metaphysical topics." See account by H. T. Colebrooke, Esq. of the Hindu schools of law in Sir Thomas Strange's Hindu Law, vol. I, p. 315 edition of 1830. See also Mr. Colebrooke on the Mimansa of Jaimini, in the transactions of the Asiatic Society vol. I, page 457. That Mr. Colebrooke in the above extract was when referring to "Bengal" applying that term not loosely, but strictly according to its true and original meaning of the country stretching south-east from Bhagalpur to the sea and was not including in that term Behar or the province of Benares is obvious from the reference in that extract to 'Bengal and Behar' and from the following passage relating to the authorities in the different schools of Hindu Law in the same account :—To these are added, in Bengal, the works of *Jîmuta váhana* and those of *Raghu Nandan,* and several others constituting a distinct school of law which deviates on many questions from that of *Mithila* and still more from those of Benares and *Dekhin* or southern peninsula." I have shown in my judgment in *Beni Prasad v. Hardai Bibi* I. L. R. 14 All. 67 that the author of the Mitakshara had construed a text of Vasiṣtha in accordance with the rules of Mimansa of Jaimini, and that the construction of that same text in the Dattaka Mimansa of Nanda Pandita was in violation of those rules. The truth is, Nanda Pandita followed no rule of construction, but construed ancient texts as it suited his fancy, or his argument."

The queer view of adoption arrived at by the majority of the Full Bench by misapplying the rules of Mimansa was very properly rejected by the Privy Council on appeal. See Bhagwan Singh v. Bhagwan Singh I. L. R. 21 All. 412.